The ESL Writer's Handbook

2ND EDITION

JANINE CARLOCK

MAEVE EBERHARDT

JAIME HORST

LIONEL MENASCHE

Pitt Series in English as a Second Language

ISBN-13: 978-0-472-03707-0

2023   2022   2021   2020   6   5   4   3

PREFACE

General Uses

The ESL Writer's Handbook, 2nd Edition, is a reference work for ESL students who are taking college-level courses. Because its purpose is to provide help with the broad variety of writing questions students may have when working on school assignments, the text focuses on English for Academic Purposes.

The Handbook complements a student writer's dictionary, thesaurus, and grammar reference book. It would be suitable as a text for an advanced ESL writing course when used together with the companion Workbook (978-0-472-03726-1).

Special ESL Features

- The **topic selection** is based on ESL writers' needs as observed by the authors over many years.
- The **coverage of topics** is more complete than the limited amount usually provided for ESL writers in first language or L1 handbooks.
- The **explanatory language** is appropriate for ESL students, in contrast to the more complex and idiomatic language of other English handbooks.
- The **level of detail** is more manageable for ESL students, compared to what is in other English handbooks.
- Many of the **examples** of paragraphs, essays, research papers, and exercise sentences were **written by ESL students**; this encourages users of the Handbook to realize that they too can become effective writers.

Structure

We have structured the Handbook in what we feel to be the most logical manner. Sections 1 and 2 provide general information about paragraph and essay structure, which students must consider when beginning to work with academic writing. These sections include topics such as how to get ideas for an assignment, how to structure those ideas into a paper, and what to check for before turning in a paper.

Section 3 is more specific. It describes five common patterns for organizing an academic essay: narrative, process, comparison/contrast, cause and effect, and argument. Here we now provide students with specific phrases and language structures that are used with these five patterns to help them build coherent sentences, and we provide models to help students build coherent paragraphs and essays. After the discussion of and exercises for each pattern of organization, sample essay topics are provided. Teachers should make use of these topics for essay assignments.

Often students are overwhelmed when given a large writing assignment. For this reason, **Section 4** guides students through the different steps they must go through to create a good research paper. The task of writing a research paper is broken into its many component parts. Understanding and experiencing this process will not only allow for a better finished product but will help students to become better overall writers as well. Teachers may wish to use this section concurrently with Sections 1–3 in the Handbook to structure a semester-long research assignment based on the steps outlined in this section. Or teachers may use this section independently, depending on their curriculum.

Section 5 addresses the grammar and style issues that ESL students writing in English seem to have the most difficulty with, helping students to recognize and correct errors at both the word level and the sentence level. This section provides clear explanations, examples, and exercises to build students' skills in these areas. Teachers may wish to assign various sections according to the needs of their particular class.

Section 6 provides basic information on punctuation, with examples for students to consult as models when they are writing, and offers some exercises as well for practice.

Section 7 provides a more visual approach to topics that ESL students commonly have difficulty with, such as verb tense and transitions. Information is provided mainly in the form of lists and charts so that students do not need to rely as much on their reading comprehension skills to understand and utilize the information.

Finally, **Section 8** provides examples of different types of writing that students will be expected to do as undergraduates in the United States. Because ESL students do not have a base knowledge of these forms, these examples should prove valuable to them. Teachers may wish to use the examples as a basis for their own assignments on these types of writing.

The handbook includes a list of common editing symbols, a glossary, and an index. Terminology that is defined in the glossary appears in color in running text for quick reference.

The Workbook Accompanying This Handbook

WB
Ex.

The Workbook that accompanies this Handbook extends the topics covered in the Handbook to enable a teacher to use the books as the core texts in an advanced-level ESL writing course or in a first-year undergraduate composition course. The Workbook provides additional exercises to facilitate students' understanding of the topics discussed in the Handbook. In the Handbook, an icon is provided in the margin next to a heading or exercise to alert the teacher or student that extra exercises on this topic are available in the Workbook. The teacher may wish to assign Workbook exercises as homework or use them in class with the exercises in the Handbook.

What's New in the 2nd Edition

We have enjoyed hearing about how useful our handbook has been over the past several years, and we are delighted to have this opportunity to participate in creating a second edition of the book. So that the book will continue to be relevant, we have incorporated changes to update it and to provide more models and practice for students. These changes include:

- **A totally revised APA and MLA guide.** We have updated to reflect the 8th edition of MLA. Also, we have provided more comprehensive coverage of types of sources in both APA and MLA styles to reflect changes in how students find information—that is, via online sources and in databases.
- **New sample research papers.** The papers have up-to-date sources and topics. Like those in the first edition, these are actual student papers (with a bit of adaptation in places to make them more helpful models) from advanced ESL

writing courses. Also as in the first edition, comments about content as well as formatting are provided on the side of the paper to indicate special features that students will want to incorporate into their own papers.

- **New organization of rhetorical pattern language.** The organization of this content in Section 3 is now more consistent across patterns to improve clarity and ease of understanding.
- **New sample writing and content within the chapters.** Much of the other content that is used as examples of certain types of writing—such as the introductory paragraph in Section 2 and the sample outline in Section 4, as well as much of the discussion and examples regarding plagiarism in Section 4— are new.
- **New additions to exercises.** Based on our own experiences teaching writing courses, we have revised some exercises to be more clear and effective. Also, many exercise items have been changed to include more timely topics.
- **A new sample resume and cover letter in Section 8.** The resume includes skills and experiences that are relevant in 2018; the resume is also from a student who recently graduated.
- **New exercises.** We have added an exercise to Section 4 on evaluating sources to reflect the changes to the way that people search for sources. With the constant developments in technology, it has become even more critical that students have the information literacy skills to evaluate online as well as print sources. An exercise has also been added in Section 5 to give students practice recognizing independent and dependent clauses, which can often be difficult for ESL writers.

Acknowledgments

We are grateful to our many students throughout the years in ESL programs and university writing courses at Duquesne University, Carnegie Mellon University, and the University of Pittsburgh who have generously given permission for their writing to be used in this project.

We thank Kelly Sippell, who continues to be an enthusiastic supporter of our work and to provide insightful editorial suggestions for the additions to this edition.

We would also like to thank our writing instructors throughout the years for instilling in us the desire to create good writing and help others create good writing as well.

All of the authors wish to acknowledge Lionel Menasche's contributions to the first edition and to thank him for the opportunity to work on the original project. We would also like to thank our families, friends, and colleagues for their support that kept us going. In addition, each author would like to thank specific individuals whose direction and guidance enabled them to feel equipped to take on this project.

- Janine Carlock would like to thank Judy Weddell, Honors English teacher extraordinaire, whose inspired teaching and personal example encouraged students to see the potential within themselves.
- Maeve Eberhardt would like to thank Christine O'Neill and Dawn McCormick—her most inspirational teachers and mentors.
- Jaime Horst would like to thank Julia Kasdorf, for showing her that writing is an art.

CONTENTS

SECTION 1

· ·

THE WRITING PROCESS

A. Overview of the Writing Process

When you write, you make something new. It is a creative process because you are presenting meaningful ideas to a reader and something that has not been expressed previously.

More specifically, your essay is new and creative because:

- it contains **information** that has never been expressed before.
- the **language** in which you express the ideas is your own.
- the **organization** of the information is your own.

Thinking about Your Composing Process

Every writer goes through a unique process to create a piece of writing. Some aspects of this process are different for each writer and different every time. Yet some elements of the **composing** (or writing) process are similar across writers and projects. Becoming aware of the composing process in general, and your own in particular, will help you to become a more skilled writer. These questions can help you to reflect on your own ways of writing and will perhaps give you some new ways to think about writing.

. . . .

Exercise 1.1: Thinking about Composing

Think about the process you have used for composing a piece of writing in the past, either in English or in your own language. Use these questions to guide your reflection. Discuss your answers.

- How do you usually get new ideas for your writing? Do you make lists? Do you make diagrams? Do you keep all of your ideas in your head until you're ready to start writing? Can you think of other possible ways to come up with new ideas? What are they?

- How do you start your writing (also called drafting)? Do you start by writing your ideas in an organized way and making a plan? Or do you start writing right away and then see how your ideas connect and develop?

- What kind of revising do you usually do? Do you add or remove ideas? Do you move ideas around and change the organization? Or do you leave your writing pretty much in its original form without making many changes?

- How do you make sure that your writing is clear and that your grammar, spelling, punctuation, and word choice are correct? Do you ask another person to read your writing and give you feedback? Do you finish your writing before the deadline so you have time to re-read it and make corrections? Do you edit and make corrections as you go along?

Exercise 1.2: Reflecting on the Composing Process

A. Think about the list of metaphors for the composing process that follows. Why is each one similar to composing an essay or academic paper? Does one of them fit with your own composing process?
B. Choose one metaphor and then discuss it with a partner or write a brief paragraph explaining how the metaphor reflects your composing process.

- constructing a building
- composing music
- solving a puzzle
- knitting a sweater
- drawing a picture
- preparing a meal

Stages of the Writing Process

The composing process is not a linear, step-by-step process. Writers usually go back and repeat several parts of the process in order to improve and refine their writing. It is important to understand the steps in the writing process so that you can easily go back and work through an earlier stage to produce an excellent piece of writing.

Stages of the Writing Process

1. Understanding the assignment
2. Thinking about audience
3. Generating ideas
4. Organizing/Outlining ideas
5. Drafting
6. Revising
7. Editing

Understanding the Assignment

An essential first step is to read the assignment carefully and make sure that you understand it. This is the point in the writing process to clarify the requirements and expectations of the assignment. If a topic has not been specified, then this step involves deciding what the topic will be, at least in general terms. If you are not given a specific topic, it is important to understand the purpose and guidelines for the assignment. It is often helpful to talk with your instructor if you are unsure about the requirements for your assignment.

For more on understanding assignments, see pages 7–10.

Examples of assignments

> When making a large purchase, such as a car or a computer, which is more important to you, high quality or low cost? Why?

> Evaluate the three main types of renewable energy: wind, solar, and geothermal. Examine the benefits and drawbacks of each energy source and discuss the development potential of each for the region where you live.

Thinking about Audience

Before writing, it is important to think about the intended **audience** for the composition. Different audiences—academic colleagues, the general public, an employer, or your instructor—influence both the content and the style of your writing.

For more on audience, see pages 11–12.

Examples of assignments for different audiences

> Describe what aspects of your previous work experience and personal characteristics make you particularly well qualified for this salesperson position. [audience: potential employer]

> Write a brochure explaining the risks of certain environmental and household toxins for pregnant women. [audience: general public]

> Examine the principal causes of the American Great Depression of the 1930s. What changes were made to the American and global economic systems as a result of this economic crisis? [audience: professor]

Generating Ideas

Once the assignment is clear, it is essential to list ideas for developing the topic. Ideas generally come from reading, discussion, listening to talks or lectures, or your own experience. New ideas often come from combining old ideas in fresh ways and doing research to discover something original. Frequently, ideas are generated by using various techniques to stimulate creativity, such as brainstorming, discussion, and freewriting.

For more on generating ideas, see pages 12–18.

<u>Examples of generating ideas</u>

Topic: When making a large purchase, such as a car or a computer, which is more important to you, high quality or low cost? Why?

Ideas for writing:

High quality → item lasts longer (positive), may cost a lot more (negative)

Low cost → can save money for other important purchases (positive), quality may be lower so item may break more quickly (negative)

→ I prefer low cost. My likes and dislikes may change anyway, so I can buy another inexpensive thing when my preference changes.

Organizing and Outlining Ideas

After generating ideas for a topic, you can begin to organize them in a possible order for the essay. You can do this in different ways, from a simple list to a more completely developed outline. A simple list is only for the order of ideas, but an **outline** shows both the order of ideas and the relationship of those ideas to each other as well as more specific ideas. Developing an outline is also a way to generate additional ideas. Numbering and indentation are used in an outline to show the idea relationships and their comparative importance. You should never feel limited by an outline that you prepare near the beginning of the writing process; you will probably change it a number of times as you get more ideas and think of new ways of organizing them. For examples of outlines, refer to pages 15–16, 28–31, and 120–121.

Drafting

Drafting refers to writing some or all of your ideas in sentences and paragraphs. Rough drafts generally do not need all the pieces to fit together nicely. In later drafts, you will organize and shape the content of your composition. This stage requires multiple versions. For more on drafting, see Section 2.

Revising

Revising involves making changes in the organization and content of a draft, continuing to improve its final shape. A few or many additional drafts are possible at this stage.

For more on revising, see pages 52–53 and 207–208.

Editing

At this final step in shaping your essay, you must focus on correcting sentence structure, spelling, and punctuation. This is also the step where you seek to make the most precise word choices. For more on **editing**, see pages 285–286.

Examples of editing

Original: Solar energy can be a good and cheap idea for power.

Revised: **Solar energy can be an economical option for electricity generation.**

Original: Many student attended last week's football game between the rival teams.

Revised: **Many students attended last week's football game between the rival teams.**

B. Understanding Writing Assignments

If, in academic courses, you write a well-expressed essay but do not follow the assignment's exact requirements for organization and focus, your essay will receive a low grade because the content does not address the topic. Therefore, the instructions, or **prompt**, for an assignment or essay examination must be examined carefully.

Certain **key words*** or **assignment cues** will tell you **how** to organize your essay or **what perspective** to take on the topic. These key words are usually **verbs** in the imperative (or command) form and appear at the beginning of sentences in the instructions, but other forms are also used.

In some cases, the key words give clues to the needed organizational pattern, like *compare, define, give examples,* or *assess.* The key words in assignment instructions are therefore very important as indicators of how you should structure your essay or paper.

Key Words* in Assignments

> **Examples of Key Words* in Assignments**
>
> Assignment instruction (political science) with only one key instructional word:
>> **Compare** *monarchy and dictatorship as systems of government.*
>
> Assignment instruction (sports & exercise science) with several key words:
>> **Describe** *the typical* **process** *of training for a professional long-distance runner and* **illustrate** *it with at least two* **examples**.

Also be sure to pay attention to phrases in an assignment that direct you to specific actions: *focus on, give special attention to, be sure to, include,* or *don't forget.*

---

*We are using this term here to convey the broad range of language used (instructional, organizational, conceptual) in assignments and prompts and are not limiting its use only to key words about the topic/content.

A list of the most common instructional words in assignments is provided in Table 1.1. <u>This is not a complete list</u>; other similar words or expressions may also be used in assignments. The words are presented in three categories:

- those that ask you to offer a **judgment** (your opinion or an argument)
- those that are **neutral** (asking you to simply describe or explain something)
- those that ask for a **specific pattern of writing** (such as defining or comparing)

WB
Ex. 1.1

Table 1.1: Key Words in Assignments		
Judgment	**Neutral**	**Specific Writing Patterns**
analyze consider the component parts of something and offer an evaluation of the strengths and weaknesses of each element	address deal with, consider, discuss	compare describe similarities and differences
assess provide a carefully considered judgment of something	clarify explain in a way that makes the ideas easy to understand	contrast describe differences
challenge present and discuss the weak points of an argument or explanation	describe provide general statements and details that present a clear picture	classify put multiple ideas into separate categories to show which ones have similarities
criticize / critique evaluate the strong and weak points	discuss consider all aspects of an issue	define describe the general class to which something belongs and how it differs from all others in that class

Table 1.1 (cont'd)		
Judgment	**Neutral**	**Specific Writing Patterns**
defend give arguments to support a position or claim	enumerate or list give a descriptive list of a series of items	distinguish describe the differences between two concepts
evaluate explain the strong and weak points and give your opinion	explain provide information to make an issue clear	illustrate give examples or an extended example
justify give reasons for doing or saying something	interpret explain the meaning	narrate tell the story of something, usually in chronological order
prove explain why something is true and provide evidence	outline or summarize provide a description that focuses only on main ideas with no details	describe a process provide general statements and details about something that is done in stages
support give arguments or evidence to show that an explanation is valid	relate explain the connections between two or among more items	
	review give a description of the issues involved	
	state say what something is	
	trace describe a series of events in sequence	

. . . .

Exercise 1.3: Identifying Key Words in Writing Assignments

WB
Ex. 1.2

These assignment instructions are from actual university courses in various subject areas. Read each assignment carefully. Underline the key words that indicate how the essay should be focused and organized.

1. Describe and identify the function of the major elements of a plant cell: cell wall, central vacuole, and plastids (including chloroplasts, chromoplasts, and leucoplasts). Compare the structure of plant cells to animal cells and explain why these differences exist. [Botany]

2. Examine a movie that was adapted from a book that you've read. List several changes that were made in adapting the book for the screen and explain why you think the director made these changes. Assess whether the book and the movie have the same impact on the audience and discuss which version you prefer. [Film Studies/Literature]

3. Choose a space telescope to investigate. Your investigation should include: (a) a brief review of the history of this telescope (launch date and lifespan); (b) a description of the telescope's components and how it works (i.e., the optics of its telescope and cameras); (c) a summary of the telescope's purpose and any major discoveries it has made; and (d) an analysis of the impact of this particular telescope on the field of astronomy. [Astronomy]

4. Compare and contrast the Italian Renaissance with the Renaissance in Northern Europe, particularly with regard to the arts. Use specific works to support your analysis. [European History]

5. Discuss the importance of memory as a brain function. Define explicit and implicit memory and explain three main stages in the formation and retrieval of memory. [Psychology]

C. Thinking about Audience

It is always important to consider your **audience** while writing. The audience refers to the intended reader(s) of your writing. In academic writing for your classes, the immediate audience is frequently the professor or instructor. Other types of writing that have a different audience may also be required of you as a college student.

Types of Writing	Possible Audience
Essays for a class	Professor, classmates
Journal article or paper for a conference	Professionals in your field
Resume/cover letter	Potential employers or supervisors

Content

As you write, think about any **technical or unfamiliar terminology** that you might need to explain for your reader. Sometimes it is also helpful to explain why a particular concept is important or to explain in the introduction why your reader should be informed about the topic at all. If your readers know little about your topic, include all the **background** and **definitions** that they need. On the other hand, if your audience is quite knowledgeable, you can leave out general background information and basic definitions.

Example of how content may vary

Technical: Oceans are the largest ecosystem in the marine biome, consisting of multiple ecological zones. Along the ocean floor, the abyssal zone is high in oxygen but low in nutrients.

General: A biome is a large group of plants and animals that shares a specific type of environment. In the ocean regions of the marine biome, the deepest waters make up the abyssal zone, where the water is high in oxygen but low in nutrients.

Style

Your intended audience may also influence the level of **formality** of your writing. For example, a brochure explaining how to apply for a driver's license will use commands and informal language, while an argument essay advocating a higher age limit for young drivers will use more formal language and grammar.

> Example of variation in style
>
> *Informal*: Remember that using a cell phone and talking with other people in the car can distract you and make you less safe as a driver.
>
> *Formal*: Numerous studies have demonstrated that young drivers are particularly vulnerable to distractions such as cell phones and passengers in the vehicle.

D. Generating Ideas

When you first approach a piece of writing, it can be difficult to find ideas for your topic. This is when using various idea-generating techniques is very useful. Such techniques can help you come up with ideas at the start of an assignment and also at any point in the writing process when you feel you need more ideas.

Idea-Generating Techniques: Points to Consider

- Most idea-generating techniques rely on the mind's strong habit of association: thinking of one thing naturally leads you to thinking of something else associated with it. This process can help you think of ideas that you might not have otherwise.
- Different writers like different idea-generating techniques. Practice using all of them to discover which ones suit your own writing process. Then use them in your future assignments. You may prefer one particular technique, or you might use several during the idea-generating process.

- Idea-generating is usually done individually, but in some cases it is useful to work with one or more other writers.
- Even if you work with others, the process of idea-generating is a personal one—the words and phrases that you list are only for your own use so that you can feel free to explore your ideas creatively.

> ## Idea-Generating Techniques
> - brainstorming
> - discussion
> - journalistic questions
> - freewriting
> - listing
> - outlining
> - visual mapping

WB
x. 1.3

Brainstorming is probably the most widely used idea-generating technique. It consists of simply letting your mind wander, following any and all thoughts related to one topic—without judging whether the ideas are good or bad, useful or useless—and listing these thoughts. You should write in whatever language you are most comfortable. By writing the ideas in a rough form (not worrying about grammar or spelling), you will not forget them, and you can go back later to your notes for more idea-generating from these thoughts. Write the ideas as single words or phrases or sentences, in the form of diagrams or lists, or any kind of notation. After brainstorming, you can make judgments about which ideas to develop and which to throw out.

WB
x. 1.4

Discussion of your topic with other writers, family members, or anyone else can help you see different points of view or learn more about your topic. The discussion may be focused, with a set time limit of five or ten minutes, or the discussion may be more casual. While talking, make a note of ideas that could be useful for your essay. This is similar to brainstorming except that it is done with a partner or in a group.

The **journalistic questions** are used by newspaper reporters when they want to be sure that they have covered all aspects of a story. Asking these questions can generate ideas because by this process you can systematically fill in gaps in the information and start thinking about various but related issues. The journalistic question words are:

Who?
When?
Where?
Why?
What?
How?

WB
Ex. 1.5

Many variations are possible for each question word. For example, using *who* you could ask: *Who was involved in X? Who initiated X? Who suffered the results of X? Who has tried to explain X?*

Freewriting is writing without any pause for a fixed time. This means you write without stopping. It is also called sometimes non-stop writing. Many writers give themselves three to five minutes to freewrite, strictly timed. This very effectively stimulates ideas by word and thought association.

WB
Ex. 1.

Example of a good freewriting procedure

- Use any sheet of paper. You will not be writing your composition in this activity, only generating ideas in a very rough form. Only you will see your own non-stop writing.
- Generate ideas and details by writing about your topic for exactly five minutes without stopping. Write any ideas and words. Write single words and phrases or parts of sentences—anything, just as it comes to your mind. Use English or your own language. **Do not stop writing, even if you think you are not writing anything sensible.** The important thing is to force yourself to continue writing all thoughts you have during this time.

- Read your non-stop writing. Circle or underline any ideas that you think might be good ones to develop further. Several of your thoughts will not be useful and may not make sense. That does not matter because you will probably find some ideas you can use during the non-stop writing. Even your main idea may be suggested by something you have written here.
- If you need more ideas after the first set of non-stop writing, try it again for another five minutes. For the second period of non-stop writing, focus on an idea generated in the first one.

WB
Ex. 1.7 **Listing** simply involves writing in list form any ideas about your topic in the order in which they occur to you. Start with a blank sheet of paper and write your topic at the top. As with brainstorming, use the power of thought association and write any ideas that come to you in a column, one under the other. Do not try to organize the ideas into groups; organizing happens later. Do not try to decide which ideas might be useful because that also happens later.

These may or may not be ideas that you eventually use in the essay. When you have completed the list, read it through several times to see if any items in the list suggest even more new ideas to you. List those also.

WB
Ex. 1.8 When you **outline**, you arrange ideas as a series of headings and subheadings showing the relative importance of each idea. You can use numbering and indentation in the outline to indicate how ideas are related. This might be a first step in idea-generating, but it can also be a useful second step to organize ideas after using any idea-generating techniques.

Start with more general main ideas. Under each one, add ideas that are more specific. Under the more specific ones, add ideas that are at the next level of specificity.

Outlines are helpful as guidelines. You can change your outlines as often as you like while writing drafts. As you outline, you might develop new ideas and different shapes for your essay. An outline can be very simple, rough, and preliminary, or it might be quite long and detailed after much idea-generating.

Example Outline: Fields of Study
  I. Introduction: Types of knowledge
     A. Observation of the external world
     B. Introspection and intuition
 II. Natural sciences
     A. Mathematics
     B. Physics
     C. Biology
III. Social sciences
     A. Psychology
     B. Sociology
     C. Education
 IV. Philosophy and Arts
     A. Fine arts
        1. Painting
        2. Sculpture
        3. Poetry
     B. Religious studies
     C. Philosophy
  V. Conclusion: Choosing a field of study

Visual mapping (or clustering) is ideal for people who like to think visually. In this process, start by writing the topic (culture shock in the example in Figure 1.1) in the center of a blank page. Then draw lines or arrows to other topics, ideas, or words that come to mind by association and seem related. Use abbreviations if you want. Include diagrams or anything else that will help you in the visual mapping.

The ideas will form groups or clusters, and the result may look like a wheel with spokes, a spider web, or a flow chart. After drawing the visual map, try to group ideas together, find a main idea or theme for the essay, or extract some points for further idea-generating.

WB
Ex. 1.

Figure 1.1: Visual Map for an Assignment on Culture Shock

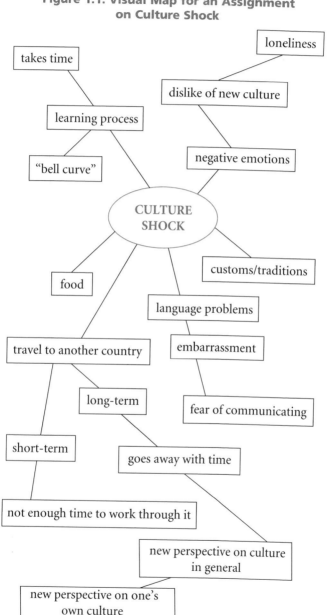

. . . .

Exercise 1.4: Generating Ideas

WB
Ex. 1.10

Choose a topic that interests you—either from this list or from your field of study—and use three idea-generating techniques to develop ideas for this topic. Answers will vary.

- natural disasters
- learning a new language
- safety in the workplace
- buying a car
- gardening
- protecting the environment

SECTION 2

. . . .

ESSAY STRUCTURE

A. Shaping a Paragraph

The purpose of expository writing is to present information on a particular topic in a clear and well-organized manner; the information may be described, analyzed, and explained, and an interpretation may be included. This is the type of writing that university students are generally expected to do in their courses. Paragraphs are one of the most important building blocks in expository writing. Although they may vary greatly in length, paragraphs usually consist of several sentences focused on one specific topic. Paragraphs in expository writing typically have a clear topic sentence and several development or support sentences. The topic sentence expresses the main idea of the paragraph and is usually placed at or near the beginning of the paragraph.

Topic Sentences

The topic sentence tells the reader about the **main idea** of the paragraph. This important sentence has two elements:

- the topic, which is the subject of the paragraph expressed in a word or phrase
- a **comment** on the topic, which is a statement or opinion

In these examples, the topic is **boldfaced,** and the comment is shown in color.

- a. **Dr. Johnson** is an excellent researcher.
- b. **A good researcher** must have intelligence and dedication to her work.
- c. Although she has the qualities of a good researcher, there are several reasons why **Paula Chan** has not yet had an opportunity to undertake a major research program.

. . . .

WB
Ex. 2.1
Exercise 2.1: Topic and Comment

Circle the topic, and underline the comment in these topic sentences.

1. Students who want to learn another language may find software programs to be very effective tools.

2. University students should be sure to make time for social activities in addition to time for studying.

3. Social media can be very distracting.

4. Engineers are working on many new technologies to improve automobile emissions.

5. Small liberal arts colleges offer many benefits to students that larger universities cannot.

Development Sentences

The **development** sentences in a paragraph **explain**, **elaborate**, and **support** the topic. This can be done in many ways, including through the use of examples, definitions, description, explanation, and outside sources.

A sample paragraph with the topic sentence in bold is shown. The development sentences, which are underlined, provide an analysis of the similarities between the task of scheduling in a manufacturing setting and in everyday life.

Sample paragraph

Scheduling is concerned with setting priorities and planning activities in relation to goals. **It may seem surprising, but there are similarities between scheduling for a manufacturing company and for the most common human activities.** In both cases, all constraints, such as resource limitations, time restrictions, and operational capabilities, must be considered. Then the same steps are taken: analysis, problem resolution, and implementation. The factory manager's goals include achieving maximum productivity with minimum costs and with no tardiness on due dates for a customer's order. The constraints might be, for example, how many workers are available and how skilled they are at their jobs. Similarly, the same manager's personal, everyday activities must be scheduled according to certain criteria—for instance, when to wake up, have meals, work, meet friends, and go to bed. In this too there are constraints such as getting all tasks done, not spending too much, and being on time when meeting with friends. Therefore, while in manufacturing the scheduling process is more complex because it is on a larger scale, the general scheduling considerations match those of most common human activities.

. . . .

Exercise 2.2: Topic and Development Sentences

WB
Ex. 2.2,
2.3, 2.4

Circle the topic sentence in the paragraph. Underline the development sentences, and discuss which type the author has used to support the topic sentence: examples, definitions, descriptions, or explanations.

Bilateral aid, the direct transfer of specific resources of money between two countries, has several key features, both for the donor country and the receiving country. Bilateral aid is rarely a grant of money. It is usually a low-interest loan. In many cases, however, it is a tied loan, which means that the recipient country is required to purchase goods and services from the donor country. For example, the United States may decide to give a tied loan for the construction of a steel mill. Under the terms of agreement the receiving government will have to buy the needed material and technical assistance from the donor country.

B. Shaping an Essay

Expository writing provides information in a clear and concise way. The information can consist of facts, theories, reasons, description, or new ideas that must be written in a formal style. For students in academic courses, compositions are usually term/ research papers, reports, essay exams, or short written assignments. A sample expository essay appears on pages 56–60.

Before you do any type of writing, consider the **content**, **purpose**, **form**, and **audience** of your writing.

- **Content** is **what you want to say** or the information that needs to be expressed in your composition.
- **Purpose** is **what you want to accomplish** in your writing. In other words, you must know whether you want to persuade your reader logically, state facts, express personal views, or amuse the reader. This will affect the style of your writing (formal or informal), as well as the content and form.
- **Form** is **how the writing will be structured and organized**; for instance, book reviews, laboratory reports, and research papers have specific types of structures.
- **Audience** is **who you are writing for.** Like purpose, this will affect the style of your wording and the content. You need to determine the knowledge your particular audience has of your topic, which will in turn determine the vocabulary you choose and how much explanation of concepts you provide.

General Structure

The shape of expository essays may vary in many ways, but these parts are clearly evident in good essays:

- introductory paragraph(s)
- development paragraphs
- concluding paragraph(s)

In a short composition, there is only one introductory paragraph and one concluding paragraph, as shown in Figure 2.1.

Figure 2.1: Structure of a Sample Essay

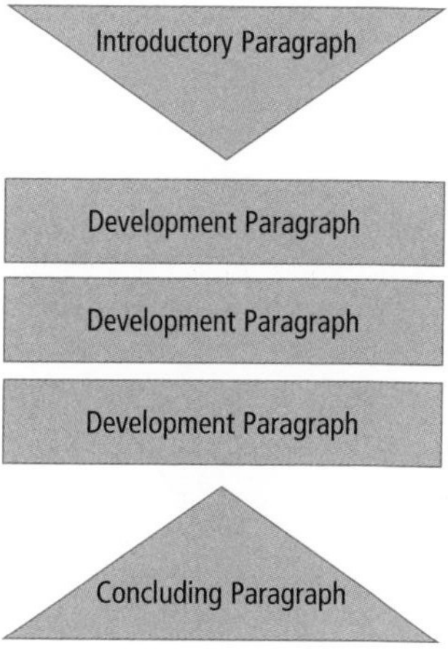

The number of development paragraphs depends on the number of key supporting ideas to be developed in the composition. It is common to have two to four main ideas (and thus, two to four development paragraphs) in an expository essay. Each paragraph has its own main idea that supports the main idea or thesis statement of the whole essay. Longer compositions may have introductions and conclusions consisting of more than one paragraph and more than four body paragraphs.

Introductory Paragraph(s)

WB
Ex. 2.5,
2.7

The first paragraph of an essay plays a very important role: It must clearly introduce the main idea of the essay and provide an idea of the direction that the essay will take, while making the topic interesting and meaningful to the reader. The **main idea sentence of the whole composition** is its thesis statement. Therefore, this main idea sentence is both a topic sentence (of the paragraph) and also a thesis statement (of the whole composition). Unlike topic sentences in the body paragraphs of the essay, which usually occur at the beginning of the paragraph, the thesis statement generally comes near the end of the introduction (see Figure 2.2).

In addition to telling readers the main idea of the composition, the first paragraph or introduction often signals **what the important supporting ideas of the essay are** and **how they will be arranged in the development paragraphs**. This foreshadows, or maps out, what readers will read in the body of the composition. In most expository essays, foreshadowing is necessary to provide the reader with a preliminary organization (or map) for what is contained in the essay.

Figure 2.2: Structure of an Introductory Paragraph

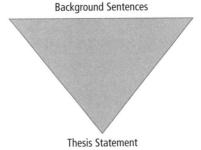

Background Sentences

Thesis Statement

Example of introductory paragraph

What is the best movie that you've ever seen? Each person who hears this question will probably have a different answer. Even if two people agree which movie is best, it may be for very different reasons. Some viewers love a particular movie because they connect with the characters in the story, while others value the artistry of the lighting and camera angles. Although people's tastes vary when it comes to deciding what makes a movie "good," certain features tend to influence people's judgment. The storyline, the lighting, the angles of the shots, and the editing all contribute to the quality of a film.

Development Paragraphs

The development paragraphs—also called the **body** of the essay—expand, support, and explain your main ideas. A shorter essay generally has two to four development paragraphs (depending on the number of main ideas) while the body of a research paper is generally much longer. **Each paragraph should focus on <u>one</u> main point that is clearly connected to the main thesis statement of the essay.** There are many ways to develop and support your ideas: examples, statistics, definitions, quotations from experts or outside sources, and explanations of your own ideas. For more explanation on developing body paragraphs, see pages 34–52.

Example of body paragraphs

A good storyline is, of course, the most obvious component to making a great movie. If you consider award-winning movies in the past—from *It Happened One Night* and *Citizen Kane* to *Gladiator*, *A Beautiful Mind*, and *The Lord of the Rings: Fellowship of the Ring*—they all share one characteristic: a good story. Whether a comedy, drama, science fiction, or action film, an excellent movie tells a story that is interesting on both an intellectual and an emotional level. Movie-goers love to be immersed in a story that begins with a conflict, rises in tension until the climax of the plot, and then comes to a resolution of the conflict by the end. People go to the movies to imagine, to be entertained, to think, and to escape, and a good storyline allows them to do all of this.

Many people don't realize that lighting also plays an important role in creating a good movie. Intensity of lighting directs the audience's attention to what the director wishes to highlight. For example, in spy movies, the actors' faces are often in shadows to highlight the theme: that these men and women work in secrecy. The direction of lighting is also important. The director can create shadows or eliminate them for a stark picture. Use of color is related to lighting and can be used to great effect, as in the movie *Hero* starring Jet Li; certain scenes were all red, seeming filled with passion, while in others, everything was white, which could symbolize purity or, in Asia, mourning, as white clothes are worn to a funeral. Lighting and color, therefore, can have a direct effect on viewers' emotions and can help create a great film.

Another important aspect of a film that may contribute to its greatness is the camera angle. In a great movie, the angles are like another character in the film: certain angles guide the audience to feel a certain way. For example, shots at eye level encourage the viewer to trust the character because it is like they are looking the viewer straight in the eye. Shots from below, on the other hand, make the character look larger than life, emphasizing his or her importance. If the audience views the character from above, the audience gets a feeling of power or omniscience. In a good movie, these angles seem natural to the audience and further the effect of the scene so that the movie has a greater impact on the audience.

Editing is a fourth aspect of a movie that can influence its quality. The director can choose to abruptly cut to the next scene, or gently lead into the next scene depending on the mood of the scene. He or she may choose to shoot the same scene from many different angles at varying distances to create a feeling of intense action, as is common in fight scenes. To show a passage of time, the director may fade in or out, or "wipe" the scene, using the image of a page turning, for example. In a film with good editing, the audience is never shocked by camera angles or scene transitions. The movie seems to flow naturally from one scene to the next. As with camera angles, editing acts as a character in the film, albeit an unseen one, to further the audience's involvement.

Concluding Paragraph(s)

WB
Ex. 2.6,
2.7

The conclusion is important because it is the last thing that your reader will remember. As a result, it should be written carefully, not quickly. The conclusion is similar in length to the introduction—just one paragraph for a shorter essay (three to six sentences, generally), but perhaps several paragraphs for a research paper or longer composition. The conclusion **restates, in different words, the ideas of the thesis statement**. Or it **summarizes** the main ideas, expresses a **logical conclusion**, or **suggests** areas for future research (if this is relevant). **It is very important not to introduce any new ideas in the conclusion.**

Example of concluding paragraph

While other aspects of a film do contribute to its success, these four elements—storyline, lighting, camera angle, and editing—are arguably the most important. A film with a strong storyline appeals to movie-goers and critics alike. The creative aspects of lighting and camera angle can add depth and emotion to the story, while careful editing aids in the flow of the story by building on the emotional intensity of each scene. All of these features work together to create a good movie. When done carefully and creatively, the result may be a truly great film that will be remembered and appreciated throughout the years.

Order of Information

In the body of an essay, the information may be presented several different ways. It is the writer who has to choose the order best suited to the purpose of the essay. **Importance, generality, familiarity,** and **chronology (time)** are essential criteria to keep in mind.

In an argument essay, for example, the writer may want to gradually build the argument with key points that get stronger, saving the most persuasive key point for last. (increasing order of importance)

Example outline: Increasing order of importance

Topic: Early education must be available free of charge to all children.

- Early education allows children to develop social skills.
- Early education teaches children academic skills that they will need in kindergarten.
- Early education helps children acquire enriched vocabulary and language skills.
- Early education results in higher achievement throughout children's academic careers.

A **classification** essay may progress from general categorization to more specific distinctions. (decreasing order of generalization)

Example outline: Decreasing order of generalization

Topic: Classification of the Swahili language

- Swahili belongs to the Niger-Kordofanian language family in Africa.
- Swahili is one of the Bantu languages (a sub-group of the Niger-Kordofanian family), which are spoken in the southern half of Africa.
- Swahili is a North-East Coastal Bantu language, spoken along the East African coast in Kenya, Tanzania, and portions of surrounding countries and islands.
- The numerous dialects of Swahili are divided into three general groups: Northern, Central, and Southern.

Or, in a **description** essay, the writer may decide that it is useful to start with an example that the reader is familiar with before continuing with less familiar aspects of the description. (decreasing order of familiarity)

Example outline: Decreasing order of familiarity

Topic: Tourist destinations in Paris
- Monuments: Eiffel Tower and Arc de Triomphe
- Museums: Musée d'Orsay and the Louvre
- Parks: Jardin du Luxembourg and Jardin des Tuileries

A **process** or **narrative** essay is usually written in chronological order, with the steps or events presented in the order in which they happen, from the first one to the last. (chronological order)

Example outline: Chronological order

Topic: The American electoral system
- Candidates register to run for an elected position.
- The field of candidates is narrowed in the primary election, usually in the springtime.
- Candidates campaign for office through advertisements, public appearances, and speeches.
- A winner is elected by the public in the general election, usually in the fall.

Or, an essay may have **neutral order**; in other words, there is no particular progression in the presentation of the ideas. The ideas in such an essay must be logically connected, but it is not necessary to place them in any specific order.

Example outline: Neutral order

Topic: How to make your home more energy efficient
- Seal around the edges of your windows and doors to maintain the temperature in your house.
- Install energy-efficient appliances and light bulbs.
- Plant trees that will shelter your house from summer sun and winter winds.

. . . .

Exercise 2.3: Ordering Information

Number these sentences to create outlines in the order that is specified.

1. **Chronological**

   The process of inventing something new

   ___ Experiment with ways to make your idea a reality.

   ___ Discover one method that is successful.

   ___ Seek out a way to produce your invention for sale to the general public.

   ___ Patent your invention.

   ___ Develop an idea that meets a need.

   ___ Experience failure in your creative experimentation.

   ___ Return to the idea phase and explore other ways of developing your idea.

2. **Importance—least to most**

   It is a good idea to carry a cell phone.

   ___ It can summon help in an emergency situation.

   ___ It can save you time and frustration when looking for a friend in a busy place.

   ___ It is convenient for staying connected with friends.

3. **Familiarity—most to least**

   A number of tools can be useful when hanging a picture on the wall.

   ___ A hammer allows you to pound in the picture hanger.

   ___ A stud-finder locates the sturdy beams within the walls.

   ___ A level helps to make sure that your picture is hung straight.

4. **Generality—most to least**

   ___ There are two main categories of trees: deciduous (which lose their leaves for part of the year) and evergreen (which keep their leaves year-round).

___ Every tree has a root system, a trunk, and branches with leaves. Its leaves absorb carbon dioxide and release oxygen into the air.

___ Red Maple, Silver Maple, and Sugar Maple are several of the varieties of maple trees that are popular for their shade and the fall colors of their leaves.

___ A small family of deciduous trees, maple trees are common in the temperate zones of the Northern Hemisphere.

Organizational Patterns

Well-written expository essays always follow the general pattern discussed so far (thesis statement, introduction, body paragraphs, and conclusion). Additionally, another element that must be considered in structuring essays is **organizational patterns related to the purpose or the type of effect the writer wants to create**. Writers may want to persuade, describe, classify, analyze, and so on. These patterns of organizing the text are often called rhetorical patterns because they deal with the art of composing effectively (rhetoric), whether in speaking or writing. The patterns reflect the ways readers think. The assignment instructions often give a clue as to the organizational pattern that the composition should follow.

Patterns of organization may include:

- **narration** (describing events in chronological order, telling a story)
- **process analysis** (describing stages or steps to complete a task)
- **comparison** (describing similarities and differences)
- **contrast** (describing differences)
- **analogy** (providing a comparison emphasizing similarities)
- **classification** (dividing and sorting into categories)
- **cause and effect** (describing what produces a certain result)
- **problem-solution** (describing a problem and explaining one or more solutions)
- **argument** (persuading a reader to agree with you)
- **analysis / logical division** (describing the component parts of something)

Other development techniques, such as **description**, **definition**, and **exemplification**, may be used along with these patterns of organization. These techniques are described on pages 34–47.

Combining Patterns of Organization

A common way to practice the rhetorical patterns in writing is to focus on a single pattern of organization for each essay. For example, a student may be asked to write a comparison essay or an essay describing a process. However, most writing does not follow just one method of organization. Essays typically combine different ways of arranging information because that is what is required to convey different aspects of the author's meaning.

That is, student papers and essays for academic classes often need to combine rhetorical patterns. Sometimes one pattern is dominant because the assignment cues indicate how the essay should be organized (see Section 3). Yet even in these cases, other patterns are also used in individual paragraphs within the essay. When writing, the writer must decide which pattern(s) to use overall for the essay, and then decide which patterns are most effective to illustrate the main point in each of the paragraphs.

See the essay on pages 95–99 for an example of an essay that combines patterns of organization, with one dominant pattern overall and other patterns evident in different paragraphs.

Examples: Combined Patterns in Essay Assignment Instructions

Comparison and contrast, classification, argument:

> <u>Compare different ways</u> of dealing with children's behavior problems in school. <u>Explain</u> which one you think is <u>best</u>, giving <u>good reasons</u> for your preference.

Analysis, process, exemplification:

> <u>What is democracy</u>? How would you explain the concept, <u>point by point</u>, to a group of young children? What <u>examples</u> might you give to help them understand?

. . . .

Exercise 2.4: Key Words* and Organizational Patterns in Writing Assignments

For each essay topic listed, underline the words that are important to doing the assignment correctly. Remember that the words used to describe the assignments offer important information about how to organize the essay. Then state which organizational patterns you would use. Explain your choices. Answers may vary depending on the emphasis a writer gives to different aspects of the topic. You may want to refer to Table 1.1.

1. **Topic:** Your company is deciding whether or not to switch to electric cars for business trips. Analyze the situation and offer an opinion as to which you would choose, being sure to support your choice with evidence and examples.

   Patterns: _____

   _____

2. **Topic:** Explain what friendship is, and give examples from your own life that reflect it.

   Patterns: _____

   _____

3. **Topic:** Professors are increasingly utilizing technology in the university classroom. Describe the changes in teaching methods, including classroom activities, that you think this use of technology is causing.

   Patterns: _____

   _____

4. **Topic:** Describe someone who has had a big influence on your life and tell how that person has influenced you.

   Patterns: _____

   _____

---

*We are using this term here to convey the broad range of language used (instructional, organizational, conceptual) in assignments and prompts and are not limiting its use only to key words about the topic/content.

Paragraph Development Techniques

Just as an essay has a thesis statement, the paragraphs within the essay each have a main idea that must be developed. Several ways to develop the main ideas—**description, figurative language, defining,** and **exemplification**—are described.

A **description** aims to create a clear, vivid picture for the reader. Although it is often used in creative writing or personal storytelling, descriptive language is also important in many types of academic writing, like historical narratives or laboratory process reports. Frequently, too, the purpose of descriptive writing is to thoroughly depict a person, place, or interesting scene.

WB Ex. 2.8

The purpose and audience of a description will influence the tone and emphasis of the description that a writer uses. Adjectives and expressions related to the human senses (taste, touch, sight, hearing, smell) and emotions are often used in description. Figurative language (comparisons using similes and metaphors) is also employed to help create an easily imagined mental picture for the reader.

- **Describing a Person.** Although there is no one way to do this, try to include information about the person's background, physical appearance, personality, occupation, and interests.
- **Describing a Place.** First, decide on the point of view of the description: think of yourself as the writer in a specific position in relation to the place (e.g., above, to one side). Provide some background, and then focus on the specific area for consideration.
- **Describing a Process.** A process is best described using chronological development, from first to last.

Suggestions for Effective Descriptions

- Be specific: avoid vague words.
- Choose formal or informal words according to your purpose and audience. Academic writing requires a formal style, but magazine or newspaper style is more informal.
- Be concise: keep your descriptions as short as possible without losing any of the meaning you want to express.
- Choose adjectives that help you create a vivid picture in the reader's mind. (See the list here and on page 36 for some examples of descriptive adjectives.)
- Use similes and metaphors appropriately for the type of writing and audience; personal writing is more suited to these than academic writing. For more on similes and metaphors, see page 37.
- In expository writing, provide direct, explicit descriptions.
- In personal writing, indirectness and hinting at extra meaning may be appropriate and effective in creating an atmosphere or mood.
- Provide sufficient relevant details and examples to build up a complete picture for the reader.

Useful Adjectives for Description

Many adjectives can contribute to making descriptions lively and clear. This is just a selection.

sight—*small, medium-sized, huge, tiny, delicate, bright, shady, tall, round, square, triangular, oval, shiny, wrinkled, dotted, green, violet, beige, dark, light, pale*

hearing—*loud, soft, harmonious, harsh, monotonous, pleasant, unpleasant, musical, noisy, grating, soothing, ear-splitting, quiet, roaring, squeaky*

taste—*sweet, sour, salty, bitter, rich, delicious, tasty, tasteless, bland, exotic, acidic*

touch—*rough, smooth, slippery, soft, hard, silky, cold, prickly, cool, warm, scratchy, damp, sticky*

> **smell**—*pleasant, unpleasant, strong, faint, scented, fragrant, acrid, rotten, sweet*
>
> **emotion/personality**—*thrilled, devastated, carefree, ecstatic, glum, sullen, reserved, gracious, contented, pompous, ashamed, dynamic, anxious, outgoing*
>
> **atmosphere/mood**—*expectant, hushed, chaotic, gloomy, cheery, somber, uncomfortable, celebratory, festive, jubilant, frenzied, tense, relaxed, awkward*

Exercise 2.5: Writing Descriptive Sentences

Write a sentence or two describing each phrase. Use specific and descriptive adjectives.

1. the moon

   _____

   _____

2. your phone

   _____

   _____

3. a favorite professor

   _____

   _____

4. a flower garden

   _____

   _____

5. your best friend

_____

_____

6. a concert

_____

_____

7. your breakfast this morning

_____

_____

Similes and metaphors are types of **figurative language** that allow a writer to provide a descriptive image of an object, person, or idea. This is accomplished through comparison of two things that are generally not alike. Similes use the words _as_ or _like_ to make the connection between the two things being compared. Metaphors generally use _is_ (or other forms of the verb _to be_) to make the comparison (but not the words _like_ or _as_).

Examples: Similes and Metaphors

simile: My art instructor, Ms. Morales, was **as beautiful as a butterfly**.

simile: When she spoke, her smile was **like the sunshine** and her voice was **like a gentle breeze**.

metaphor: Her bright, billowing dresses **were her wings** as she moved gracefully around the room.

. . . .

Exercise 2.6: Description: Similes and Metaphors

A. Write a simile or a metaphor for each topic in the space provided.
B. Develop one of these topics into a descriptive paragraph that includes similes, metaphors, and descriptive adjectives. Then write the paragraph on a separate sheet of paper.

1. my hometown _____

_____

2. the forest _____

_____

3. a family celebration_____

_____

4. war_____

_____

5. the internet _____

_____

6. children playing_____

_____

7. grief_____

_____

8. language_____

_____

Example Paragraphs: Personal Description

In these examples of personal writing, notice that many similes and metaphors are used. Adjectives are used to create a vivid emotional picture. Indirectness creates atmosphere and mood. Word choice is specific and informal. Details and examples build a complete, concise picture. Similes, metaphors, and descriptive adjectives are in bold.

From an essay on living in another country

I come from a country that has **little** variation in the seasons: one season is **hot** and **wet**; the other is **cool** and **dry**. Coming to a place with four seasons has been a particularly **wonderful** experience because I love walking. I consider walking my hobby: I did it a lot in my country and I do the same here. It is **like a medicine** for me, protecting my **mental** and **physical** health. I am very **lucky** because I now live in an area that is **perfect** for walking, so I often walk between my apartment and the university for my English classes. In this city, the **rich** colors of the different seasons are fascinating. Most of all, I love the fall when I watch the leaves gradually change from **green** to **brown**, **red**, **orange**, and **yellow**. Then in winter the **blanket of sparkling snow** and the **white cotton puffs** on the **dark**, **leafless** tree branches make me feel **as if I am in a different world**, especially when I take an **early morning** walk as the **gentle** light of dawn **creeps up the sky**. As winter moves into spring I keep a close watch on the **fresh green** colors that start off **light green** and become **darker** as summer arrives. Even in the summer heat when the humidity is **high** and the rain soaks my skin **like a bath**, I feel **relaxed**. The changing seasons are **food for my busy thoughts and tired eyes**. Because of my love of nature I observe carefully; I see a **new universe in each gradual change** throughout the seasons. I am a traveler in a **strange** world where everything is always **being born again** in nature.

From an essay about a family member

I remember watching her as she carefully bent over to remove the bread pans from the oven that she had used for fifty years. As she set the bread on the counter to cool, the light would shine through her **soft**, **white** hair, making it look **like a halo**. Every year more wrinkles appeared on her **thinning** face; every year she walked a **little** more slowly and got up from her chair with a **little** more difficulty. But her **sapphire** eyes still shone with love whenever she looked at me, her only grandchild. Patiently, she watched as I carefully helped her measure ingredients for the bread she made every week, **smiling like an angel**. She would put her hand, with its **hard** and **ropy** veins, on my **small** child's hands as I stirred. Then we would knead the dough together. With a "slap, slap" on the table, laughing softly, we would mold the dough, mixing it, allowing the yeast to begin its work. The warmth of the oven **was a blanket that wrapped us in comfort**. Because of these days with my grandmother, baking bread is even now not the **boring** task it could be, but an act of love.

Example Paragraphs: Academic Description

In these examples of expository writing, notice that the writing is formal and direct. Similes and metaphors are not used. Adjectives are neutral in feeling. Word choice is specific and formal. Details and examples build a complete, concise picture.

From an essay on the history of the French language

During the nineteenth century, a period of **internal struggle** over the establishment of French as a nationally used language, the European elite was adopting the language as its own. French became a status symbol of sorts, representing a **high level** of education, **refined** culture, **distinguished** heritage, and **elegant sophistication**. The European aristocracy, in its desire to appear **educated** and **forward-thinking**, **eagerly embraced** the philosophical and political ideals of the French Revolutionary era, along with the language in which they originated. Essentially, the European acceptance of French as the **preeminent** language of Western culture, and the subsequent radiation of the language beyond Europe, were **significant** elements in the formation of French linguistic identity.

From an essay on national identity

The combination of the concepts of nation and identity creates the **complex** and **comprehensive** notion of national identity, a term that has found its way into social science with **increasing frequency** in recent years. By associating the idea of identity with that of nationality, it becomes clear that the nation is a **significant** source of identity for most humans, particularly since both concepts involve a sense of **commonality** and **uniqueness** with respect to other persons. The sense of uniqueness provided by a strong national identity is **closely connected** to a **prevalent** sense of superiority that stems from pride in one's **exclusive** heritage. Once a community has recognized itself as **distinct** from surrounding groups, it has established an identity, in this case, a national identity.

In much of your academic writing, you will have to **define** terms or concepts. You may define a word or you may provide an extended definition of a complex idea. Always keep in mind that there are two key elements in a definition: (1) a statement about the **general category** that the word or concept belongs to and (2) a description of **how the word or concept is different** from others in the general category.

WB
Ex. 2.9,
2.10

Example: Simple Definition

Definition of *pencil*
General category: an instrument
Differences:

- used for writing or drawing (unlike a hammer, for example)
- can be held in one hand (unlike a computer keyboard, for example)
- uses a thin rod of graphite or colored wax as the marker (unlike a pen or paint brush, for example)
- usually in a cylindrical casing made of wood or plastic

Simple definition:
   A pencil is a writing instrument with a cylindrical casing made of wood or plastic that contains graphite as a marker.

Example: Complex Definition

Definition of *monarchy*

General category: a type of government

Differences:

- rule by one person or royal family
- ruler's power inherited from a parent (unlike an elected leader, for example)
- ruler has absolute power (unlike democratic rule, for example)
- ruler's position is held for life (unlike an elected president, for example)
- possible variations and combinations of the following: absolute monarchies, with all power in the hands of one person; parliamentary monarchies, with some power in the hands of an elected governing body; constitutional monarchies, in which the monarch's function is more ceremonial.

Complex definition (a paragraph from an essay on systems of government):

Monarchy is one of the oldest systems of government in the world. This system places absolute power in the hands of one person, usually for life, which is much different from democratic forms of government. The monarch generally inherits the position from a member of his or her family, known in most cases as the royal family. There are many forms of monarchy, ranging from absolute monarchy to parliamentary and constitutional monarchy. The latter share a portion of power with another governing body such as a parliament.

Exercise 2.7: Writing Definitions

A. Write a simple definition for these words. Then choose one word and develop a one-paragraph complex definition for it. Write the paragraph on a separate sheet of paper.

1. library _____

2. failure _____

3. music _____

4. relaxation _____

5. culture _____

B. Choose a term from your field of study or a class you are currently taking. Write a simple definition for this term, and then write a one-paragraph complex definition. Write your definition, but write the paragraph on a separate sheet of paper.

Simple definition:

_____

_____

Providing effective **examples in writing** is very important. In an argument paper, for instance, good examples may help to reinforce your position and persuade the reader. In an expository essay, well-chosen examples clarify your presentations of facts and ideas.

Illustrations are lengthy examples and usually require several sentences rather than a few words or phrases.

WB
Ex. 2.11

> ▸ ▸ ▸ **Usage Note**
>
> In a different sense, **illustrations** can also refer to graphics, such as photographs, charts, diagrams, or drawings; these also clarify and support what is written in the text.

Useful Words and Expressions for Introducing Examples

Transitions

> Certain rapidly spreading plants, _____ knotweed and bamboo, are not native to the northeastern United States.

> **such as**
> **including**
> **for example**
> **for instance**

Whether used in the middle or at the beginning of a sentence, the phrases *for example* and *for instance* must always be followed by a comma. These two phrases can also be used at the beginning of a sentence:

> _____ , the very popular butterfly bush has been planted so extensively that it commonly invades other habitats and displaces native plants.

> **For example**
> **For instance**

> Barberry, _____, was introduced by European settlers as an ornamental plant in the late 19th century and is now considered invasive.

> **for example**
> **for instance**

Sentence Beginners

> Some non-native invasive plants are so widespread that they are commonly seen in the wild. _____ bristled knotweed, orange daylily, and Canada thistle.

> **These include**
> **Examples include**

. . . .

Exercise 2.8: Writing Example Sentences

Write an example to support each of these sentences using the phrase indicated in bold.

1. If you want to make your diet healthier, there are several simple changes you can make._____

   _____

   _____ [**for example**]

2. Mass transportation, _____

   _____

   [**such as**], is an important part of any major city's infrastructure.

3. The East African savannah is home to several large predatory animals. _____

   _____

   _____ [**for instance**]

4. Serious illness has a significant impact not only on the ill patient's life, but also on the lives of her immediate family and close friends. _____

   _____

   _____ [**for example**]

5. It is not difficult for college students to integrate volunteer activities

   _____

   _____ [**such as**] into their lives.

When writing examples, consider these features:

- **Appropriateness of Examples (Relevant or Representative Examples).** The key point to remember is that it must truly represent the larger group that the example belongs to and must directly support the point you want to make. That is, it must be appropriate or relevant.
- **Number of Examples.** It is important to think about how many examples to use. Sometimes long lists of examples lose their force because they overwhelm the reader. Typically, readers prefer to be given fewer well-chosen and relevant examples rather than a list of many.
- **Order of Examples.** When presenting several examples in a paragraph or an essay, start with the least familiar or most interesting one to get the reader's attention. Alternatively, if the essay introduces an unfamiliar or complex topic, begin with the most familiar point.

Example Paragraph: Presenting Examples

From an essay on politics and citizenship

These dynamics and features determine not just the role that every actor would play in domestic policies, but also the informal and real socio-political framework in which citizens and state interact and exchange goods and services, as well as values and principles. On the one hand, the implicit role of citizens consists of a variety of activities. **For instance**, citizens may help to build social policies, channel social problems and solutions, practice civil and political rights, and control the state's performance. On the other hand, the role of the state is stated formally in the National Constitution and it is an extension of the power of the citizens. However, the state, without a very well-developed citizenry with a proper discretionary power, can drift away from its natural role. Its performance can then be inefficient regarding its capacity to govern, as, **for example**, in the correct use of the military, management of the economy, and organizing elections.

. . . .
Exercise 2.9: Using Examples in a Paragraph

Write a paragraph on a separate piece of paper that uses examples to demonstrate the importance of the internet in the world today.

Unity and Coherence

Expository paragraphs and essays achieve their purpose most effectively when they have the qualities of unity and coherence. Writing that has these qualities leaves a clear, single impression in the mind of the reader. A text that has unity and coherence is meaningful and logical in its arrangement of ideas.

An essay has **unity** when the main idea of each development paragraph is clearly connected to the thesis statement expressed in the first paragraph or introduction. The main ideas of the development paragraphs should be more specific than the thesis statement (the main idea of the whole essay), and they should all be clearly related to the thesis statement. Similarly, the development sentences in a single paragraph are more specific than the topic sentence of that paragraph, and they need to all clearly support the topic sentence of that paragraph.

WB
Ex. 2.12

When the sentences in a paragraph follow logically from each other, the paragraph has **coherence**. When the parts of an essay (paragraphs) are linked in a way that is logical and meaningful, the essay has coherence since it makes good sense as a whole.

WB
Ex. 2.13,
2.14

Paragraphs and essays can be made more coherent by use of effective **transitions** (like *however* or *in addition*), repetition of key words, and clear use of **reference words** (such as *it, they, these, most of which*). Note that transitions may be single words, phrases, clauses, sentences, and paragraphs. **Transition sentences** connect paragraphs in longer essays by referring to a previously mentioned idea and indicating what the next paragraph will discuss. **Transition paragraphs** connect sections of longer papers in a similar way.

Transitions

- **Transition Words or Phrases between Sentences.** Some transitions for creating different logical relationships between sentences are listed. More detailed lists of useful expressions are provided with various organizational patterns in Sections 3 and 7. Using transitions effectively makes your writing flow logically and therefore makes it more easily understood by your reader. Use these words accurately, and be careful not to overuse them.

Useful Transitions for Unity and Coherence

sequence—*now, first, second, third . . . , next, then, prior to, before, last, finally*

comparison emphasizing similarities (analogy)— *in the same way, similarly, likewise*

comparison emphasizing differences (contrast)—*yet, however, nevertheless*

cause and effect—*therefore, thus, as a result, consequently*

emphasis—*in fact, indeed, again*

addition—*also, furthermore, in addition*

exemplification—*for example, for instance*

concluding and summarizing—*in conclusion, to sum up, finally, in short, in brief, all in all, last*

- **Transition Sentences between Paragraphs.** Just as the sentences within a paragraph must follow logically from one to the next, the paragraphs that make up the entire essay should also have a logical progression. To achieve this, use transition sentences in between paragraphs to show how one paragraph is related to the next.

Examples: Transition Sentences

There are three more issues to consider. The first issue. . . .

While it's true that there are advantages to this situation, there are also disadvantages. . . .

This is a difficult problem to address, but there are several viable solutions. . . .

. . . .

Exercise 2.10: Transition Words and Phrases

WB
Ex. 2.15,
2.16

Use transition words or phrases to link each pair of sentences. Add commas where necessary. Answers will vary.

1. **sequence**

   When I decided to study in the U.S., there were many things I had to do. _____ I had to decide on a university. _____ I filled out an application. _____ I had to wait to be accepted.

2. **addition**

   Caffeine can impact the quality of your sleep at night. _____ it can cause your body to crave it so that if you don't drink it, you will get a headache.

3. **cause and effect**

   So many people are eating out nowadays. _____ restaurants are always busy, so service is often poor.

4. **exemplification**

   Companies who sell products online often send customers surveys to maintain customer service. _____ a week after you make a purchase online, you may receive an email asking you to answer questions about your satisfaction with the website, the delivery, and/or the quality of the product.

5. **emphasis**

The governor said that the news reporter had called him a liar. _____ the journalist had said no such thing; he had only claimed that the governor's statement should be carefully evaluated.

6. **comparison expressing similarity**

An increasing number of people are calling Uber® if they need a ride rather than a taxi company. _____ people are also calling Lyft.®

Example Paragraph: Unity and Coherence

This paragraph has the qualities of unity and coherence. It has a clear main idea and all the development sentences provide information or opinions that are relevant to that main idea. The paragraph therefore has unity. In addition, each sentence is logically and clearly linked to the ideas expressed in the sentences that come before and after it, making the paragraph coherent.

From an essay on culture shock

If you have studied in a foreign country, chances are you have experienced some form of **culture shock. This phenomenon** generally progresses through **several stages**. Becoming familiar with **the stages** can help you deal with each stage more easily. **The first stage** is the "honeymoon" stage. At **this stage**, everything about the foreign country is appealing. The differences between your country and the country you are visiting make the new country seem fresh and exciting. **Second, however**, is the rejection stage. During **this period**, what seemed charming only days or weeks before is now frustrating. You get tired of having to live your life the way people do in the new culture you are living in. You may think, "Why can't they just act like people from my culture?" If you remain abroad, though, you will reach the **third stage**, adjustment. You will begin to adapt to the new culture and see that it is not all bad. **Finally**, you will reach the acceptance stage. **At this point**, you will realize that the foreign country is different from your home country, but those differences, instead of seeming alien and unacceptable, will seem interesting. You may even come to prefer some things about the foreign country you are visiting. In conclusion, if you are studying abroad, **culture shock** is unavoidable, but familiarizing yourself with **these stages** can help you to adjust to your new home with less stress.

C. Re-Reading and Revising the Essay

Once your essay is finished, it is important to take time to read it carefully and to make revisions that will improve the content, clarity, unity, and coherence of your writing. (Be sure to allow enough time for this step! Finishing your first draft just a few hours before it is due will usually not allow sufficient time to effectively re-read and revise your essay.) Some guidance to help in the revising process follows (see also Step 7 in the 10-Step Guide to the Writing Process):

- Set your essay aside for a while—a few hours, or even a day or two—before you read it again. Taking some time to not think about your writing can help you look at it with a fresh perspective when you sit down to re-read and revise it.
- Look at your composition from an outside point of view— imagine that you are a professor, colleague, or reviewer as you read. This will help you to evaluate your ideas, organization, and clarity in a more impartial way.

- If you find that you need to re-read a sentence or a paragraph because it was confusing, take another look at it. Do not skip it. Confusion is probably a sign that there is a problem with the ideas, the grammatical structure, or the logical connections in your writing.

- Ask someone else to read your composition—a friend, a colleague, or perhaps a tutor in the Writing Center at your university. Input from another reader can be helpful in identifying aspects of your writing that are confusing, repetitive, or awkward. Keep in mind that a friend's feedback may be different from a Writing Center tutor's or a professor's (who are experts in evaluating writing). Think about each comment or suggestion you receive, and make changes based on what you, the writer, think is appropriate.

- Think about the overall main idea of your essay, and look at how the body paragraphs support that main idea. To evaluate the connection between the ideas in your writing, write the main idea(s) of every body paragraph in the margin, and then look at how the ideas relate. (This is sometimes called **glossing** or **back-outlining**.) Again, if you find yourself confused or unsure about how an idea connects, think carefully about how you can revise that section to make it clearer. This technique is also a good way to check for good transitions between your ideas.

- Editing for mechanics (grammar, spelling, punctuation, and formatting) can be quite challenging and tedious, but it is an important step in writing a great composition. Once you are confident that the content and organization are satisfactory, read your essay line by line, sentence by sentence to check the mechanics (not thinking about meaning unless you find a sentence confusing for some reason). Keep in mind that an outside reader is often better at finding mechanics errors than the writer.

D. A 10-Step Guide to the Writing Process

Use this guide as you work on any writing assignment.

1. Read the assignment carefully. Notice the key words, and decide which organizational pattern(s) you should use.

2. Generate ideas using a technique of your choice.

3. Organize your ideas into a preliminary outline.

4. Evaluate whether you have enough ideas and whether your ideas fulfill the assignment. If not, use idea-generating techniques to expand or improve your ideas.

5. Create a more developed outline for your essay.

6. Write a complete draft of your essay.

7. Use this checklist to evaluate the content and organization before going on to the next step, the final draft.

    _____ a. Are your ideas well developed? Is there enough content?

    _____ b. Is your organization logical? Are your ideas arranged clearly using appropriate patterns of development?

    _____ c. Is there balance among the introduction, body, and conclusion? Is the body much longer than the introduction and conclusion?

    _____ d. Is there a clear thesis statement in the introduction?

    _____ e. Is there foreshadowing in the introduction that signals specific main points of the development?

    _____ f. Is there a clear topic sentence expressing the main ideas for each development paragraph?

    _____ g. Are there effective transitions between paragraphs?

    _____ h. Are there effective transitions between ideas within paragraphs so that the sentences are clearly connected?

    _____ i. Does the conclusion restate the main idea and offer a logical conclusion for the composition?

8. Re-read and revise your essay for the final draft. Check for clarity, unity, coherence, and organization now that you have finished revising based on your checklist in Step 7.

9. Edit your draft for correct mechanics. Check the grammar, spelling, punctuation, and formatting.

10. Finally, give your essay a title that concisely expresses its topic.

E. Sample Essay

The student essay on pages 56–60 provides good examples of many of the structural and organizational points mentioned in this unit. Some are indicated in the margin notes. Notice also these features of the essay:

- Order of information: neutral order (not specifically ordered by importance, generality, or familiarity)
- Development techniques: description and examples
- Unity and coherence: All paragraphs relate to the main idea of the essay; development details relate to the topic sentence for each paragraph; and many transition words and one transition sentence are used.
- Organizational patterns:
  › contrast—main pattern of the whole essay (Chinese vs. American educational systems)
  › process analysis—basis of Paragraphs 4 and 5 (teachers' procedure in explaining concepts)
  › analysis / logical division—in thesis statement of the introduction (analysis indicates several areas of difference, and the author selects two as focus of essay)
  › narration—first sentence of the introduction (author mentions sequence of education in China and then in U.S.)
  › cause and effect—in Paragraph 3 and in the topic sentence of the conclusion (culture causes the differences in educational approaches)

University Classes in China and the United States

I received my university education in my country, China, and now I am studying at a university in the United States. **I have found that the two university systems have significant differences in several areas, including the interaction between teachers and students, and the amount and type of in-class explanation by teachers.** It is not surprising that the classroom practices in each of these countries reflect important contrasts between Eastern and Western cultures.

Overall, classes in China are still and quiet. Desks are set in straight rows, and students sit silently during class listening to the teacher and taking notes. It is very rare to see a hand raised in a classroom in China. Students do not ever question or confront their teachers in class. Even when students have questions, they refrain from asking them, because doing so is seen as being disrespectful to the teacher. *Instead*, if students have a question, they usually wait until after class to talk to the teacher individually. The teacher is *therefore*

INTRODUCTION

Context given in first sentence (author's personal experience)

Thesis statement giving **main idea** of essay (*educational differences*) and **foreshadowing key issues** of development paragraphs (*interaction, explanation*)

DEVELOPMENT (4 PARAGRAHS FOLLOWING INTRODUCTORY PARAGRAPH)

Topic sentence (*classes in China overall*)

Paragraph development (desks in rows, no questions during class, testing, respect)

Transition

Transition

never questioned or challenged in class. *In addition,* in order to check students' understanding of concepts introduced in class, teachers often use tests and quizzes instead of asking and answering questions. *Thus,* students do not receive feedback in class on their comprehension of the material. Chinese students are taught from a very young age to respect their teachers, and part of that respect is remaining quiet in class and not putting the teacher in a position in which he or she will feel challenged in front of the students.

In contrast, **the environment of classrooms in the United States is dynamic and animated.** One can often find desks in a U.S. classroom arranged in a circle, as opposed to in rows. Students frequently raise their hands while the teacher is speaking, so the teacher's lecture is often interrupted with students' questions. Sometimes, more than one student speaks at a time, to express their opinions on the topic of the class. Not only are students able to ask the teacher questions during the lecture when they do not understand, but they may even openly disagree with the teacher. *Moreover,* teachers do not become angry when students

[margin notes]

Transition

Transition

Transition + **topic sentence** (classes in U.S. overall)

Paragraph development (desks in circle, student questions in class)

Transition

do this, and even encourage them to ask questions and state their opinions during class. International students may find classrooms in the U.S. to be loud and disorderly. *However*, just as the quietness of Chinese classrooms reflects cultural values in China, so does the liveliness of U.S. classrooms reflect American culture and beliefs. Students learn that it is acceptable, even desirable, to question or challenge their teachers because it shows that they are able to form their own opinions and think for themselves.

Chinese teachers and the United States teachers also diverge in the amount of in-class explanation. **In Chinese culture, a teacher is viewed as another parent to the students; therefore, teachers must be detailed and patient.** Normally, before starting a new unit, Chinese teachers ask the students to preview it and ask questions about it to check their understanding of the new concepts. *However*, in class, teachers still explain the text in detail, because part of the job of the teacher in China is to explain everything clearly to the students. *Thus*, students frequently do not preview the new unit because they know that the teacher will explain the

Margin annotations:

Transition

Transition sentence

Topic sentence (teacher's role in China)

Transition

Paragraph development (teacher explains everything for students)

Transition

important information to them in the following class.

On the other hand, **in the United States, teachers are not expected to explain the material in-depth to the students to the extent that their Chinese counterparts are.** Teachers in the U.S. also ask students to preview the text before class and often assign homework to help them understand the new concepts. *However,* when they begin the new material in class, teachers in the U.S. do not spend a great deal of time explaining the concepts. *Instead,* they choose a select number of important points and ask students about them in class in order to check both that the students have done the assignment and that they have understood the material. For the remaining portion of class, after the students have asked questions about what they have not understood, the teacher tries to begin a discussion about the students' opinions and feelings. It is believed that it is more efficient for the teacher and the students if the students have already read the material before class. This way, class time is not spent explaining the text in detail, but addressing the confusion that students may have about it.

> Transition +
> **topic sentence**
> (teacher's role in U.S.)

> Transition

> Transition
>
> **Paragraph development**
> (teachers explain important points only, teachers question students in class, students ask questions in class, discussion)

In conclusion, **within the two educational systems, the ways in which teachers and students differ in the U.S. and China are a result of important contrasts between Chinese and American culture.** As mentioned, the first important difference is the relationship of teacher and students, in which students' respect for the teacher leads to a quiet atmosphere. *The second important contrast* is in the depth, amount, and style of explanation, with American teachers expecting students to prepare outside of class and to think critically about the new information. Both approaches may have advantages and disadvantages for the students and the teacher, but neither way of conducting class is superior to the other. Individuals may prefer one system or the other, but overall each style is reflective of and appropriate for its cultural setting.

CONCLUSION

Transition + **topic sentence** restating main idea of essay

Key issues of essay development mentioned again (interactions, explanations)

Transition

Author ends with **opinion** (neither educational system is superior; each is culturally appropriate to its setting)

PATTERNS OF ESSAY ORGANIZATION

3

Most essays and papers combine patterns of development (see pages 31–33), but there are several types that are especially useful in academic writing: narrative, process, comparison and contrast, cause and effect, and argument. You should study these carefully in order to improve your skill in using them separately or in combination with each other. The patterns are described and expressions associated with them are listed with sample paragraphs and related exercises.

> **▸ ▸ ▸ Usage Note**
>
> The useful words and expressions for each writing pattern are organized according to grammatical function. Pay careful attention to the **punctuation** used in example sentences because some connecting words are followed by a comma, while others are not. Also, sometimes connecting words such as *of* or *that* are key elements of a phrase.
>
> It is helpful to remember these ways that certain grammatical terms are used:
>
> **Conjunctions** are used to connect two independent clauses.
>
> **Transitions** are used at the beginning of an independent clause.
>
> **Subordinating conjunctions** begin a dependent clause. The dependent clause must be connected to an independent clause.

A. Narrative Essay

WB
Ex. 3.1

Purpose: To tell a story, often about things that happened in the past; to guide readers through past events

Organization: Chronological. Usually from past to present, but may move from present to past

Verb Tenses: Mostly past tenses:
1. simple past
2. past continuous
3. past perfect

Types of Narrative Writing:

General—describes a sequence of events or actions

Biography—tells about the life of someone other than the writer

Autobiography—tells about the writer's own life

Useful Words and Expressions for Narrative

Transitions

_____ we had a barbecue in the park.

To start with,   **Second,**
First (of all),   **Third,**

_____ we walked along the edge of the lake.

Next,   **Later,**
Then   **After that,**

Fireworks started going off. _____ the band began to play music.

Simultaneously,   **Suddenly,**
At the same time,   **Finally,**
Immediately,   **At last,**

Subordinating Conjunctions

_____ we watched the fireworks, we had a barbecue in the park.

Before
After
While

Adjectives

The _____ week we had bought some of our own fireworks.

previous   **preceding**

The _____ day we went on a picnic and set off our fireworks.

following

. . . .

Exercise 3.1: Connecting Ideas in Narrative Writing

Fill in the blanks with the most appropriate word from the Useful Words and Expressions box on page 63. Answers may vary.

Let me tell you about a scary day in the chemistry lab. It was the first experiment my partner and I had ever done. ① _____ we performed the experiment, we checked all of our equipment to ensure it had been properly cleaned. ② _____ we poured our first solution into a beaker. ③ _____ adding this solution, we heated it. ④ _____ we added a second solution to the first. ⑤ _____, the color changed from yellow to green. ⑥ _____, it began to emit smoke. ⑦ _____, we dumped it down the sink, scared that it might explode! Unfortunately, we had obtained the correct reaction, but we got an F on the assignment since the professor had not seen our work. In the end, this was not only a scary day, but an unhappy one as well.

Ordering Events: Using *When* and *While*

When indicates that two things happened in the past in a particular order—one happened **before** the other (although the two events may have occurred almost simultaneously).

<u>Examples</u>

> When I graduated from college, I <u>decided</u> that I wanted to be a teacher.
>
> *The writer first graduated from college. Later the writer decided to become a teacher.*
>
> He <u>wrote</u> his autobiography when he retired.
>
> *First, he retired. Then he wrote his autobiography.*

> ▸ ▸ ▸ **Usage Note**
>
> **Whenever** may also be used when an action happens many times:
>
> **Whenever** my uncle came to visit, he would bring us gifts from exotic places.

While indicates that two actions happened **in the same time frame,** sometimes with both happening at the same time.

<u>Examples</u>

> She <u>rode</u> her bicycle in the park while the others <u>played</u> soccer.
>
> *She rode her bicycle. At the same time, others played soccer.*
>
> While she <u>was riding</u> her bicycle in the park, the others <u>were playing</u> soccer.
>
> *She was riding her bicycle. During the same period of time, the others were playing soccer.*
>
> While she <u>was reading</u>, she <u>heard</u> a loud noise outside the window.
>
> *She was reading. During that same time, she heard the noise.*
>
> The doorbell <u>rang</u> while he <u>was cooking</u> dinner.
>
> *He was cooking dinner. At the same time he was cooking dinner, the doorbell rang.*

Verb Tense Consistency in Narrative Writing

Narrative writing in the form of a personal or historical example may be used to demonstrate a point the writer is trying to make. Generally the verb tense used is past tense, as narrative is a story that took place in the past. What comes before the narrative and/ or after the narrative may be in a different tense if the narrative is not the main focus of the writing. You must be sure to use tense accurately as you move into and away from the narrative to avoid confusing the reader.

Some general guidelines are:

1. If you are talking about an **event in the past**, use the **past tense.***
2. If you are talking about a **fact**, something that is true in the past, present, and future (so far as you know), use the **present tense.**
3. If you are talking about something that was **true in the past** and is **still true now** (without considering the future), use the **present perfect tense.**

Example Essay: Narrative

[adapted from a student essay; useful expressions are in **bold**]

Topic: Communicating in a second language

When communicating in English with my American friends, sometimes a serious misunderstanding occurs. Though I know such misunderstandings are natural since I am a non-native speaker of English, I am embarrassed each time it happens. The most recent example of miscommunication happened just last week.

It began when I went out to lunch with an American friend of mine, Jennifer. We had a good time and enjoyed the food

---

*Sometimes an idea may *still be true*, but you are focusing on a past example of that idea, so you should use the past tense.

very much. **When the bill came**, I saw that it was $15. Since I had only a $20 bill, I thought I would pay for lunch, and later she could give me half of the total. I said to her, "I'll pay, because I have big money." I saw her expression change from smiling to confused. She had taken her wallet out of her purse, but **after I said this**, she put her wallet back into her purse and seemed very uncomfortable. **When we left the restaurant**, I was just about to ask her for half of the bill when she said, "Well, Chiharu, thank you for the meal." **Now** I was confused. I had not intended to treat her to lunch, but **at that point**, I thought that it would have been rude to ask her for the money.

On my way home, I kept thinking about what had happened, and I was wondering about my saying, "I have big money." **As soon as** I got back to my apartment, I called a good friend of mine, Chris, to tell her what had happened. **After I told her the whole story**, she burst out laughing and said, "Chiharu, if you say 'I have big money,' that usually means 'I am rich.'" **At that moment**, I could feel my face turning red with embarrassment.

After Chris and I got off the phone, I decided that I had to clarify what I meant with Jennifer, no matter how ashamed I was. **The next day**, I called Jennifer to explain what I meant. Just like Chris, Jennifer laughed and said, "I thought that was what you wanted to say. I wanted to pay for half of the bill, but **when you said that**, I didn't know if it was because that's what you meant, or if you actually meant something else." Although I was still sorry that my mistake had caused all of this confusion, I was very relieved to know that she understood and that it was not so serious after all. **Then** it was my turn to laugh **when Jennifer said on the phone**, "Next time I'll treat you to lunch, Chiharu. Maybe on payday, because then I'll have big money!"

Write a Narrative Essay

Now it's your turn. Using the suggested phrases and expressions, organizational strategies, and verb tenses, write a narrative essay. Choose one of these topics, or come up with your own topic (with your instructor's approval).

1. Describe how you spend a typical weekend.
2. Describe what happened during a time of your life that was very important to you.
3. Tell the story of how you decided on your field of study or area of work.
4. Describe your experiences when learning another language.

B. Process Essay

Purpose: To give instructions on how to carry out a particular process, generally informal; to describe or explain how a process works

Examples: recipes, instruction manuals, and travel directions

Organization: Chronological/step-by-step

Verb Tenses: Can vary:

1. imperative verbs (commands), modals for advice (*should, must, ought to*), and second-person pronouns (*you*) to give instructions
2. present tense to describe how a process works
3. past tense to describe a process that happened in the past

Types of Process Writing:

Instructional or How To—often used in non-academic situations; generally informal

Examples: recipes and instruction manuals

Explaining or Describing—frequently used in a variety of academic fields; more formal

Examples: **how** a volcano is formed (geology), **how** the modern nation-state emerged (history/politics), **how** a child learns to speak (linguistics/psychology)

WB
Ex. 3.3

Useful Words and Expressions for Process

Nouns

_____ was the centralization of political power.

The first step
The final stage

Transitions

_____ the feudal socio-economic system of Medieval Europe began to disintegrate.

Firstly,	**Before that,**
First (of all),	**After that,**
In the first stage,	**Then**
During the first stage,	**Finally,**
Second,	**Lastly,**
Next,	

_____ the Magna Carta limited the king's power and strengthened the rights of nobles.

To start this process,
To begin with,
At first,

_____ a centralized government was established in England.

At the end of this process,

Subordinating Conjunctions

_____ the French monarchy was overthrown, the French Republic was established.

After	**When**
Before	**As soon as**
Once	

Adjectives

The _____ stage was a significant one in the development of the modern nation-state.

initial	**subsequent**
following	**previous**
succeeding	

Exercise 3.2: Connecting Ideas to Describe a Process

WB
Ex. 3.4

Part 1. Put the steps about the formation of a hurricane in logical order by numbering them 1–5. The first one has been done for you as an example.

_____ a.   The hurricane moves over land or cooler water: it loses strength and its winds decrease until it is no longer considered a hurricane.

__1__ b.   A tropical depression takes warm air from the surface of the ocean and pushes it upward, causing rotating wind patterns to develop.

_____ c.   The hurricane continues to gain strength as it pulls moisture from the surface of warm waters (80 degrees F or warmer).

_____ d.   Winds reach 39 mph, and the system is labeled a tropical storm and given a name.

_____ e.   The storm takes a cyclonic form, with an eye of moist, hot air in its center, and winds of at least 74 mph. It is now considered a hurricane.

Part 2. Using the sentences from Part 1, write a paragraph on a separate piece of paper. You will need to put the sentences in the correct order and use words or phrases from the Useful Words and Expressions box on page 69 so that ideas flow smoothly and are connected logically.

Example Essay: Explaining a Process

[adapted from a student essay; useful expressions are in **bold**]
Topic: An archaeological procedure

Commonly, archaeologists around the world create models about cultures that have already evolved into other forms or that disappeared a long time ago. However, many people ask themselves how archaeologists are able to talk with such confidence about people that do not exist anymore.

First of all, the archaeologist has to define the problem to investigate and limit the area of interest. **At this beginning stage,** the archaeologist reviews all the information already known about the topic. This information may contain contemporary data as well as facts about the past. The range of the topics to cover could vary from soil composition to ethnohistorical data of the area and the period to investigate.

The second step is the most well-known one done by archaeologists, the fieldwork. **During fieldwork**, the archaeologist has to be very rigorous about the proceedings. Each part of the area to investigate is excavated, photographed, and mapped. The exact position and depth where each artifact or piece of evidence of a past culture is found has to be carefully documented and recovered (if possible).

The next step is data analysis in the laboratory. Through techniques developed over the past two centuries, archaeologists order and process the information collected. **Finally,** using statistical tools of prediction, anthropological models, and ethnohistorical and historical data, archaeologists are in a position to interpret the artifacts and evidence found and elaborate on hypotheses about the ancient societies that they are investigating.

It is important to remember, however, that the work of archaeologists is not simply going into the field, excavating, and creating interesting stories about the objects that they have collected. Archaeology is a social science, and therefore an archaeologist's main goal is to try to understand our past through a complex and thorough investigative process.

Write a Process Essay

Now it's your turn. Using the suggested phrases and expressions, organizational strategies, and verb tenses, write a process essay. Choose one of these topics, or come up with your own topic (with your instructor's approval).

1. How to prepare a traditional food of your country.
2. Give advice to someone to deal with the process of adapting to a new culture.
3. Discuss the stages that someone must go through to achieve personal success.
4. Explain a scientific or technical process that you are familiar with.

C. Comparison/Contrast Essay

Purpose: To describe differences and/or similarities between physical objects or abstract ideas to show how two or more are related to one another

Verb Tenses: Vary depending on the topic of the essay

Organization: Two patterns

1. **AB/AB or Point-by-Point Pattern.** Pick one specific point you want to compare and/or contrast, and then present information about **A** regarding **that point**, followed by information about **B** for **the same point**. Do this for each point you would like to focus on. Use this pattern when there are many aspects to be compared in a long essay to make it easier for your reader to remember the differences for each point.

2. **All-of-One/All-of-the-Other Pattern.** Discuss **A completely** and then **B completely**, making sure to keep the points discussed in the same order in both the A and B sections for a more consistent comparison/contrast. Use this pattern when there are only a few specific points of comparison to help the reader more easily remember all the points about A before going on to read about B. Sometimes, you may want to make a general comparison or contrast without giving too much attention to the details; in this case, the all-of-one/all-of-the-other pattern is also more appropriate.

Examples

Topic: Attending a large university (A) vs. a small college (B)

Points of comparison: Class size, facilities, environment

AB/AB	**All-of-One/All-of-the-Other**
1. Class size, A Class size, B	1. A, class size, facilities, environment
2. Facilities, A Facilities, B	2. B, class size, facilities, environment
3. Environment, A Environment, B	

WB
Ex. 3.5,
3.6

Useful Words and Expressions for Comparison

Comparison: Showing Similarities

Verbs

The cold and the flu _____ with both you
feel achy and may have a bad cough.

   Is/are alike in that . . .   **Is/are similar in that . . .**

Transitions

When you study, finding a comfortable place to work is
very important. _____ turning off your cell
phone to avoid distraction is important.

   Also,   **In the same way,**
   Similarly,   **Likewise,**

Comparison Word + Preposition

_____ humans, the whale is a mammal.

British English is _____ American English
in many ways.

   Similar to   **similar to**
   Like   **like**

Useful Words and Expressions for Contrast

Contrast: Showing Differences or Unexpected Result

Verbs

The cold and the flu _____ severity of symptoms.

differ with respect to   **are different with respect to**

The cold and the flu _____ one experiences much more severe symptoms with the flu.

differ from each other in that

Transitions

My chemistry professor assigns homework every night. _____ my public policy professor never assigns homework.

However,

My chemistry professor assigns homework every night. My public policy professor, _____, never assigns homework.

on the other hand

_____ my chemistry professor, who assigns homework every night, my public policy professor never assigns homework.

In contrast to/with

My chemistry professor assigns homework every night. My public policy professor, _____, never assigns homework.

in contrast

Some people describe him as being cooperative. _____, he is uncooperative.

On the contrary*

*refers to opposites or contradictory statements.

The weather was cold and stormy. _____ we still went to the beach.

> **Nevertheless,***   **However,***
> **Nonetheless,***

Subordinating Conjunctions

_____ bioengineering is the study of the application of engineering principles and techniques to problems in medicine and biology, bioinformatics is the sum of the computational approaches to analyze, manage, and store biological data.

> **Whereas**   **While**

_____ much research continues to be done on cancer, we still do not have a cure for this disease.

> **Although****   **Though****
> **Even though****

Coordinating Conjunctions

They said Amy was absent today, _____ I saw her near this room only five minutes ago.

> **but**   **yet**

The prime minister says he is not playing politics, _____ he continues to react to opinion polls about it.

> **but**   **yet**

Contrast Word + Preposition

_____ cell phones 10 years ago, the newest smartphones have many more capabilities.

Pittsburgh, Pennsylvania, is a sunny city _____ London, England.

> **Compared to**   **compared to**
> **In contrast to**   **in contrast to**
> **Unlike**   **unlike**

---

*shows unexpected result and a contrast between what we might expect and what is actually true.

**shows unexpected result and a contrast between what we might expect and what is actually true.

Useful Words and Expressions for Simple Comparison/Contrast

Similarity

Joe is _____ tall _____ his sister.

   as . . . as
   (adjective or adverb)

I enjoy watching _____ baseball _____ basketball.

_____ baseball _____ basketball are interesting to watch.

   both . . . and   **Both . . . and**

_____ the governor _____ the president was prepared for the storm of protest that arose after their failure to deal with the crisis.

She liked _____ the food _____ the entertainment at the party.

   neither . . . nor

Differences

Statistics is _____ difficult to learn ___ microeconomics.

   not as . . . as   **more/less . . . than**

▸ ▸ ▸ Usage Note

An **analogy** is a comparison of two objects or ideas that have similar qualities. The purpose of an analogy is usually to clarify or explain a theory, principle, or way of operation. For example, you might explain how blood flows in a human body by drawing an analogy between blood flow and traffic flow in a city. Another example is the novel *Animal Farm* by George Orwell, which makes an implied analogy between the story he tells about animals and totalitarian governments.

. . . .

Exercise 3.3: Expressing Comparison or Contrast

WB
Ex. 3.5
3.6

Fill in the blanks with words or phrases from the Useful Words and Expressions boxes on pages 74–77 to express comparison or contrast. Answers may vary.

1. _____ Professor Harrison _____

   Professor Dukovich give very difficult examinations at the

   ends of their courses.

2. Ali and Ahmed are twins, _____ they do not behave

   _____ in all respects.

3. As forms of entertainment, watching television and going to the

   theater are _____ in some ways and _____

   in others.

4. _____ engineers are concerned with the soundness of

   a structure, architects are concerned with the aesthetic design.

5. Traveling to foreign countries to study the customs has many

   advantages; _____, I want to point out some of the

   disadvantages.

Example Essay: Comparison and Contrast

[adapted from a student essay; useful expressions are in **bold**]

Topic: Korean society

Koreans suffered through many wars and poverty in the past. This and the fact that Korean society has rapidly developed over the last twenty years have led to large **differences** in life values **between** those of the older generation and those of the new generation. Specifically, the two generations' views on lifestyles, on having and raising children, and on ways of spending and saving money are very **dissimilar**.

First, generally speaking, those of the older generation value diligence and sincerity. They tend to prefer seriousness. **On the other hand,** those of the younger generation do not want to be serious. **On the contrary,** they have an inclination towards flightiness, preferring to do things on the spur of the moment. Moreover, they **too** have a passion for life, but in **a totally different way from** their parents' generation. That is, those of the older generation pursue happiness for the future **while** those of the younger generation focus on happiness in the present.

With respect to children, those of the older generation expect to have children soon after marriage, and as parents they easily give up their own desires to satisfy their children's. Those of the younger generation, **on the other hand**, want to keep their married life interesting by devoting time to their spouse instead of having children right away. Also, their own or their spouse's desires may be **more** important to them **than** anyone else's, including their children's.

With respect to spending habits, those of the older generation in Korea suffered through periods of poverty and war, and so they save money rather than spend it. For example, they are content with housing that they can afford to pay for up front. **In contrast**, those of the younger generation spend money rather than saving. **Unlike** their parents, those of the younger generation are not afraid of long-term loans for housing and cars. They want more luxurious houses and cars, even though they may end up with mountains of debt.

While each generation does things differently, those of the older generation need to understand that those of the younger generation do their best to manage their life in their own way; **likewise**, the young generation needs to understand and respect the old generation's diligence and sincerity toward life. In this way, they can learn from each other and so live in better harmony.

Write a Comparison/Contrast Essay

Now it's your turn. Using the suggested phrases and expressions, organizational strategies, and verb tenses, write a comparison/contrast essay. Choose one of these topics, or come up with your own topic (with your instructor's approval).

1. Compare an aspect of your culture that you are familiar with (for example, food, lifestyle, raising children) with that of another culture.
2. Compare and contrast living with your parents, living with a roommate, and living alone.
3. Compare and/or contrast your personality with the personality of someone you know well.
4. Compare two or more energy sources that may be able to replace coal or oil, for example, wind turbines, solar power, hydrogen power, or ethanol.

D. Cause-and-Effect Essay

Purpose: To describe the causes or reasons for an event; to describe the effects or consequences of an event

Organization: Three main types

1. **Cause.** If you want to show **why** something happened, then you will discuss **causes**. There may be **direct causes** and/or **indirect causes**. **Direct causes** are those that are clearly linked to the event that occurred. **Indirect causes** are those that may not seem obviously connected to an event but that the writer may choose to focus on to reveal to the reader a more in-depth explanation of why something happened.

   Topic: ozone depletion

   Direct cause: too many CFCs in the atmosphere

   Indirect causes: volcanic release of carbon monoxide into the air, automobile emissions, appliance emissions

2. **Effect.** If you want to show the results of an occurrence, then you will discuss **effects**. These too may be direct or indirect, depending on the desire of the writer.

   Topic: drug use

   Direct effects: negative impact on the body, negative impact on relationships

   Indirect effects: higher crime rate, weaker social structure, higher health care costs

3. **Causal Chain.** Sometimes causes and effects may be linked in a **chain**. In this case, the writer must show a situation chronologically, moving from cause to effect to cause to effect to cause, and so on.

Topic: effects of stress

Causal chain: example of stress → inability to sleep → poor health → inability to concentrate → difficulty working → more stress → serious health problems → unemployment → financial problems

---

WB
Ex. 3.7,
3.8

Useful Words and Expressions for Cause and Effect

Cause

Nouns (+ Preposition)

One _____ insomnia is stress. Another _____ may be eating too much before going to bed.

cause (of)	**reason (for)**

Verbs + Preposition

Serious health problems can _____ stress.

be caused by	flow from
derive from	arise from
originate in	be related to
spring from	result from

Subordinating Conjunctions

_____ you are not getting enough sleep, you will likely have trouble concentrating.

Since	As
Because	If

Transition + Preposition

Financial problems can occur _____ health issues.

due to   **because of**
as a result of

Effect

Nouns

One _____ of stress is an inability to sleep.

effect   **result**
outcome   **consequence**

Verbs

Insomnia may _____ one's concentration.

affect   **have an influence on**
impact   **have an impact on**
influence

Stress often _____ serious health problems.

results in   **leads to**
contributes to   **gives rise to**
brings about   **is the reason for**

Transitions

Mood can be affected by the weather. _____
many people feel sad when there is a long period of
rainy days.

Consequently,   **Therefore,**
As a consequence,   **Thus,**
As a result,   **Hence,**

▸ ▸ ▸ **Usage Note**

Be careful! Use **effect** as a noun to mean "outcome or result." Use
affect as a verb to mean "have an influence on."

- -

Exercise 3.4: Creating a Cause-and-Effect Paragraph

Create a cause-and-effect paragraph on a separate sheet of paper explaining the effects of having too many cars on the road. Use this information to develop your paragraph. Be sure to include transitions from the Useful Words and Expressions box on pages 82–83.

- Too many cars on the road
- Roads need maintenance and expansion more often → taxes go up to help pay for these
- More carbon monoxide released → increase in depletion of the ozone layer → climate changes
- More individuals driving → funding for public transportation goes down → those without cars are negatively impacted
- Prices for public transportation go up → routes are cut → people cannot get where they need to go

Example Essay: Cause and Effect

[adapted from a student essay; useful expressions are in **bold**]

Topic: Chinese society

A tradition of being thrifty is one feature of Chinese culture that **affects** the Chinese consumer's behavior. Most Chinese people spend money only for necessary living expenses—including food, rent, clothes, and insurance—and deposit their remaining money in a savings account.

This situation is partly **because** there is no sound social welfare system, health insurance, or retirement plan in China. **Therefore,** people in China have to save money for the future.

This means spending is cut down as much as possible. Nice clothes and entertainment are seen as luxuries. **Consequently**, few people spend money on them.

This tradition of thriftiness has also **given rise to** another feature of Chinese consumer behavior: Chinese consumers do not like any debt in their lives. **As a result**, they do not like to purchase or buy anything that is beyond their financial capacity. For instance, most Chinese do not buy a car or house until they are able to pay for it in full.

Thriftiness **has also led** the Chinese to be conservative with spending. They have a low tolerance for risk. This is displayed in the Chinese behavior of saving extra money in a bank rather than taking the risk of investing it in the stock market. **In order to** make their lives more stable and safe, Chinese people usually watch over their money carefully.

In summary, Chinese spend money cautiously and do not like to take financial risks. Being careful with money makes them feel more certain about their future.

Write a Cause-and-Effect Essay

Now it's your turn. Using the suggested phrases and expressions, organizational strategies, and verb tenses, write a cause-and-effect essay. Choose one of these topics, or come up with your own topic (with your instructor's approval).

1. Analyze the effects of an unexpected action taken by someone you know.
2. Present the causes of a significant historical event in your country.
3. Explain the causes of a specific social conflict or an example of social cooperation.
4. Describe the causes and effects of a community problem.

E. Argument Essay

Purpose: To inform an audience of an opinion in an effort to convince them to adopt that point of view

Support: logical argument, evidence such as facts that are widely accepted, relevant statistics, or opinions of experts on the subject

Organization: Three main types

1. **Present your arguments and evidence** to support them, without addressing the opposing side.

2. **Briefly state the opposing view**, and then say why it needs to be altered or in what way(s) it is incorrect. The remainder of the essay is focused on argument and evidence in support of your view.

3. **Alternate between the opposing arguments and the supporting arguments for each point** if there are several points that need to be addressed.

Order of Arguments

1. Present the arguments according to order of their importance.

2. Present the strongest or most important argument first to attract the reader's interest.

3. Present the best argument last to provide a final, firm impression of reasoning.

> ▸ ▸ ▸ **Usage Note**

To argue in response to another person's opinion, be careful to avoid arguing against **the person** and to only argue against **his or her ideas and reasoning**.

How to Construct a Logical Argument

1. Make a list of the main supporting and opposing arguments.

   Topic: Gun Control

   Supporting arguments:

   Harder for criminals to get guns → reduces assault crimes

   → mentally unstable people will not be able to go on shooting sprees

   Fewer people will get accidentally shot, especially children.

   Opposing arguments:

   People have a right to own a gun to defend themselves.

   If people take proper security measures, accidents won't happen.

2. Include your opponents' main arguments in the essay with a **rebuttal**. A rebuttal addresses either why the opponents' main arguments are not valid or why your argument is stronger or more valid. This is similar to when you are having a conversation and say "Yes, that's true, but. . . . "

   Example A:

   While it's true that the U.S. constitution does grant citizens the right to bear arms, this was to ensure that they could defend themselves if the government turned into a dictatorship and threatened the safety of citizens. This is not likely to happen in today's world.

   Example B:

   It's true that proper security measures would reduce the number of accidental or rampage shootings by children or relatives of gun owners. However, who can guarantee that a gun owner will take the proper precautions when storing a weapon?

3. Use **logical reasoning**. This takes two forms: deductive or inductive.

   A. Deductive reasoning

   In its simplest form, a **deduction** is based on a general statement expressing a truth or a belief followed by a second statement linking another idea to the first one. Then a logical conclusion may be drawn:

   Example A:

   Statement A: All the students in Mrs. Matoko's class work very hard.

   Statement B: Krishin is in Mrs. Matoko's class.

   Deductive Conclusion—Therefore, Krishin works very hard.

   In this example, Statement A is given as a fact or accepted truth, and Statement B says something about Krishin that connects him to the idea in the first statement. If we accept Statements A and B as being accurate, then we can correctly make the conclusion above using deductive reasoning.

   B. Inductive reasoning

   Induction is a kind of reasoning that we use every day in many fields. It involves making a generalization based on several or many specific instances. Consider these two examples:

   Example A:

   1. A scientist conducts an experiment in which an unknown liquid boils at 95 degrees Celsius.

   2. The unknown liquid boils at the same temperature each of the 15 times the experiment is done.

   Inductive Conclusion—The liquid will always boil at 95 degrees Celsius.

Example B:

1. Many tourists go to the same resort on vacation.

2. They all report that it is a wonderful place.

Inductive Conclusion—Future visitors will also think the resort is a wonderful place.

In both of these examples, evidence from previous experience (experimental trials or personal reports) leads to the conclusion that, if the evidence held true in all of these instances in the past, it will hold true for all instances in the future as well.

By presenting the arguments of the opposing side, you will strengthen your argument as this allows you to address what your reader may already have in his or her mind. You will be letting your reader know that you have thought about the **evidence** against your point of view, but you have stood by your opinion because you believe it is more valid, and you believe that your arguments are stronger.

▸ ▸ ▸ **Usage Note**

Be sure to address your opponent's arguments.

Useful Words and Expressions for Argument

WB
Ex. 3.9

Sentence Beginners Indicating a Position

_____ many non-smokers are aware of the risks of smoking and therefore choose not to smoke.

It is logical to think that
It is reasonable to assume that
It seems evident that

_____ second-hand smoke is just as dangerous as first-hand smoke.

It can be concluded that
We can deduce that
It can be inferred that

_____ smoking and non-smoking sections in restaurants effectively shield non-smokers from second-hand smoke.

It is inconsistent with the evidence to say that
It is unreasonable to assume that
There is little evidence for the argument that

_____ second-hand smoke is harmless _____.

The argument that . . . is erroneous.
The claim that . . . is fallacious.
The proposition that . . . is easily refuted.

Transitions Indicating Personal Conclusion

_____ smoking ought to be banned in indoor public spaces.

Therefore,   **Thus,**
Hence,   **Consequently,**

Exercise 3.5: Expressing Arguments

Create sentences about the ideas using words and phrases from the Useful Words and Expressions box on page 90.

1. Temperatures on earth have been rising for the last decade.

   _____

   _____

2. Making civilian ownership of guns illegal will help lower the amount of violent crime in the United States.

   _____

   _____

3. Women and men who do the same job should make the same amount of money.

   _____

   _____

4. The family of murder victims should determine the punishment of the murderer.

   _____

   _____

Example Essay: Argument

[adapted from a student essay; useful argument expressions are in **bold**; cause-and-effect expressions that support the writer's argument are underlined.]
Topic: Technology in the classroom

Nowadays we have SmartBoards in many classrooms, on which teachers can write or display PowerPoint presentations and digital files or websites. Numerous software packages allow teachers to tailor programs to their own curricular needs, and laptops can be easily connected to a display screen for easy viewing of material. As a result of these technologies, many more resources are available to teachers than before. This has led to the belief that using technology in the classroom can only enhance education. **However,** if not used carefully and in moderation, technology can actually be detrimental to educators and students alike.

First, **it is logical to assume that** the availability of more resources leads to better education. **After all**, the more input and examples students get, the better they can understand a subject. **However**, while technology may lead to more resources being available, searching for materials can be an extremely time-consuming process due to the large number of possible resources available. **Moreover**, the search for resources using various forms of technology often causes teachers to become distracted. The large amount of information available may cause teachers to focus on their search and lose sight of the purpose of the activity they are trying to develop. In addition, teachers may find a good resource but have to take a lot of time adapting it to the particular lesson they have in mind. This means they may be led astray by focusing more on materials development and less on student learning. **In the same way,** students could spend so much time looking for information for an assignment that, <u>as a consequence</u>, the quality of the assignment itself suffers. Hours that a student could have spent in completing the assignment and checking it for correctness may instead be spent in searching and following interesting items on the internet that are not related to the assignment.

Second, **it is true that** software such as PowerPoint and Microsoft Word enable both teachers and students to produce high-quality output. **However**, the availability of these resources <u>leads to</u> another negative <u>consequence</u>: more is expected of teachers and students, sometimes to an unreasonable degree. For example, thirty or forty years ago when typewriters were in use, it would take hours to prepare an error-free document. <u>Therefore</u>, focus was less on the form of the document and more on its content. Since the advent of advanced word processing programs and PowerPoint, however, emphasis has moved to include form as well. <u>As a result</u>, output by teachers and students may be visually appealing but not necessarily of good quality. Unfortunately, if readers are attracted by the format, this <u>may lead them to believe that</u> the document is automatically of high quality. <u>Therefore</u>, evaluations of documents sometimes are not an accurate reflection of the quality of content. **It seems that** the ability to think critically and express thoughts well is taking a back seat to creating something that is attractive to look at.

In the end, **it seems evident that** technology can indeed be a benefit to learning in that it does make available resources that can improve student understanding. **However**, those involved in education need to be aware of the pitfalls technology can bring to education and make others aware as well. Otherwise we will become a society that is very good at finding information and displaying it, but without having a true understanding of the information or being able to critically analyze it.

Write an Argument Essay

Now it's your turn. Using the suggested phrases and expressions, organizational strategies, and verb tenses, write an argument essay. Choose one of these topics, or come up with your own topic (with your instructor's approval).

1. Discuss the idea that space exploration should be stopped so that the huge amounts of money spent on it can be used to alleviate hunger in the world.

2. Argue for or against allowing complete freedom of expression on the internet.

3. Present arguments in support of the idea that all citizens should be provided health care by their government.

4. Present the arguments for and against the position that parents should be punished by society when their children under the age of 21 years commit crimes.

F. Combining Patterns of Organization

While an essay may have one primary pattern of organization, most essays use more than one pattern throughout.

Example Essay with Combined Patterns

In the sample essay, the student has used **cause-and-effect** and **argument** patterns as the basis of the essay. This flows naturally from the fact that she is taking one side in an argument about smoking and discussing its effects on health. In addition, she uses a **contrast** pattern to express the differences between the two sides of the argument and a brief **narrative** pattern (which she calls a *scenario*) to support a specific point in the third paragraph.

Notice also that this essay's development includes effective use of description, definition, and examples. The coherence and unity of the essay are achieved by means of transitions, repetition of key words, and clear use of reference words.

No Smoking in Public Areas

Recently there has been an argument raised in this country about a burning issue: whether we should forbid smoking in all public areas. **People who support the idea that we should forbid smoking in public areas claim that smoking is harmful to health for both smokers and non-smokers and that smoking in public areas has a bad influence on children. In contrast, people on the other side of the argument complain that a smoking ban would eliminate the individual liberties of smokers.** As the daughter of a father who smoked heavily, I know how difficult it is for a smoker to struggle with his habit. **However, I still agree with the position that we should completely forbid smoking in public areas because smoking could have serious consequences for both individuals and society.** There is a **negative health effect** on smokers themselves, people near them, and youth. Moreover smokers interfere with the **freedom** of others.

From the individual point of view, smoking negatively impacts health. Evidence shows that smoking

INTRODUCTION

Context given in first sentence (a social issue)

Argument and **contrast** patterns combined (two opposing positions in the argument)

Thesis statement near end of introduction, giving author's opinion

Key ideas of development paragraphs **foreshadowed** in last two sentences of introduction (health, freedom)

is a habit that kills more than 480,000 Americans each year (Campaign for Tobacco-Free Kids). Among those unlucky persons, some of them are non-smokers who are categorized as second-hand smokers, also known as "environmental tobacco smokers." According to research results from the American Cancer Society's Cancer Action Network, heart, lung, and other diseases caused by second-hand smoke result in more than 40,000 deaths annually. I would like to share this information with those smokers who light a cigarette in public areas like work environments, public buildings, public transportation vehicles, and public family areas where their spouses or children are. Although they will not be sued in the same way as the person who directly brings about someone's death, they are playing the role of potential murderer when they are breathing out smoke in any public area.

In addition, smoking in public areas gives rise to some negative outcomes for adolescents. I believe that everybody has realized the negative effects of cigarette advertising: this kind of propaganda tries to equate smoking with the American Dream, maturity, success,

DEVELOPMENT (3 PARAGRAPHS FOLLOWING INTRODUCTION PARAGRAPH)

Two body paragraphs focusing on key issues foreshadowed in introduction

Cause-and-effect pattern to develop argument in these two paragraphs (health effect on individuals and negative results for young people)

Transition connecting this paragraph to the previous one

and athleticism in efforts to attract the young generation to smoke. This is the main reason for the government to stop any TV advertising of cigarettes and forbid the sponsorship of popular sports by the cigarette companies. However, we can infer that adults who are smoking in public areas are launching another kind of advertising for adolescents. In society, adults are logical role models for children. **You can imagine this scenario: when students from a middle or high school walk through the bar areas on a university campus, they may see a group of university students who are smoking inside a crowded bar, talking, and excitedly playing games with each other. What do they think? It is reasonable to assume that they see smoking as cool, as an adult behavior that they would like to emulate.** This, too, then acts as vivid advertising to show those children how smoking can be related to university life, maturity, friendship, and excitement. I do believe that this is more persuasive to them than any TV advertising.

> **Narrative** pattern to support cause-and-effect argument (scenario of university students as model)

There is, furthermore, a more general social issue to consider. Smokers may complain that by promoting the cessation of smoking in public areas, we are

> **Body paragraph** focusing on second key issue foreshadowed in introduction (freedom of non-smokers to breathe clean air)

recommending a rule that will destroy their individual freedom. I cannot agree with this opinion. **They are misinterpreting the definition of individual liberties. I agree that everybody has his or her individual liberty, but such freedom is based upon the fact that he or she is not taking away other persons' liberties.** Forbidding smoking in public areas is not denying smokers' individual liberties. In fact, it protects the liberties of non-smokers. Everyone has the right to breathe clean air and have a healthy environment. While this point of view will probably not change smokers' lifestyles, hopefully it will encourage them to use only private areas to smoke in.

Defining pattern to support author's argument (individual freedom)

To conclude, I would suggest that forbidding smoking in public areas, which protects not only the right to *health of non-smokers* and future generations but also *individual freedom*, must be a national program of all countries for the long-term benefit of their populations. These areas include work places, public buildings, public transportation vehicles, and even the places at home where non-smoking family members gather. It follows that we need to provide

CONCLUSION

Conclusion restates essay's **main idea**

Key issues mentioned again, with ways to achieve author's goal (education, restriction of advertising)

education programs so adolescents realize the risks mentioned above, we need to continue to forbid smoking in public areas, and we need to restrict advertising of tobacco products. Otherwise, we will pay for it in the near future with rising health costs and more deaths as a result of cigarette smoking.

Author ends with **prediction** (warning about consequences)

Campaign for Tobacco-Free Kids. "Toll of Tobacco in the United States." 26 July 2017. www.tobaccofreekids.org/facts_issues/toll-US

Cancer Action Network. "Secondhand Smoke." American Cancer Society. www.acscan.org/sites/default/files/Facts-About-Secondhand-Smoke.pdf

Write an Essay that Uses Different Patterns of Organization

Now it's your turn. Using the suggested phrases and expressions, organizational strategies, and verb tenses, write an essay that uses different patterns of organzation. Choose one of these topics, or come up with your own topic (with your instructor's approval).

Combining Narrative and Process

Academic topics:

1. Explain a scientific process that is familiar to you. Include a personal experience with this process.
2. Discuss the process of becoming an adult, focusing on cultural and social aspects of the transition to adulthood.
3. What do you believe are the stages one must go through to achieve personal success? Use personal examples to state your case.

Personal topics:

1. Discuss your experience at learning another language. What steps did you have to go through? Have you been successful?
2. We all have a process we follow when making appropriate choices in a given situation. Discuss a situation where you had to make an important decision. What steps did you have to go through to make a choice? Do you think you made the correct choice?
3. For you, what is the best process to follow in order to create a good essay? Use personal examples to prove your point.

Additional topics:

1. Discuss the process of adapting to a new culture. How did you succeed at overcoming culture shock? If you are still in the process, describe what you have been through so far and the stages you expect to go through in the future.
2. Have you or someone you know had to adapt after entering a new group (such as peers at a new school, co-workers at a new job, or in-laws in a new family)? Discuss the process of adapting to this new role.

Reaction essay topic:

Consider these statements:

- *Creative inspiration, rather than careful planning, often results in the best solution to a problem.*
- *The process of solving a problem must begin and end with careful planning.*

Think about how you solve problems. Which of these statements do you think apply to your problem-solving process? Is one better than another in certain situations?

Combining Comparison/Contrast and Description

Academic topics:

1. Compare two or more sources of revenue that governments can use to fund public projects.
2. Compare the effects of two 20th-century inventions on modern society. (For example, commercial airplanes, personal computers, air conditioning, traffic signals, mobile phones, credit cards, etc.)
3. Compare and contrast your own process of writing in English and writing in your native language.

Personal topics:

1. Compare one or more of your special interests or hobbies with those of someone else you know well.
2. Compare and contrast two or more experiences that have been very important to you.
3. Compare and/or contrast two ways that you deal with stress.

Additional topics:

1. Compare and contrast three different countries where you might like to live, work, or study in the future.
2. Compare procrastinating (waiting until the last minute to get things done) with doing things in a timely manner.

SECTION 4

. . . .

RESEARCH PAPER

4

Writing a research paper is necessary to being successful in the academic world. Students at both the undergraduate and graduate levels are expected to write research papers and follow certain conventions and guidelines, which will be described.

Research papers vary greatly in length, but they all require a significant amount of work that can take weeks or months. Breaking up the process into steps makes the project more manageable and generally produces a better paper in the end.

Review pages 2–6 for an overview of the process, and then refer to it for guidance as you write your papers.

A. Choosing a Topic

- Choose a topic you are knowledgeable about or that you want to learn more about. Your topic should be broad enough to fulfill the requirements of the assignment (if the paper is 12–15 pages, your topic must be complex enough for that length), but it must be narrow enough to provide you with a specific focus for the paper (a topic like sports is too broad for a research paper).
- Generate ideas about this topic. (See pages 12–18 for idea-generating techniques.)
- Find some sources (books, articles, websites) related to these ideas.
- Using information from your sources and, for an argument paper, your own ideas, shape your general topic into a focused research question from which you can develop a thesis statement or argument for the paper.
- The research question or thesis for your paper should not be fixed at this point. As you find sources and read more about the topic, your understanding and point of view will develop, and you will get a better idea of what you want to say. Like most researchers, you are likely to change your original plan based on your reading and research.

Important Terms

Research Question: a question focused on the key information that you want to learn about: *What evidence supports the idea that surveillance cameras should be allowed in all public areas of cities and towns to reduce high crime rates?* Answering this question is the reason for writing the research paper.

Thesis Statement: one or more sentences expressing the main idea of the research paper: *Although many people believe they violate personal privacy, surveillance cameras should be allowed in all urban areas because their use reduces crime rates.*

Argument: the evidence and logical reasoning you use to make your reader agree with your point of view about the research question. For the thesis statement, the central argument is that *surveillance cameras should be allowed in all urban areas,* supported by the reasoning *because their use reduces crime rates.*

B. Finding Sources

When you write a research paper, use **sources** of various types to provide background information on your topic and, for an argument paper, to support your position. Once you have chosen your topic, start looking for such sources. Keep in mind that the available sources—or the information that you find—may help you narrow or even shift your topic. This kind of change is not a problem; it is a normal part of the process of writing a research paper.

Where to Find Sources

- The **library** is filled with paper resources—books, newspapers, maps, journals—and it provides access to a wide variety of electronic sources there as well (online journals, databases, indexes). People who work in the library can be a very valuable asset to your search for sources. Don't be afraid to ask a librarian for assistance at any point in your research; a librarian can help you narrow your topic, choose appropriate key words for a computer search, find a specific journal article, or navigate the bookshelves in search of useful books.

- The library's online catalog lists the books and journals that the library owns or has access to through other institutions. To search any electronic reference, you will need to use keywords or phrases that are related to your topic. A librarian can help you to find keywords to make your search more efficient.
- Make use of electronic databases that list articles in specific fields from a variety of sources. These databases are generally available on the Internet or through the library's online resources.

Be sure to allow plenty of time to thoroughly explore each type of collection. It takes time to search electronically; you may have to sort through the many results that you find, determine which sources look useful, and then actually locate the resources, which may be in print or electronic form.

Types of Sources

Many types of sources, both print and electronic, can be useful when researching an academic paper. These include newspapers, brochures, newsletters, conference papers, dissertations, theses, journal articles, and technical reports. If you are unsure about what types of sources to use, ask your instructor to explain what is appropriate or expected for the research paper.

- The information in **books** tends to be well researched and complete. A single book often has a fairly broad focus, which means only one or two chapters might fit any one topic. Books are good sources for background information.
- A **journal** is generally published by a professional or academic organization on a monthly or quarterly basis. The articles contained in a journal are usually focused on many aspects of one academic field. Although one overall field unites the articles in a journal, a particular volume of a journal generally only includes one or two articles that relate to a specific topic.

- A **magazine** is usually published on a weekly or monthly basis and contains a variety of articles and advertisements. Magazines are often aimed at a more general audience and are usually <u>not</u> the best sources for academic writing. Generally speaking, magazine articles are written more simply than journal articles, so they are easier to understand, but they also do not examine topics as thoroughly as professional journals do.
- The **internet** contains a vast amount of information, and websites exist for almost any topic imaginable. Some of this information is reputable and useful as a source for a research paper. However, there is also a large body of false, misleading, or unsupported information that should not be used as a source in academic writing.

Evaluating Sources

Before using any source in your paper, use the criteria listed to ensure it is valid.

1. **Author**
   - Is the name of the author available? If an article is posted without a name, look at it carefully before assuming that it contains valid information.
   - If you can find the name of the author, what credentials or information about the author (academic degrees, affiliation with an academic institution, position in a company, etc.) are listed?

2. **Source**
   - What type of organization hosts the site where the article appears? Academic and governmental institutions (.edu and .gov) are generally neutral, reliable sources of information. Other organizations, businesses, and sometimes even governments may present good information on their websites, but think carefully about how these organizations' perspectives may bias the information that they present. Non-profit organizations (usually .org) and for-profit companies (.com) may present accurate information, but their perspective may lack objectivity. For example, political or religious organizations will typically give information reflecting their own points of view.

3. **Relevance**
   - What is the relationship between the information provided in the source and your research topic? The information may be too general for you to use or may not be closely related.

4. **Accuracy of information**
   - Does the information originally come from another source? Is this source clearly indicated? Are there links to other related sites?
   - Does the author cite other sources and give a bibliography?
   - Does the information seem complete, or does it seem to be missing some aspects of the discussion?

5. **Purpose**
   - What are the goals of this site? (To inform? To sell something? To persuade?) Look carefully at the location of the information (On an organization website? In a peer-reviewed journal? On a personal website, like a blog?) and the type of language (emotional or neutral) that an author uses to help you to recognize the author's purpose for writing the article.

6. **Currency**
   - How recent is the source? Is it recent enough to be useful? Electronic sources are frequently updated, but many are left online long after the information is no longer valid.

Exercise 4.1: Evaluating Sources

Imagine that you are writing a paper on internet addiction. Use Google, Google Scholar, and/or your library's online research databases to find one of each source type listed. Provide brief notes for each. Decide whether you would use it in a research paper and explain your answer.

1. **An online journal**

Title of journal:_____

Title of article: _____

Author: _____

Source: _____

Relevance:_____

Accuracy of information: _____

_____

Purpose: _____

Currency: _____

Use of this source?   Yes / No / Maybe_____

_____

2. **A website**

URL and title of website (or part of website): _____

_____

Author: _____

Source: _____

Relevance:_____

Accuracy of information: _____

_____

Purpose: _____

Currency: _____

Use of this source?   Yes / No / Maybe_____

_____

C. Taking Notes

For the great majority of writers of research papers, taking notes is an important part of the process. Taking notes achieves more than one valuable purpose:

- It allows the writer to record, in a convenient and accessible form, the information that might become part of the research paper. Although it may seem time-consuming, the value of such notes becomes clear once you start to draft the paper itself. Good notes provide quick access to information and quotations already judged to be of direct value to your paper, eliminating the need to re-read through piles of sources when the due date for the paper approaches.
- The process of taking notes can provide ideas for possible organizational structures for a research paper.
- Notes written on cards or in an electronic file can easily be rearranged when the writer is experimenting with different ways to organize ideas and sections.
- The act of reading carefully plus writing the main ideas, details, and good sections for quotations encourages a deep understanding of the subject matter. This can generate new and original ideas in the mind of the note-taker, especially by allowing fresh connections between ideas from different sources.

Guidelines for Taking Notes

- Note the source of your information. For all your notes, be sure to write the details about where they come from: the author, the title of the book or article, and the publication information. Then, if the ideas are used in the paper, this information is easily available for the bibliography and citations.

- Be sure to differentiate between exact quotations, summaries, or paraphrases and the notes that are your own ideas. This prevents plagiarizing, and you will remember to cite the quotations and paraphrased sections.

- Develop a system of word or phrase abbreviations for quickly taking notes. These are very useful as time-savers since some words are very common and may appear frequently in texts on the same subject. No one will see your notes, so your personal abbreviations can be of any kind and can be the same as those you use in taking notes during a lecture. Some examples are:

alt (alternative)	♂ (males/men)
b/c (because)	♀ (females/women)
cat (category)	? (doubtful, unknown),
def (definition)	> more than
emph (emphasis)	⟵ (comes from)
ex (example)	⟶ (goes to, becomes)
req (required, needed)	// (parellel, similar to)
wk (week)	∴ (therefore/as a result)
w/o (without)	∵ (because/due to)

D. Summarizing, Paraphrasing, and Using Quotations

Most of your research paper must be written in your own words. Only a small proportion of it may be **direct quotation** (no more than 5 percent). Since you will report information from many sources, you need to be able to **summarize** that information, paraphrase it, and use quotations in an appropriate way. Doing these things correctly will help you avoid plagiarism (described on pages 116–119).

WB
Ex. 4.2

Summaries express only the main ideas of a passage or long text and are of two kinds:

- A paraphrased summary gives the essence of a text in your own words. Almost all your notes for a research paper should be paraphrased summaries because this is what creates most of your paper.
- An **abstract** provides the main ideas in brief form at the beginning of a paper (usually a published paper or journal article). The purpose of the abstract is to allow the reader to see the main ideas of a paper in order to determine if the content is of interest. The assignment for the paper will tell you if you have to write an abstract.

Paraphrasing is using your own words to explain or describe something that another person has explained or described. This is an extremely important skill for academic writing since research papers and term papers contain information from various sources, much of which is paraphrased. When paraphrasing a passage from another source, you must find a new way to express the author's main ideas without changing the meaning of the original text. To achieve this, you must use:

- your own words
- your own phrases
- your own grammatical structures
- different order of information

Any section of a text that is not paraphrased and is copied directly is a quotation and must be formatted as such. This rule also includes summaries and parts of sentences, or short phrases (even as short as two or three words).

Tips for Paraphrasing

- Use **synonyms** as often as possible. It is rare for any two words to be exact synonyms in a language; there are usually different nuances of meaning and the words may be typically used in different contexts with, for example, different degrees of formality. However, there are many words that do have similar meaning, and these are the ones that must be used whenever possible in paraphrasing. For instance, the word *tired* might be replaced by *fatigued, exhausted,* or *weary.* For help in finding such words of similar meaning, you can use a reference book of synonyms, called a thesaurus, which is a valuable resource for all writers. Inexpensive thesauruses are available in most bookstores, and they are also available on the internet.

- In some cases, technical or specialized words from the original cannot be changed; using these in paraphrasing is acceptable. For example, if you are paraphrasing information from an article about weather conditions, you will have to use words or phrases that are also in your sources, such as *storm, fog, precipitation, high pressure,* and *low pressure.*

- It is essential to avoid using groups of words—phrases—from the source passage. Even if you think the phrasing of the original expresses the intended meaning very well, some other way of stating the meaning must be found to successfully paraphrase. Therefore, do not use any phrases from the original unless they are essential words that cannot be expressed in another way (such as technical words).

- When paraphrasing, it is not acceptable to change only specific words and phrases while at the same time copying the grammatical structure of any of the source sentences. The sentence structure must also be changed. For example, passive voice may be used where the original had active sentences, subordination and coordination may be varied, and clauses may be reduced to phrases.

- The specific order of information of the original passage should be changed in a paraphrase so that it is clearly not copying the original. For instance, if the main idea of a paragraph is at the beginning of the original, it can be placed somewhere else by the paraphrase writer.
- If the author's phrasing has expressed an idea in such a way that a paraphrase cannot equal the clarity of the original, a quotation may be the only choice.
- When information from a source is not paraphrased, it must be in quotation marks. A longer quotation of four or five lines or more is block indented with no quotation marks (see page 240 for more information and an example).

For more information on using quotations and citing sources, see pages 128 and 231–234.

> ▶ ▶ ▶ **Usage Note**
>
> Remember, quotations should form only a very small part of research papers.

Paraphrased Summary Example

Note that this example of a paraphrased summary is about one-fifth the length of the original. The length of a summary may vary according to how much of the original information you wish to use.

Original text [Semuels, A. (2017, May 28). Making the machines that replace humans. *The Atlantic*. Retrieved from www.theatlantic.com]

Robots and algorithms are proving themselves better than humans at a number of tasks, both physical and mental. [. . .] Foxconn, the company that builds electronic devices for companies including Apple and Samsung, is reportedly replacing tens of thousands of factory workers with more-efficient robots. [. . .] Evidence suggests that industrial robots [. . .] have cost thousands of American jobs. The number of industrial robots, which are automatically controlled, multipurpose, reprogrammable machines, increased fourfold between 1993 and 2007, according to a recent study by MIT economists Daron Acemoglu and Pascual Restrepo. The authors found that one such industrial robot in a metropolitan area reduced employment by about six workers, costing the U.S. economy 670,000 jobs between 1990 and 2007. But there are positives too. The MIT economist David Autor has emphasized that automation also complements labor, making workers more productive. There are certain tasks that robots can't do, he writes, and humans will always be needed for those. [. . .] (Semuels, 2017)

Paraphrased summary

Robots can accomplish many tasks more quickly, efficiently, and accurately than most humans, and are therefore replacing human workers in industrial settings. However, this new technology is also creating new employment opportunities for humans (Semuels, 2017).

Plagiarism

Plagiarism is a serious academic offense. To avoid plagiarism, you must be familiar with the two types:

Plagiarism of language is when you copy words, phrases, or sentences from a source without indicating with quotation marks or a citation that you are quoting directly from the original. (See also pages 231–234.)

Plagiarism of ideas is based on the view that some ideas are owned by the person who first thought of them. Ideas that are new in a field of study are of this kind, but they may gradually become common knowledge. When the idea is new, the originator must be given credit for it in a citation. When ideas have been widely accepted for a long time (such as the information in an introductory textbook), there is usually no need to cite the source.

Plagiarism of ideas can be judged only by someone who knows the field, but plagiarism of language can easily be seen by comparing the original wording with the uses that are made of it. The examples and exercises that follow focus only on plagiarism of language. The examples show acceptable (not plagiarized) and unacceptable (plagiarized) language uses of an original passage from an article about mosquito bites.

Original text [Stromberg, J. (2013, July 12). Why do mosquitoes bite some people more than others? *Smithsonian. com*. Retrieved from www.smithsonianmag.com]

Not surprisingly—since, after all, mosquitoes bite us to harvest proteins from our blood—research shows that they find certain blood types more appetizing than others. One study found that in a controlled setting, mosquitoes landed on people with Type O blood nearly twice as often as those with Type A. People with Type B blood fell somewhere in the middle of this itchy spectrum. Additionally, based on other genes, about 85 percent of people secrete a chemical signal through their skin that indicates which blood type they have, while 15 percent do not, and mosquitoes are also more attracted to secretors than nonsecretors regardless of which type they are (Stromberg, 2013).

Example 1:

Plagiarism (missing quotation marks and citation):

One study found that in a controlled setting, mosquitoes landed on people with Type O blood nearly twice as often as those with Type A.

Not plagiarism (quotation marks and citation included):

According to one study, "In a controlled setting, mosquitoes landed on people with Type O blood nearly twice as often as those with Type A" (Stromberg, 2013).

Example 2:

Plagiarism (a few key words have been changed but the original sentence structure is the same):

Moreover, based on other genes, about 85 percent of people emit a chemical signal through their skin that is unique to the blood type they have, while 15 percent do not, and mosquitoes appear to be more attracted to those who secrete this signal than those who do not, regardless of which type they are (Stromberg, 2013).

Not plagiarism (full paraphrase, with new word choice, new sentence structure, and changed order of information):

A chemical signal, unique to each blood type, is emitted through the skin. Most people—about 85 percent—emit this signal, which attracts mosquitoes regardless of people's blood type (Stromberg, 2013).

. . . .

Exercise 4.2: Recognizing Plagiarism of Language

WB
Ex. 4.3

An excerpt from an article about Manu National Park in Peru follows. For each of the uses, give the description (A, B, C, or D) that correctly describes it.

Original text [James, C. H. (2016, June). Peru's world apart. *National Geographic*, 30–57.]:

At 6,627 square miles, the park covers the entire watershed of the Manu River, from grasslands at nearly 13,000 feet, on the eastern flank of the Andes, down through moss-draped cloud forest to the lowland rain forest of the westernmost Amazon Basin. It's a sumptuous, extravagant, overwhelming landscape. The region is traversed by tapirs, crowned by flights of scarlet macaws, veined with snakes. Ninety-two species of bats own the night sky; 14 species of primates swing through the trees, pursued by harpy eagles with six-and-a-half-foot wingspans. Butterflies are everywhere: scarlet knights; giant blue morphos; tiny, transparent glasswings. And on every surface, vertical and horizontal, there are ants. At night the foliage sparkles in your headlamp with what looks like pixie dust—the shining eyes of hundreds of thousands of insects. (James, 2016, p. 42)

Descriptions:

A. Not plagiarism: Original words quoted with quotation marks and with citation

B. Not plagiarism: Complete paraphrase with citation

C. Plagiarism: Original words quoted but with no quotation marks

D. Plagiarism: Some paraphrase but with unchanged sentence structure and some original words quoted but with no quotation marks

Uses:

1. Manu National Park, comprising over 6,000 square miles, covers the entire watershed of the Manu River, from high-altitude grass-lands, on the eastern flank of the Andes, down through damp cloud forest to the rain forest in the lowlands of the westernmost Amazon Basin. (James, 2016, p. 42) _____

2. Butterflies of all sizes and colors flutter through the forest, and nearly one hundred species of bats fill the air at night. (James, 2016, p. 42) _____

3. Insects are so abundant in Manu National Park that at night, "the foliage sparkles in your headlamp with what looks like pixie dust" as the light hits the hundreds of thousands of insect eyes. (James, 2016, p. 42) _____

4. Peru's Manu National Park is a sumptuous, extravagant, overwhelming landscape traversed by tapirs, snakes, primates, and insects. (James, 2016, p. 42) _____

5. Tapirs, macaws, and snakes are among the species that fill Manu National Park, which comprises several habitats, from grassy highlands in the West to rain forest in the East. (James, 2016, p. 42) _____

E. Outlining

WB
Ex. 4.4

Before writing the first draft of the paper, develop an outline. Outlining helps you organize your thoughts, determine the relationships between ideas, arrange topics in a logical order, and generate new ideas.

Here are some general guidelines for creating an outline:

1. Decide what your main topics are within the research paper. These will be the main sections of your research paper.
2. Within each of these main topics, identify what subtopics you will address. These are the specific points about each main topic that you will address in your paper.
3. Structure the ideas on the page the way they are structured in the paper. Do this by using a numbering system and indentation to show the relationship between ideas.

An example outline for a research paper is shown on page 121. The main topics, which are general, are numbered with roman numerals (I, II, III). The subtopics, which are more specific, are indented and labeled with letters. The subtopics have more detail and are more specific and are labeled with numbers.

Notice that the topics in the sample outline are not complete sentences. They are just the main ideas that the writer will discuss in each section. In addition, the example is a formal outline, with a numbering system and indentation. You can use this system or a more informal one with no numbering or indentation. Either format helps the writer represent the relationships between ideas.

The first draft of an outline is often not the final product. It's common for writers to change their outlines because they find a better way to organize their ideas or they see how pieces of their paper fit together in a different way. Also, listing all of the possible topics creates new ideas. Therefore, create an outline early in the writing process and be willing to change it as your ideas develop. If you wish, list the names of sources you have found for each section.

Schooling Options for Children in the United States

I.   Public School
   A. Advantages
      1. Many learning opportunities and activities
      2. Free
   B. Disadvantages
      1. Sometimes large class sizes
      2. A lot of required testing of students
II. Private School
   A. Advantages
      1. Small class sizes
      2. Unique opportunities
   B. Disadvantages
      1. Financial cost for parents
      2. Sometimes not as diverse a student population
III. Home School
   A. Advantages
      1. Curriculum tailored to child's individual interests
      2. Many opportunities for learning & enrichment
   B. Disadvantages
      1. Burden of education falls on parents
      2. Students might be less academically challenged

F. Writing Thesis Statements

In its introduction, a research paper typically includes a sentence that expresses the main idea of the whole paper. This is its **thesis statement**. If the introduction consists of only one paragraph, the topic sentence of that paragraph is also the thesis statement of the entire paper. As you take notes, think about the main idea of your paper and how you might express it in one sentence. Initial attempts to formulate this sentence will likely be revised as you continue to read, take notes, and think about your topic.

A research paper may be one of two types, a report or an argument paper, and its thesis statement must be appropriate to that type.

A report research paper presents known information about a certain topic to acquaint the reader with all aspects of that topic, providing a comprehensive view. **Report thesis statements** are usually straightforward descriptions of generally accepted facts or points of view.

Examples of report thesis statements

> Computer technology has changed significantly in the last thirty years.
>
> Smoking contributes to cardiovascular disease.

An argument research paper is one in which the author takes a position and argues in support of it. Facts are presented about the topic, but the focus of the paper is on convincing the reader that the author's point of view is the correct one. The author will use literature from other writers and show how it supports the argument and refute the arguments of others to help convince the reader of the validity of the argument.

Argument thesis statements, therefore, make a claim and indicate the opinion or point of view that will be supported in the paper. Certain words and phrases are often used in argument thesis statements to indicate that the opinion of the author is being expressed. Some examples are:

although	*need to*	*most useful*
while	*have to*	*most efficient*
however	*cannot*	*most important*
must	*better*	*most significant*
should	*best*	*more useful than*
ought to	*only*	*more effective than*

Examples of argument thesis statements

> Universities need to consider seriously the disadvantages of online classes before continuing to increase the number of online courses offered each semester.
>
> While it is possible to benefit from eating organic products, eating organic is not necessary to have a healthy diet.

Exercise 4.3: Thesis Statements: Argument or Report?

Examine each sentence to determine whether it could be the main focus for a report (R) paper or an argument (A) paper. If the sentence presents an argument, underline the key words that indicate it is an argument. The first one has been done for you as an example.

1. While nuclear energy is an economically viable way of decreasing electricity production costs, the potential <u>hazards</u> associated with using this form of energy <u>make it too dangerous</u> to consider using. [A] R

2. Recycling methods have undergone many changes in the past ten years. A R

3. Online education is not as effective as classroom education. A R

4. The rapid rise in smartphone use has been shown to have a positive impact on public safety. A R

5. Selecting a good CEO is the most crucial element in determining the success of a company. A R

6. Schools need to do more to encourage children to exercise to decrease obesity in the U.S. A R

7. New medical procedures are proving valuable in increasing the lifespan of humans. A R

8. Many claim that any use of technology in the classroom enhances learning; however, to be used effectively, it must be used appropriately. A R

9. Although some may argue that it violates the principle of free speech, if we do not set strict limits on the realism of graphics in video games and on television, children will become desensitized to violence, resulting in negative impacts on society. A R

10. Several studies seem to indicate that owning pets is likely to increase a person's lifespan. A R

G. Writing Complete Drafts

The suggestions for drafting and revising in Section 1 (page 6) and Section 2 (pages 52–55) are also generally applicable to writing research papers. However, the style, length, and format requirements of research papers involve special considerations.

There is no one best way to write a draft. Write the sections in the order in which they will appear in your paper, or write them in a different order in the first draft and revisions. Because writers discover new ideas while drafting, many prefer to write body paragraphs first, and then, toward the end of the process, to write the introduction and the conclusion to incorporate the new ideas.

During all writing, and especially when starting longer works like research papers, writers may get stuck and not be able to think of anything else to write. This is very common and is called **writer's block**. If this happens to you, do not get frustrated. Simply set aside the section you are working on and move on to work on a different section of the paper. You may find that new ideas will come to you once you return to that portion of your paper. To get past writer's block at any stage of the process, you can also make use of the idea-generating techniques mentioned in Section 1 (pages 12–18).

Structure

Information about general essay structure, which also applies to research papers, can be found in Section 2 (pages 22–27). Some structural considerations specific to a research paper are described.

Abstract

An abstract is a summary of the main points of a research paper, published article, or other longer kinds of writing such as graduate theses and dissertations. Its function is to inform the reader very briefly about the key points in the paper or other work. In many cases, especially for undergraduates, instructors do not require an abstract with a student paper, but if one is required, it is usually about one paragraph (100 words) in length.

Introduction

The introduction is an important element in the research paper because it provides the reader with some background, the main idea as expressed in the thesis statement, and a preliminary mental organization for what will be found in the body of the paper.

An introduction typically starts broadly and ends narrowly. In other words, you should start with the most general ideas and information about the subject to orient your reader to your topic. The information then gets increasingly more specific, leading to the thesis statement. The most specific information—the foreshadowing of points to be developed in detail in the body of the research paper—usually comes at the end of the introduction. It is helpful to think of a research paper introduction as having the shape of an inverted triangle, as shown in Figure 4.1.

Figure 4.1: Structure of an Introduction

Body

The development paragraphs of a research paper (the body) are vital as support for the main idea of your paper. Because a research paper is more extensive than an essay, its organization needs careful thought. Refer to Section 3 for different ways to organize your paper. Remember that most papers, especially long ones, combine various organization patterns.

Conclusion

The conclusion of a well-constructed research paper should not present any surprises to the reader because its main idea has been stated in the introduction and the body paragraphs have provided support for that idea. The conclusion, therefore, restates the logical outcome of the paper—the idea expressed in the thesis statement—but it does not do so in exactly the same words as the thesis statement. The main points of the body are also briefly mentioned again in the conclusion, and some discussion of the importance of the main research idea or a possible direction for future research are often included. A quotation that effectively sums up the paper might be included if it is closely related to the thesis statement.

Transitions and Headings

The sections of your paper should be properly connected and flow smoothly from one idea to the next. This is done using effective transitions such as *however, in addition,* and *as a result.* For more examples of transitions, refer to Section 2 (pages 48–50), Section 7 (pages 244–248), and the sample essays and research papers in this section. Transitions are often a word, a phrase, or one or two sentences. In a research paper, you may need to write a separate, short paragraph to act as a transition to a new idea or section.

Some writers add headings before sections of their paper to guide the reader. This is standard practice in some academic fields, but not in others. Discover whether or not section headings are used in research papers in your field.

Integrating Sources

Incorporate sources into your research paper by paraphrasing or by directly quoting the authors (pages 112–116). Direct quotations can be helpful support, but you should use only a few; they should not make up more than 5 percent of the entire paper. Try to use direct quotations only when the author has said something in a very effective manner, when the strength of it would be lost if you paraphrased it.

For example, these sentences, from the book *Glass: A World History* published by the University of Chicago Press, express an idea so well that it would be better to quote rather than para-phrase them: "We tend to become too familiar with the world around us. The mirror, by reversing it, throws it into a new light and, in a curious way, makes it more intense" (Macfarlane and Martin, 2002, p. 201).

Whenever you use a source, either by paraphrasing or by including a quotation, explain why you have used it and provide a connection to the rest of your paper. For instance, you might say that the author has done the most recent research, or that many think that the author is an authority on the topic, or that the author has expressed a view opposing that held by others as in these statements:

- Ferranti and others have recently conducted experiments to investigate this problem and have found that . . .
- According to the International Institute for Population Studies, widely considered to be a reliable source of information, there are two major influences on . . .
- A very different point of view is presented by Jones and Omar, who assert that . . .

Reporting Verbs

When incorporating information from outside sources into your paper, choose from various **reporting verbs** to express the different ways of presenting information in the sources. The words *say* and *state* are basic and useful (for example: *In a recent article, Morrison states that . . .*), but there are many others that express different shades of meaning. A list of some of the words (with their meanings) that can be used to report the ideas of your sources follows.

advocate: publicly promote
assume: accept as true without proof
concede: accept unwillingly
emphasize: give special importance to
point out: draw attention to
remark: make a comment or statement
suggest: propose an idea for consideration

Citing Sources

You must be sure to properly **cite** every source that you include in your paper (see the advice on plagiarism on pages 116–119 for more information). Within the text of your paper, give credit to the authors of the sources that you use. In an in-text citation, the information you must include is the author's name and the year of publication.

There are a number of ways to cite authors in the text of your paper. Try to vary the way that you cite sources in your paper to make your writing more mature and sophisticated. Some general guidelines when citing sources within the main text follow, with examples.

- Put parentheses around anything in the citation that is not a part of the sentence.

  A recent study (McKenzie, 2017) has shown that. . . .

- If you are citing a specific part of the research from your source or using a direct quote from the source, include the page number where the reader can find the information or quotation.

  Raval (2015, p. 178) asserts that. . . .

- If you are referring to general information provided by the source, you do not need to include the page number.

  As proposed by Thomas (2016), . . .

  As early as 1975, Johnson and Carter were claiming that. . . .

H. Proofreading

The last thing that you should do before handing in your research paper to your instructor is to proofread. This is a crucial step in the writing process because there are generally specific require-ments of correctness and format for research papers. Proofread-ing focuses on format, sentence structure, and vocabulary. Ask these questions when proofreading your paper:

- Are there any typographical errors?
- Are there any grammar mistakes?
- Is the word choice appropriate?
- Is the references/citations list complete, citing all informa-tion from other sources?

- Is the page numbering complete?
- Is the format consistent in following a single style guide (APA, MLA, or some other)?

I. Citation Style Guides

Each source that you cite in the text of your paper must be added to your references list. The most common citation styles are the **APA (American Psychological Association)** and the **MLA (Modern Language Association)**, which are described in *Publication Manual of the American Psychological Association* and *MLA Handbook*. Less used but required in some fields is *A Manual for Writers of Research Papers, Theses, and Dissertations* by K. L. Turabian, based on the *Chicago Manual of Style* published by the University of Chicago Press. The style that you use depends on your field. Scientific and technical fields frequently use different styles. Check with your instructor to see which style is preferred.

Note that the official style guides are updated periodically, so you should consult them as needed for the latest editions and guidelines.

The reference list at the end of a research paper includes several pieces of information. APA and MLA are slightly different, but some pieces are required for both:

- author (or editor if a collection)
- chapter title or journal article title
- title of book or journal name
- year of publication
- publisher
- page numbers, for journal articles and chapters in books
- volume and issue number for articles

For all entries in both styles, use a **hanging indent**—all lines after the first one are indented half an inch.

> ▸ ▸ ▸ **Usage Note**
>
> These guidelines are adapted for student research papers. For other types of citation and for more detailed information on formatting papers, consult the latest edition of the complete style guide that you follow.

Bibliographic examples are given for APA and MLA styles for some of the most commonly cited types of sources. You must not mix styles: follow one style consistently. The differences between the two styles are sometimes small but important and may include elements such as:

- ordering of information
- use of italics
- use and placement of punctuation (such as periods and quotation marks)

J. APA Style: References, Format, and Sample Paper

Non-Electronic Sources

1. Book with one author

Svendsen, A. (2017). *Intelligence engineering: Going beyond the arts and sciences.* Lanham, MD: Rowman & Littlefield.

2. Book with two or more authors, edition other than first

Aliber, R. Z., & Kindleberger, C.P. (2015). *Manias, panics, and crashes: A history of financial crises* (7th ed.). London: Palgrave Macmillan.

3. Book by a group (corporate) author

American Psychological Association. (2010). *Publication manual of the American Psychological Association* (6th ed.). Washington, DC: American Psychological Association.

4. Edited book, no author

Zipes, J. (Ed.). (2017). *The sorcerer's apprentice: An anthology of magical tales.* Princeton, NJ: Princeton University Press.

5. Journal article

Park, S. Y. (2012). Stitching the fabric of family: Time, work, and intimacy in Seoul's Tongdaemun market. *The Journal of Korean Studies, 17*(2), 383–406.

6. Article or chapter in an edited volume

O'Leary, A. O. (2017). Undocumented Mexican women in the U.S. justice system: Immigration, illegality and law enforcement. In C. Datchi & J. Ancis (Eds.), *Gender, psychology, and justice: The mental health of women and girls in the legal system* (pp. 254–279). New York, NY: New York University Press.

Electronic Sources

1. ebook

Barr, D. (2007). *Introduction to U.S. health policy: The organization, financing, and delivery of health care in America.* Retrieved from http://search.ebscohost.com. ezproxy.uvm.edu/login.aspx?direct=true&db=nlebk&AN =249411&site=ehost-live&ebv=EB&ppid=pp_Cover

2. Journal article

Hisschemöller, M. (2016). Cultivating the global garden. *Challenges in Sustainability, 4(*1), 28–38. doi: 10.12924/ cis2016.04010028*

3. Article from online periodical

Wild, S. (2017). Ghana telescope heralds first pan-African array. *Nature, 545.* Retrieved from http://www.nature. com.ezproxy.uvm.edu/news/ghana-telescope-heralds-first-pan-african-array-1.21958

4. Online news article

Alderton, B. (2017, May 5). Laguna council to consider extending citywide smoking ban. *LA Times.* Retrieved from http://www.latimes.com/socal/daily-pilot/tn-dpt-me-lb-council-preview-20170506-story.html

---

* Journals now routinely assign a DOI, which stands for Digital Object Identifier. This sequence of numbers and letters allows a reader to find the exact version of a journal article that you read, so you should always include it. If there is no DOI, provide the URL of the journal's homepage.

5. Non-periodical web document

> The United States Census Bureau. (2017). *U.S. population and world clock*. Retrieved from https://www.census.gov/popclock/

6. Online encyclopedias and dictionaries

> Intersectionality. (2017, Feb. 27). In *Oxford English dictionary online*. Retrieved from http://www.oed.com.ezproxy.uvm.edu/view/Entry/429843?redirectedFrom=intersectionality#eid

Exercise 4.4: APA References: Correcting Errors

WB Ex. 4.6

Fix the one error in each APA bibliographic entry.

1. Book with one author

Gennett, P. (2015). *The benefits of walking: what your doctor never told you.* New York, NY: Pringle Press.

2. Book with two or more authors, edition other than first

Salesh, B., and Jounell, G. (2017). *Giving up technology may just make your day* (2nd ed.). Chicago, IL: University of Chicago Press.

3. Book by a group (corporate) author

World Bank. (2017). *Doing Business: Equal Opportunity for All.* Washington, DC: World Bank.

4. Edited book, no author

Concueso, L. (Ed.). 2016. *Critical thinking: A collection of essays.* Stanford, CA: Stanford University Press.

5. Journal article

O'Toole, R.S. (2017). The bonds of kinship, the ties of freedom in colonial Peru. *Journal of family history, 42*(1), 3–21.

6. Chapter in an edited volume

Neruda, Pablo. (2017). If you forget me. In M. Strand (Ed.), *100 great poems of the twentieth century* (pp. 21–22). New York, NY: W.W. Norton & Company.

7. **ebook**

Kranz, M. (2017). *Building the internet of things: Implement new business models, disrupt competitors, transform your industry.* From http://eds.a.ebscohost.com.authenticate.library.duq.edu/eds/ebookviewer/ebook/bmxlYmtfXzE0MDk4MDdfX0FO0?sid=78bd74b6-1bd3-4ebf-a41d-c5da0fdce15c@sessionmgr4009&vid=0&format=EB&rid=1

8. **Journal article (electronic)**

Thomas, R. G. (2013). How to achieve world security. Annual Review of Political Science, 6, 205–232. doi: 10.1146/annurev.polisci.6.121901.085731

9. **Article from online periodical**

Grossman, Lisa. (2017). Milky Way's loner status is upheld. *Science News, 64.* Retrieved from https://www.sciencenews.org/article/milky-ways-loner-status-upheld?tgt=nr

10. **Online news article**

Davis, N. (2017, Jun. 7). Suppressing the reasoning part of the brain stimulates creativity, study finds. Retrieved from https://www.theguardian.com/science/2017/jun/07/thinking-caps-on-electrical-currents-boost-creative-problem-solving-study-finds

11. **Non-periodical web document**

Edmunds. *2016 hybrid buying guide.* (2016). Retrieved from https://www.edmunds.com/hybrid/buying-guide/

12. **Online encyclopedias and dictionaries**

Fuel cell. (2017, Apr. 10). *Encyclopaedia Britannica Online.* Retrieved from https://www.britannica.com/technology/fuel-cell

APA Format for Student Research Paper

A **cover page** is the first page of your paper. This information should be centered on the page:

- title of paper
- name
- course number and/or name
- instructor's name
- date that you are handing in the paper
- page number in the upper right-hand corner (this is page 1)

Include an **abstract** on a separate page after the cover page if required by the instructor.

The **main text** of your paper should:

- be double-spaced
- have 1-inch margins on all sides of the page
- have page numbers in the upper right-hand corner following an abbreviated paper title or topic
- have indented new paragraphs (not an extra space between)
- be written in a standard font, such as Times New Roman, in 11 or 12 point size

In the text of your paper, when citing a work by more than one author, you should:

- cite both authors if there are two
- for 3 to 5 authors, the first time you cite, include all author names. After that use the first author's last name and **et al.**
- for 6 or more authors, always cite the first author's last name followed by et al.

Your **references** should begin with the centered heading References and:

- begin on a new page after your conclusion
- include only the sources mentioned in your paper
- number pages as a continuation of those in the text
- be double-spaced
- use hanging indent format for each entry

APA Sample Student Research Paper

The Deep Web 1

Include a shortened version of the title and page numbers at top right of all pages.

The Deep Web and the Dark Web:

The Other Side of the Internet

Cover page: Full title, student's name, course information, instructor's name, and date are all centered.

Capitalize main words of title.

Gustavo Sanchez

Course: English Writing 001

Instructor: Dr. Diane Jarvis

Date: April 14, 2017

The Deep Web 2

The Deep Web and the Dark Web:
The Other Side of the Internet

Title centered at top of page

All words are capitalized except for smaller words such as *in, on, at, the.*

Did you know that every time you get on a computer, you are using only a small part of the Internet? The Internet is much larger than people believe. In fact, the Internet can be divided into two big sections, one bigger than the other. The first section and the smallest one is the surface web, which has the web pages that we commonly use. It includes Google, Facebook and any other web page starting in "www." However, the much bigger section that most people do not know about is the Deep Web. This is the part that browsers cannot access. It includes items such as, "all user databases, webmail pages, registration-required web forums, and pages behind paywalls" (**Egan, 2017**). In 2000, studies by BrightPlanet web intelligence found that the Deep Web contains 7550 terabytes of information compared to the 19 terabytes contained in the surface web. *Furthermore*, the Deep Web contains 550 billion individual documents against the one billion of the

Citation (author, date)

Transition: adding information

The Deep Web 3

surface web (**Bergman, 2001**). Many businesses employ the Deep Web to get more information to improve their businesses. *However, most people also are unaware that a small portion of the Deep Web exists called the Dark Web, which is used for illegal purposes.* As Bartlett (2015) defines it, the deep web is "a catchall term for the myriad shocking, disturbing, and controversial corners of the net – the realm of imagined criminals and lurking **predators**" (**p. 5**).

The Dark Web, like the Deep Web, is not navigable from a common browser like Google Chrome or Firefox, which can navigate only an estimated .03 % of the total Web (**Segev, 2010**). To navigate on the Dark Web, you need to use the browser TOR (The Onion Browser). This makes possible the idea of diving into the dark side of the web. The surface web uses ".com" or ".co" pages but this web browser was made to navigate in ".onion" pages, which comes from the idea of layers, or skins, where people can dig deeper, looking for more information than what is visible from the surface (**Segev, 2010**).

Citation

Thesis statement near end of introduction

Direct quotation with page number following the quote, and the punctuation after the page number (not inside the quotation marks)

Transition sentence between paragraphs with citation

Citation

The Deep Web 4

The Dark Web browser Tor was created in the 1990s by the U.S. navy, specifically by military naval programmers led by Paul Syverson, Michael G. Reed and David Goldschlag, with the purpose of supporting government spying operations and protecting U.S. intelligence communications online (**Smith, 2013**). Its development started in 1995 by The U.S. Office of Naval Research with the name "onion routing" and later in 1997, was helped by The Defense Advanced Research Projects Agency (DARPA). Years later, in 2004, Tor became part of a new project, "The Tor Project" (**Babatunde, 2013**). Since then Tor has been opened to the world wide public and is now accessible for anyone who wants to make their internet navigation private (**Bartlett, 2015**).

As the security specialist and certified ethical hacker Pierluigi Paganini (**2012**) explains, Tor anonymity works by basically sending encrypted information between several connections. In simple words, imagine that you send a message to a friend that says "hello." This word is going to be changed or

Citation

Citation

Citation

Citation (author's name part of the sentence, not in parentheses)

The Deep Web 5

encrypted while your friend is receiving the message,
and if someone else tries to get this information he
will receive something like "ehlol." The information
is going to be disorganized while it is being sent,
and later reorganized on your friend's computer. In
that way, only you and your friend can see the real
message (**Rouse, 2014**). With regards to routing,
Citation
the information is disorganized and passed through
different computers between you and a web page server
several times and then organized in the right order
when the information arrives to your computer. Using
these several connections makes it harder for people to
find your personal information, such as the IP address
of your computer, adding an extra layer of privacy
(**Paganini, 2012**).
Citation

However, since opening Tor and the Dark Web
Transition: unexpected result
usage to the world, Tor and the Dark Web have come
to be used for illegal purposes. Commonplace illegal
activities in the Dark Web include fake identification
vending, illegal gun and drug sales, hitman contracts,
and even child porn (**Komarov, 2012**).
Citation

The Deep Web 6

But how do people exchange money for such illegal services inside the Dark Web? The answer is using bitcoin. It is a new digital currency, invented by Satoshi Nakamoto in 2009, that is used to buy any kind of product or service through the internet (**Yellin, Aratari, & Paglieri, 2016**). It has no bank intervention, no middle man and no fees like normal currencies. It is becoming more popular for its internationality; *in fact,* it is accepted in many countries as a payment method on online stores. *Additionally,* it makes sales completely anonymous. The transactions are done through a public log where buyers and sellers' names are never revealed, keeping bitcoin users' identities private.

The abuse of these tools has brought *consequences,* such as the usage of online drug markets through Tor. Teenagers are using Tor to buy drugs online. Believe it or not, there are Amazon stores created just for drug selling. A good example of this is "Silk Road 3," an online store that sells any type of drug secretly (**Nelson, 2015**). It is hard for the police to catch the customer

Rhetorical question used as transition

Citation. Note the use of the ampersand instead of *and* with multiple-author citations.

Transition: example

Transition: adding information

Effect indicator

Citation

The Deep Web 7

and the seller of these illegal substances because there is
no record of who the seller and buyer are.

As mentioned above, there are also hitmen services
on the Dark Web. People can easily find hitmen or
hire assassins through the Deep Web. There are many
pages with the purpose of paying, usually in bitcoin,
to maintain the anonymity on both sides for such
transactions. One of the better known hitman pages on
the Dark Web is "The Hitman Network," where people
can find a person who will be paid to do the crime
for them (**Bartlett, 2015**). The only conditions for the
customer are that his target has to be over 16 years of
age and not a major politician (**Lake, 2013**). This has
maligned the name of Tor and the Deep Web, making
them look like a source just for illegal activities.

*Unfortunately, even if you want to use Tor for non-
illegal purposes*, such as searching for information
for a research paper or for learning, there is another
negative aspect to Tor and the Dark Web. It is not safe.
There are many chances for people with no experience

Transition phrase

Citation

Citation

Transition
from previous
paragraph

The Deep Web 8

navigating the deep waters of the internet to get into
the dark side of it, which is full of viruses and hackers.
Thus, people are taking the risk of being infected or
hacked by using this browser.

In conclusion, there is much more information on
the Internet than most people are aware of. The Deep
Web can be used to hide user information and protect
confidentiality. *However,* there are parts of the Deep
Web that are used for illegal purposes, which is why
it is called the Dark Web. Navigating the Dark Web
can be dangerous. People must be made aware of the
Dark Web and its usage. In this way, people can make
a more informed choice of whether they will use the
Dark Web or not. Yes, privacy is important, but not at
the cost of putting your information at risk.

Transition:
conclusion/result

Transition:
showing
conclusion

Transition:
unexpected result

Main idea of
paper is stated
again (in different
words) in
conclusion.

The Deep Web 9

References

Babatunde, J. (2013). *The armed forces: Instrument of peace, strength, development and prosperity.* Bloomington, IN: AuthorHouseUK.

Bartlett, J. (2015). *The dark net: Inside the digital underworld.* Brooklyn, NY: Melville Publishing House.

Bergman, M. K. (2001, Aug.). *The Deep Web: Surfacing hidden value.* Retrieved from http://quod.lib. umich.edu/cgi/t/text/text-idx?c=jep;view=text;rgn =main;idno=3336451.0007.104

Chandler, N. (n.d.) *How the Deep Web works.* Retrieved from http://computer.howstuffworks.com/ internet/basics/how-the-deep-web-works.htm

Egan, M. (2017, Apr. 6). *What is the Deep Web and Dark Web?* Retrieved from http://www.pcadvisor. co.uk/how-to/internet/what-is-dark-web-deep-web-3593569/

Komarov, A. (2014, Sept.). *So what is this "Dark Web" I keep hearing about?* Retrieved from http://blog. infoarmor.com/category/privacy-prevention/

References list starts on a new page at the end of the paper.

Center the heading.

Use hanging indent format for each entry: first line not indented, second and following lines indented.

References are listed in alphabetical order by author last name.

The Deep Web 10

Lake, E. (2013, Oct. 17). Online hitmen. *The Daily Beast.* Retrieved from http://www.thedailybeast. com/articles/2013/10/17/hitman-network-says-it-accepts-bitcoins-to-murder-for-hire.html

Nelson, S. (2015, Oct. 2). Buying drugs online remains easy, 2 years after FBI killed silk road. *U.S. News.* Retrieved from https://www.usnews.com/news/articles/2015/10/02/buying-drugs-online-remains-easy-2-years-after-fbi-killed-silk-road.

Noack, D. (2001, Sep./Oct.). Web sites hidden from view. *Link-up, (18)*5, 26. Retrieved from https://search-proquest-com.authenticate.library.duq.edu/docview/210232536?accountid=10610

Paganini, P. (2012). *The good and the bad of the Deep Web.* Retrieved from http://securityaffairs.co/wordpress/8719/cyber-crime/the-good-and-the-bad-of-the-deep-web.html

Rouse, M. (2014, Nov. 21). *Encryption.* Retrieved from http://searchsecurity.techtarget.com/definition/encryption

The Deep Web 11

Segev, E. (2010). *Google and the digital divide: The bias of online knowledge.* Oxford: Chandos Publishing.

Smith, G. (2013, Aug. 19). *Meet Tor, the military-made privacy network that counts Edward Snowden as a fan.* Retrieved from http://www.huffingtonpost.com/2013/07/18/tor-snow den_n_3610370.html

Yellin, T., Aratari, D., & Paglieri, J. (2016). *What is Bitcoin?* Retrieved from http://money.cnn.com/info graphic/technology/what-is-bitcoin/

Multiple authors. Note the use of the ampersand (&) in the reference list.

K. MLA Style: Works Cited, Format, and Sample Paper

Samples of specific types of sources are included as models to help with structuring your own Works Cited sources. Note that access dates are not included. If the access date is required for your assignment, refer to the format shown.

Non-Electronic Sources

1. **Book with one author, edition other than first**

   Steinbeck, John. *Of Mice and Men*. 4th ed., Penguin Books, 1993.

2. **Book with two authors**

   Raustiala, Kal, and Christopher Jon Sprigman. *The Knockoff Economy: How Imitation Sparks Innovation*. Oxford UP, 2012.

3. **Book by a group (corporate) author**

   Center for Chemical Process Safety. *Guidelines for Engineering Design for Process Safety*. 2nd ed., Wiley-AIChE, 2013.

4. **Edited book (no author)**

   Allergies and Asthma: What Every Parent Needs to Know, edited by Michael J. Welch, American Academy of Pediatrics, 2011.

5. **Work in an anthology, reference, or collection / chapter in an edited volume**

   Williams, Joseph M. "Defining Complexity." *Style in Rhetoric and Composition*, edited by Paul Butler, Bedford/St. Martin's, 2010, pp.186–201.

6. **Journal article, more than two authors**

   Odden, Michelle C., et al. "The Impact of the Aging Population on Coronary Heart Disease in the United States." *The American Journal of Medicine*, vol.124, no. 9, 2011, pp. 827–833.

Electronic Sources

1. ebook

> Massengill, Rebekah P. *Wal-Mart Wars: Moral Populism in the Twenty-First Century.* NYU Press, 2013. *eBook collection (EBSCOhost).*

Note: For an ebook, the database and URL (or doi if available) will be included at the end for location. The database is in italics, but the URL or doi is not.

2. Journal article with doi, obtained from a database

> Noel, Valerie A., et al. "Barriers to Employment for Transition-age Youth with Developmental and Psychiatric Disabilities." *Administration and Policy in Mental Health and Mental Health Services Research,* vol. 44, no. 3, 2017, pp. 354–358. *ProQuest Central,* doi:10.1007/s10488-016-0773-y.

3. Article from online periodical

> Eaton, Elizabeth. "Spray-on Mosquito Repellents Are More Effective Than Other Devices." *Science News,* 28 Mar. 2017, www.sciencenews.org/article/spray-mosquito-repellents-are-more-effective-other-devices?mode=magazine&context=193019.

4. Online news article

> Pérez-Peña, Richard, and Sheryl Gay Stolberg. "Prosecutors Taking Tougher Stance in Fraternity Hazing Deaths." *New York Times,* 8 May 2017, www.nytimes.com/2017/05/08/us/penn-state-prosecutors-fraternity-hazing-deaths.html?ref=todayspaper&_r=0.

5. Non-periodical web document, without author

> "Asthma Health Center." *WebMD,* www.webmd.com/asthma/default.htm.

6. Non-periodical web document, with author

> Fritz, Joanne. "Online Fundraising: A Startup Guide." *The Balance,* 16 Oct. 2016, 1:00pm, www.thebalance.com/online-fundraising-a-startup-guide-2502433.

7. Chapter/section of a web document

Occupational Safety and Health Administration. "Guidelines for Employers to Reduce Vehicle Crashes." *US Department of Labor,* www.osha.gov/Publications/ motor_vehicle_guide.html.

8. Online encyclopedias and dictionaries

Rafferty, John P. "Is the Ozone Layer Finally Healing Itself?" *Encyclopaedia Britannica,* 21 Apr. 2017, www.britannica.com/demystified/ is-the-ozone-layer-finally-healing-itself.

9. Video located in an online journal

Connected Learning Alliance. "Elizabeth Lawley: 'Just Press Play'—Adding a Game Layer to the Undergraduate Experience." *The International Journal of Learning and Media,* vol. 4, no. 3–4, ijlm.net/node/13215.

10. Blog/Listserv/Discussion Group

Muza, Sharon. "Maternal Mental Health Matters!" *Science & Sensibility,* 2 May 2017, https://www. scienceandsensibility.org/blog/maternal-mental-health- matters.

11. Email

Cicchinelli, Amanda. "Re: Innovations in 3D Printing." Received by Gerry Kort, 1 Jun. 2017.

12. YouTube video

"History Channel Documentary—Who Really Discovered America?—Documentary 2016." *YouTube,* uploaded by Discovery World, 25 Oct. 2016, www.youtube.com/ watch?v=d_8aYdOPs3g.

WB
Ex. 4.7

Exercise 4.5: MLA Works Cited: Correcting Errors

Fix the one error in each MLA bibliographic entry.

1. **Book with one author, edition other than first**

   Renfrew, Stephen. Tell Me a Story. 3rd ed., Scribner, 2015.

2. **Book with two authors**

   Springfield, Janice, and Manchester, Simone. *A History of Immigrants in the US.* W.W. Norton and Company, 2012.

3. **Book by a group (corporate) author**

   NASA. *A History of NASA.* 2nd edition, NASA, 2016.

4. **Edited book, no author**

   Ghost Stories from the Gore Orphanage, James Pierce (ed.), Ohio UP, 2014.

5. **Work in an anthology, reference, or collection / chapter in an edited volume**

   Vaira, Louis. "Some Aspects of Pittsburgh's Contributions to the Civil War." *Industry and Infantry: The Civil War in Western Pennsylvania,* edited by Brian Butko and Nicholas Ciotola, Historical Society of Western Pennsylvania, 2003, p. 60–70.

6. **Journal article, more than two authors**

   Martinez-Austria, Polioptro F. et al. "Temperature and Heat-Related Mortality Trends in the Sonoran and Mojave Desert Region." *Atmosphere,* Vol. 8, No. 3, 2017, pp.1–13.

7. **ebook**

   Houston, Edwin J. *The Wonder Book of Volcanoes and Earthquakes.* Bolster Press, 2016. *http://www.gutenberg.org/ebooks/43320.*

8. Journal article with doi, obtained from a database

Clennett-Sirois, Laurence. "It's Complicated: The Social Lives of
Networked Teens." *Canadian Journal of Communication*,
vol. 39, pp. 663–665, 2014. *ProQuest Central*, dx.doi.org/
10.22230/cjc.2014v39n4a2917.

9. Article from online periodical

Lee, Robert. "Accounting for Conquest: The Price of the Louisiana
Purchase of Indian Country." The Journal of American History,
Mar. 2017, http://jah.oah.org/issues/march-2017/#articles.

10. Chapter/section of a web document

The MLA Style Center. Works Cited: A Quick Guide. *Modern
Language Association,* https://style.mla.org/works-cited-a-
quick-guide/.

11. Email

Crettering, Kimberly. "Re: How to Find the Best Internships."
Received by Humberto Gonzalez, May 5, 2017.

What's New in MLA, 8th Edition?

MLA, 8th Edition, is slightly different from previous editions. It is a little more flexible than APA and previous MLA editions. The general order of information (and punctuation) that you should include is:

> Author. Title of Source. Title of Container, Other Contributors (Edited by first name last name, etc), version (2nd edition, abridged edition, etc), volume (vol.), number (no.), Publisher, Publication date, Location (pages (pp.), URL (begin with "www"), or doi).
> 2nd Container's Title, Other Contributors, version, number, Publisher, Publication date, Location, Date of Access (if applicable).

In MLA, 8th Edition, a **container** is something that holds something smaller. For example, for an article in a journal, the article is the smaller part within the larger container—the journal. New technologies such as streaming video may mean you have more than one container.

Some general changes:

- Some publisher names are now abbreviated: Cambridge University Press is now Cambridge UP. City of publication is not required.
- Access date may be included if required by the instructor. If it is required, it comes at the end of the citation and is in the form:

  > Accessed day month year: Accessed 21 Jan. 2017.

- Listing more than one author follows this format:

  > <u>2 authors:</u> Last name, First name Middle name or initial, and First name Last name, as in:
  >
  > > Smith, John H., and Margaret Pullman.
  >
  > <u>3 or more authors:</u> Last name, First name Middle name or initial, et al., as in:
  >
  > > Renquist, Alan, et al.

MLA Format for Student Research Paper

There is no **cover page**. This information should be written, double-spaced, in the upper left corner of the first page:

- name
- course number and/or name
- instructor's name
- date that you are handing in the paper

Your last name and the page number should be on all pages in the upper right-hand corner (a **running head** in word processing).

The **title** and **text** of your paper continue on the first page and should:

- start with the title, centered
- be double-spaced
- have 1-inch margins on all sides of the page
- have your last name and page numbers in the upper right-hand corner
- have indented new paragraphs (not an extra space between)
- be written in a standard font, such as Times New Roman, in 11 or 12 point size

Include an **abstract** immediately after the title and before the text if required by the instructor.

When citing a work by more than one author, you should:

- cite both authors if there are two
- for three or more authors, cite only the first one followed by the abbreviation **et al.** (with a period at the end of the abbreviation but not after *et*)

Your **Works Cited** list should begin with the centered heading Works Cited and:

- begin on a new page after your conclusion
- include only the sources mentioned in your paper
- number pages as a continuation of those in the text
- be double-spaced
- use hanging indent format for each entry

MLA Sample Student Research Paper

Shen 1

Barbara Shen

Professor Robert Michaels

English 109

4 May 2017

The Challenges of Reducing Car Emissions

in China to Improve Air Quality

Every winter, a thick haze descends on eastern China for one to two months, a blanket of smog so thick that it is visible from space. In the winter of 2013, instruments at the U.S. Embassy in Beijing registered record-breaking levels of air-borne pollutants, which brought global attention to China's haze problem (**Toon**). In mid-December 2016, as a result of the poor air quality, officials issued pollution alerts for more than 40 cities in Northern China—schools and offices were closed, and citizens were urged to stay indoors (**Hilaire**). **Scientists and government authorities have been striving to determine the most significant causes**

Margin annotations:

Write your last name and the page number in the top right corner of all pages.

At the top left margin, write your name, instructor's name, course name, and date.

Double space the whole paper.

Center the title.

Capitalize all words in title except smaller words like *of, in, on, at.*

Citation: last name of the person quoted in parentheses. No page numbers given in source text.

Citation

Shen 2

of this serious problem and are working to find ways
to reduce the level of pollutants entering China's air,
but it is neither simple nor easy to convince people
to make lifestyle changes in order to improve the air
quality.

*Because China has gone through rapid urbanization
and motorization in recent decades, it is not surprising
that automobile emissions have played a significant
role in degrading the nation's air quality.* China has an
enormous population (1.39 billion and growing) which
contributes to the enormous need for personal vehicles.
As of 2015, 56% of China's population resided in cities,
making urban areas particularly susceptible to air
pollution problems, for where there are a lot of people,
there are also a lot of cars (**"Urban Population"**). **Feng
and Li** *report on* the dramatic increase of automobiles
in China in the past two decades, with the number of
registered automobiles in Beijing from 2001 to 2011
rising from 100 per 10,000 people to 470 per 10,000
people. **The Chinese newspaper *Global Times* reports
that between 1998 and 2013, the number of cars**

Thesis statement near end of introduction

Indicates pattern of organization: causes

Citation: First few words of the title in quotation marks is used for the citation as no author is available for this source.

Citation of author in text

Reporting verb

Shen 3

in Beijing grew approximately 303%, confirming Beijing's dramatic rise in number of automobiles ("Beijing to Cut Number"). *Thus,* in major urban centers such as Beijing—home to nearly six million private vehicles—air pollution *is caused* primarily *by* vehicle emissions. *As one scholar reports*:

> Research conducted by a special team studying 'causes and controls of atmospheric haze' at the Chinese Academy of Sciences indicates that automobile emissions are the greatest contributor to the PM2.5 pollution in Beijing, accounting for almost one-fourth of the total pollution. (Wang)

Obviously, the large number of vehicles—especially in China's urban areas—produces a great deal of emissions, which has a strong negative effect on air quality.

Vehicle emissions are dangerous in terms of air pollution *for several reasons*. PM2.5 is the main factor of air pollution in Beijing. **Jeng and Yu** explain the matter as follows:

Margin annotations:

Paraphrase, using an introduction with the type of source used, including a citation at end of paraphrase

Transition

Indicates pattern of organization: cause

Connecting phrase

Quotation 4 lines or longer: entire quote indented .5 in. from left margin

Citation after end of quote punctuation

Indicates pattern of organization: reasons

Citation in text, so not needed at end of quotation

Shen 4

Airborne particulate matters (PMs) consist of a mixture of solids or liquids suspended in the air. PMs are conveniently classified based on their aerodynamic diameter sizes, ranging from nanometers to 100μm. Thoracic particles (PM10) are those with aerodynamic diameters less than 10μm, with similarities applicable to coarse particles (PM2.5–10), fine particles (PM2.5), and ultrafine particles (PM0.1).

According to Shah and Wang, the fine PM 2.5 particles will go directly to the alveoli of the lungs, causing major health hazards such as angiocardiopathy, respiratory tract infection and restricted growth in children. **Moore** *reports that* "studies by the World Bank, WHO, and the Chinese Academy for Environmental Planning on the effect of air pollution on health concluded that between 350,000 and 500,000 people die prematurely each year as a result of outdoor air pollution in China." **Moore** also *points out that* in 2011 twice as many people in Beijing had lung cancer as in 2002. This is clearly a serious problem for China,

Phrase connecting source to the text

Citation of author in the text

Reporting verb

Citation of author in the text

Reporting verb

Shen 5

with deadly consequences for hundreds of thousands
of people, not to mention those who suffer respiratory
problems on a regular basis. *Since a great deal of air
pollution is caused by car emissions, and considering
the huge population and the need for personal vehicles
in China, it is necessary to find a way to meet people's
transportation needs while decreasing emissions.*

 In order to combat the pollution problem, the
government has implemented several policies to reduce
the number of private vehicles on the roads. An odd-
even license plate policy was introduced in Beijing in
2008 that allows "cars that have an even last number of
their license plates to be able to drive on roads in one
day while the cars that have an odd last number of their
license plates are able to go on the road the next day in
order to improve air quality in the city" (**"Road Space
Rationing"**). These restrictions are put into effect
when pollution in the city reaches (or threatens to
reach) unhealthy levels. *Thus* the number of cars on the
road—and *therefore* the amount of emissions—is cut
in half for a period of time. While this approach has a

Concluding
sentence for
section on causes
of air pollution

Transition phrase

Citation

Transition

Transition

Shen 6

noticeable effect on the air quality in a time of crisis, it
is a short-term solution to a long-term problem, and it
is an unpopular policy as well. Clearly other solutions
must be sought.

Another approach to reducing vehicle emissions — Transition phrase
is that the government has also asked citizens
to give up using private vehicles and instead use
public transportation more often. Beijing has a very
convenient public transportation system, which
includes a subway system with 18 lines and a bus
system of more than 700 routes served by 20,000
buses. There are even 40,000 public bicycles available
for rent, for people who want to use their own energy
to transport themselves around the city (**"Beijing** — Citation
Transportation"). *Nonetheless,* many people still — Transition
would like to have a private car, especially middle-aged
people, many of whom regard private vehicles as the
sign of social position and personal power. Although
they don't necessarily need a car, many middle-aged
people would like to purchase a vehicle as soon as
they have money to afford one. *Additionally,* as for the — Transition

Shen 7

young generation of people who live in megacities, life is quite busy and taking public transportation has the drawback of following the set transit schedules. People who have private vehicles have freedom to control their time and choose when to travel: they don't need to follow the public transportation schedule. In both of these cases, people would rarely consider the connection between environmental consequences and private vehicles. Rather than being concerned with environmental protection, they prefer to use a private car for social status or convenience. It is not a popular solution to ask people in Beijing to give up their private vehicles. It is *therefore* very difficult to make | Transition
a significant improvement to this serious pollution problem by asking people to change their means of transportation.

Since reducing the number of vehicles on the roads and asking people to use more public transportation are solutions with limited effectiveness, other solutions must be found. New automotive technologies that have been emerging in recent years—like electric

Transition sentence connecting previous ideas about "government solutions to reduce air pollution" to new idea of *other solutions*

Shen 8

cars—hold the promise of significantly reducing
vehicle emissions. *According to* an article in *LiveScience*,
"whereas conventional vehicles burn fuel in an internal
combustion engine, battery-powered electric vehicles
don't have an engine. Instead, they use energy stored
in batteries to power one or more electric motors"
(**Lewis**). *Compared with* traditional vehicles with
gasoline engines, electric cars don't have emissions at
all, and could therefore be an effective solution for air
pollution problems in places like China. The Chinese
newspaper *Shanghai Daily proposes that* with the
serious air pollution in Beijing, there are more potential
buyers seeking electric cars (**"Pollution"**). When a red
alert is issued in the city due to high pollution levels,
there are restrictions on which gasoline cars can drive
at certain times. But electric cars are free to drive at
any time, and are *therefore* very appealing to drivers.
Drivers are interested in the freedom that electric cars
may bring, along with the possible environmental
benefit. *Moreover*, the Chinese government is offering
many incentives for people to buy electric cars:

Margin annotations:
- Phrase connecting source to the text
- Citation
- Indicating relationship: comparison
- Phrase connecting source to the text
- Citation
- Transition
- Transition

Shen 9

exempting them from certain taxes and fees, which can
save buyers a lot of money. *According to* one Beijing
business-owner, electric cars are a hopeful way to save
the air quality in the city and also bring people benefits
beyond just the air they breathe (**"Pollution"**).

Phrase connecting
source to the text

Citation

To conclude, automobile emissions are the main
contributor to Beijing's air pollution, a serious
problem that is a threat to people's health and long life.
Ordinary people can contribute to purifying air quality
by reducing how much they drive (as sometimes
required by the government during pollution "red
alerts"), and by taking public transportation rather
than driving private vehicles. Yet many people prefer
not to give up the comfort or convenience brought
by private vehicles, so these are insufficient solutions
to an enormous problem. The growth of the electric
car market in China is encouraging, with regard to
improving air quality by reducing vehicle emissions.
The government is encouraging people to buy and
drive electric cars by providing incentives and by
building charging stations. *However*, it is important

Transition phrase

Conclusion
states the main
idea and topics
mentioned in the
introduction.

Transition

Shen 10

to remember that these cars are charged by electricity, and over 70% of the electricity in China is produced by coal-powered plants (**Deb**). This means that charging an electric car actually produces air pollution in a different location. So while electric cars may be beneficial for air quality in cities, widespread use of electric cars might actually increase air pollution in the places where coal is burned to produce electricity. Clearly, there is no simple solution for the problem of air pollution in China. **The best path to better air quality is for the government to continue to strengthen its policies, and for citizens to gain a greater sense of personal responsibility for the environment, so that they are willing to drive their cars less, to take public transportation, and to make use of new technology that reduces vehicle emissions.** In this way, they will ensure a healthier and more beautiful future for themselves and their children.

Citation

Suggestion for future course of action. Common content in a conclusion

Shen 11

Works Cited

"Beijing to Cut Number of New Cars." *Global
Times*, 25 Oct. 2016, www.globaltimes.cn/
content/1013607.shtml. Accessed 1 May, 2017.

"Beijing Transportation." *Travel China Guide*,
www.travelchinaguide.com/cityguides/beijing/
transportation/. Accessed 27 April 2017.

Deb, Anrica. "Why Electric Cars are Only as Clean as
their Power Supply." *The Guardian*, 8 Dec. 2016,
www.theguardian.com/environment/2016/dec/08/
electric-car-emissions-climate-change. Accessed 25
April 2017.

Feng, Suwei and Qiang Li. "Car Ownership Control
in Chinese Mega Cities: Shanghai, Beijing and
Guangzhou." *Journeys*, Sept. 2013, pp. 40–49.
www.lta.gov.sg/ltaacademy/doc/13Sep040-Feng_
CarOwnershipControl.pdf. Accessed 26 Apr. 2017.

Hilaire, Eric. "Satellite Eye on Earth: December
2016—in Pictures." *The Guardian*, 4 Jan 2017,
www.theguardian.com/environment/2017/

Works Cited list
begins on a new
page at the end
of the paper
(insert a page
break after the
text of the paper).
Note that it is
Works, never
Work.

Center the
heading.

Use hanging
indent format for
each entry: first
line not indented;
second and
following lines
indented.

Works cited
are listed in
alphabetical order
by author last
name.

Shen 12

jan/04/satellite-eye-on-earth-december-2016-in-pictures#img-6. Accessed 25 April 2017.

Jeng, Hueiwang Anna Cook and Liang Yu. "Particulate Matter." *Green Health: An A-to-Z Guide*, edited by Oladele Ogunseitan, SAGE Publications, Inc., 2011, pp. 351-53, doi: http://dx.doi.org/10.4135/9781412974592.n109. Accessed 27 April 2017.

Lewis, Tanya. "Electric vs. Fuel Cell Vehicles: 'Green' Auto Tech Explained." *LiveScience.com*, 28 Jan. 2015, www.livescience.com/49594-electric-fuel-cell-vehicles-explainer.html. Accessed 25 April 2017.

Moore, Malcolm. "China's 'airpocalypse' kills 350,000 to 500,000 each year." *The Telegraph*, 7 Jan, 2014, www.telegraph.co.uk/news/worldnews/asia/china/10555816/Chinas-airpocalypse-kills-350000-to-500000-each-year.html. Accessed 1 May 2017.

"Pollution a Boost for Electric Car Industry." *Shanghai Daily*, 11 Dec. 2015, www.shanghaidaily.com/business/auto/Pollution-a-boost-for-electric-car-industry/shdaily.shtml. Accessed 27 April 2017.

Shen 13

"Road Space Rationing in Beijing." *Wikipedia*, 23
Feb. 2017, en.wikipedia.org/wiki/Road_space_
rationing_in_Beijing. Accessed 25 April 2017.

Shan, Juan and Qian Wang. "Exposure to Smog is
Severe Hazard." *China Daily Europe*, 6 Dec. 2011,
europe.chinadaily.com.cn/china/2011-12/06/
content_14216539.htm. Accessed 1 May 2017.

Toon, John. "China's Severe Winter Haze Tied to
Climate Change." *Georgia Tech News Center*, 15
March 2017, www.news.gatech.edu/2017/03/15/
chinas-severe-winter-haze-tied-climate-change.
Accessed 25 Apr. 2017.

"Urban Population (% of Total)" *The World Bank*,
data.worldbank.org/indicator/SP.URB.TOTL.
IN.ZS?locations=CN. Accessed 1 May 2017.

Wang, Tao. "Impact of Automobile Emissions to
Beijing Smog Might Be Underestimated." *Carnegie-
Tsinghua Center for Global Policy*, 28 Feb. 2014,
carnegietsinghua.org/2014/02/28/impact-of-
automobile-emissions-to-beijing-s smog-might-be-
underestimated-pub-55286. Accessed 1 May 2017.

SECTION 5

GRAMMAR AND STYLE

5

AT WORD LEVEL

A. Word Form

Words in a sentence must be in the correct form. Errors in **word form** may include wrong choices with respect to singular or plural, part of speech (noun, verb, adjective, adverb), pronoun form (male or female), or verb form.

<u>Examples</u>

Wrong (verb form): Chung **walking** very quickly along the street.

Correct: Chung **was walking** very quickly along the street.

Wrong (adverb form): Chung was walking very **quick** along the street.

Correct: Chung was walking very **quickly** along the street.

Exercise 5.1: Recognizing Word Form Errors

Each of these sentences has one or two word form errors. Correct the errors. The first one has been done for you as an example.

1. The inventions of tool use was a huge step in human development. [*inventions* should be singular to agree with the singular verb *was.*]

2. Progress in agricultural are essential for all societies.

3. The industrial revolution was based on learning how to harnessed the power of machinery.

4. They were speaking so loudly that I could not concentration.

5. The impact of writer systems was profound because it allowed humans to communicate easy across great distances of time and space.

6. Oral history is part of many culture, but written history is said to be the foundation of civilize.

7. Some experts claiming that computer technology, as compared to all other inventions, has had the great influence on world history.

8. Electronic calculators have enable modern commerce to progress in unexpected ways.

9. The astonishingly advances in modern telecommunications will enable a new revolutionary to occur.

10. Technology today allows us to communicate instantaneous.

11. The most important question is whether humans can learn to using technology for peaceful purposes.

12. Inventions that we have not yet even dream of will be part of the normal life of future generation.

B. Articles

Terms to know

Indefinite article: *a* (or *an* if the noun begins with a vowel sound)

Definite article: *the*

Count (countable) noun: A noun that can be made plural or counted (*book, books, three books*).

Non-count (uncountable) noun: Nouns that usually cannot be counted or made plural (*furniture, flour, weather*).

Zero article: This refers to use of a noun with no article before it, as in *Snow is white.*

To decide which article to use, determine what type of noun is being described.

Count and Non-Count Nouns

- Use **a** or **an** with a singular count noun (never with a non-count or plural noun).

Examples

> Give me **a** pen.
> (referring to an unspecified pen)
>
> **An** elephant damaged this tree.
> (referring to an unspecified elephant)

- Use **a** or **an** if someone (or something) is one in a group of many.

Example

> I discussed it with Dr. Martin, **a** professor in the Philosophy Department.

> ▸ ▸ ▸ **Usage Note**
>
> Many nouns can be non-count or count **depending on the context.** In these cases, the meaning of the noun may be different according to whether it is non-count or count.

Nouns with General Reference

- Use **no article and the singular form** of the noun to refer to a general type of something.

Examples

> I went there by **bus**.
>
> **Time** flies when you're having fun.
> (general idea of time)

- Use **no article and the plural form** of the noun when you mean all things or persons referred to by that noun.

Examples

> **Students** often come here to see me.
> (refers to all types of students)
>
> I've been to that restaurant many **times**.
> (a specific number of different times)

- Use **a** or **an** or **the** for the general meaning of all types, species, or items referred to by the noun, especially to a species or type of something (a more formal usage).

Examples

> **A lion** is an interesting animal.
>
> **The lion** is an interesting animal.

Nouns with Definite Reference

- Use **the** with count or non-count nouns, in singular or plural, when the reader (or listener) knows what definite or specific thing is being referred to by the noun. Often an *of* phrase or *that* clause is used to make something specific.

> ▸ ▸ ▸ **Usage Note**
>
> Some adjectives can also make a noun unique and definite.

Examples

> Give me **the** pen.
> (referring to a specific pen that the reader/listener knows)
>
> **The development** of this system is recent.
>
> **The information** that he gave me was wrong.
>
> **The medicines** in my cabinet are effective.

Examples

> Give it to **the first person** to arrive.
>
> **The only way** to do the job is to work hard.
>
> Talk to **the next customer.**

- Use the with many specific geographical features or regions when there is an adjectival form in the name.

  <u>Examples</u>

  > It sank in **the Allegheny River**.
  > We went to **the Rocky Mountains**.
  > My sister vacationed in **the Hawaiian Islands**.

- Use the when the noun is something specific because it is unique.

  <u>Examples</u>

  > **The earth** revolves around **the sun**, and **the moon** revolves around **the earth**.
  > I left my coffee cup in **the kitchen**.
  > (when there is one kitchen in the house)

- Use the when you want to point out a particular group and exclude other groups.

  <u>Example</u>

  > **The bus drivers in this city** are very friendly.
  > (specific contrast with other groups)

Nouns Using Zero (No) Article

- Use no article before the noun with non-specific, non-count nouns, plural count nouns, and names or titles (such as movies, people, or books).

  <u>Examples</u>

  > There was **evidence** to prove it.
  > (non-specific, non-count noun)
  > I need **money**.
  > (non-specific, non-count noun)
  > I don't like **raisins**.
  > (plural count noun)
  > Take the patient to **Wilkins Hospital**.
  > (name of a hospital)
  > **_Great Expectations_** is a great novel.
  > (title of a book)

. . . .

WB
Ex. 5.3,
5.4, 5.5,
5.6
Exercise 5.2: Using Articles

Fill in the blanks with **a/an, the,** or **0** for zero article. Some items may have more than one possible answer.

1. She would like to borrow _____ pencil on the desk.

2. _____ student sitting in _____ corner has an extra pencil.

3. Would you like _____ coffee or _____ tea?

4. He took _____ only maps that were left.

5. Our director announced, "_____ play has been cancelled."

6. She went to _____ Heinz Hall to listen to the symphony last night.

7. I bought _____ rice, _____ broccoli, and _____ pan at the store.

8. My daughter is learning to play _____ violin at school.

9. That restaurant is on _____ Fifth Avenue.

10. Seoul is _____ capital of Korea.

11. _____ President Costa defeated all his _____ opponents in the election.

12. I had an appointment with Ms. Aldali, _____ accountant who works for _____ Baker, Zelie, and Sons, Ltd.

13. Marie ate some of _____ candy that I gave her.

14. _____ human being is a mammal.

C. Prepositions

Prepositions are best learned in context because they can vary in meaning, depending on which other words they are used with. They are often idiomatic, and, in many cases, they do not have translation equivalents in other languages. The most common prepositions in English are *at, by, for, from, in, of, on, to,* and *with.* However, there are many others. Give special attention to their use in what you read and hear, and try to give them repeated attention in order to gradually learn their usage.

Note these important points:

- Prepositions usually indicate relationships of **time, place, movement, and logical connections between ideas.** Prepositions connect a noun (or pronoun or noun phrase) with another word, usually a noun, verb, or adjective.
- A preposition has a **noun (or noun phrase, pronoun, or gerund) as its object.** Use the object form of pronouns after prepositions. A verb that follows a preposition as object must be in the gerund form (V + *-ing*), its noun form.
- There are many **verb + preposition** combinations—phrasal verbs—in which the preposition does not have its usual meaning and the meaning of the phrasal verb is not clear from its parts. Phrasal verbs must be learned as whole phrases.

<u>Examples</u>

> I think you should arrive **before** 12:30 PM. (time)
>
> Lionel will stay **in** the house. (place)
>
> Walk **along** the street. (movement)
>
> After some time, I **gave up**. (phrasal verb)
>
> Bill walked **around her**. (object form following preposition)
>
> She tried to **talk** me **into going** to see the movie. (phrasal verb + gerund)
>
> **After speaking**, Ahmed left the room. (gerund following preposition)

WB
Ex. 5.7,
5.8, 5.9,
5.10

Exercise 5.3: Using Appropriate Prepositions

Insert the correct preposition in each gap in the paragraph.

① _____ my opinion the most important and useful everyday device ② _____ present is a computer. There are several reasons why I would suggest buying a computer first when you would like to furnish your apartment ③ _____ technical devices. Modern computers have enough multimedia and computational capabilities to perform all functions that such devices ④ _____ televisions, audio players, and video equipment can. In relation ⑤ _____ computer games, a computer can become the entertainment center ⑥ _____ your world. The internet as a source ⑦ _____ most news information, e-business, e-shopping opportunities, email, and videoconference communication is an advantage you can obtain only ⑧ _____ means ⑨ _____ a home computer. Finally a great deal ⑩ _____ hiring ⑪ _____ modern jobs is done ⑫ _____ using computers. Having a computer ⑬ _____ home helps you to get the necessary practice if you are a novice. If you are an experienced user, all these arguments are redundant because you know the reasons! I am sure you will agree ⑭ _____ me.

D. Word Choice in Formal Writing Style

It is important when writing in a formal, academic style to choose words that are very specific in meaning. This will give the reader an exact idea of what is being expressed. Vague or general words such as *thing* or *get* should be avoided. Be careful when choosing alternates because some words that are similar do not always have the same meaning or connotation when used in different contexts. For instance, *proficient* and *beneficial* can both substitute for *good*, but they have different meanings and must be used accordingly. A **thesaurus** (reference list or book of synonyms) can be very helpful in finding alternates, but use a dictionary as well to help you select the most appropriate words.

Words that are usually too general or too informal, followed by examples of alternate words that might be used instead:

give → donate, provide, offer

get → obtain, acquire, achieve

lots → much/many, numerous, multiple

nice → kind, pleasant, enjoyable

good → proficient, beneficial, decent

let → allow, enable, permit

thing → element, factor, entity

people → individuals, citizens, inhabitants

make → compose, formulate, create

Common **phrasal verbs** that are too informal for academic texts, followed by examples of alternate words that might be used instead:

talk about → discuss

go into → enter

cut back → reduce

drop by → visit

ask for → request

WB
Ex. 5.11

Exercise 5.4: Using More Specific Words

Replace the underlined words with words that are more specific.

1. I am planning to <u>get</u> a new car this year. _____

2. Eating nutritious food and getting enough exercise are the most important <u>things</u> for a healthy lifestyle. _____

3. From the time she was a child, she has been a <u>good</u> soccer player. _____

4. I believe that Apple should add some new <u>things</u> to the next version of the iPhone. _____

Exercise 5.5: Using More Formal Words

Replace the underlined words with words that are more formal.

1. For her research, she will <u>look at</u> the effects of carbon monoxide emissions on the environment. _____

2. In order to <u>get</u> a driver's license, you have to take a computerized test and a driving exam. _____

3. The third chapter of the book <u>talks about</u> the role of stereotypes in speech processing. _____

4. Mrs. Romero was a <u>great</u> person; she always gave money to charities and helped individuals financially whenever she could. _____

E. Reference Words: Pronouns and Synonyms

Accurate use of reference words helps writers create coherence and avoid unnecessary repetition. The most common reference words are personal pronouns (*he/him, she/her, you, it, we, you, they/them*), possessive pronouns (*mine, yours, his, hers, its, ours, theirs*), and demonstrative pronouns (*this, that, these, those*).

Synonyms also help writers avoid repetition when used together with *this, that, these, those*. By using synonyms, previously mentioned ideas can be referred to without using the same words too many times.

Using Pronouns to Avoid Repeating Nouns

<u>Examples</u>

Weak: My husband's mother is a very courageous woman. *My husband* admires *his mother* because *my husband's mother* worked extremely hard throughout *my husband's* childhood in order to support the family.

Better: My husband's mother is a very courageous woman. **He** admires **his** mother because **she** worked extremely hard throughout **his** childhood in order to support **her** family.

However, make sure it is clear which noun a pronoun refers to. You might have to repeat a noun rather than using a pronoun.

<u>Examples</u>

Unclear: Doctors and patients must have good relationships. *They* must be friendly and relaxed so that *they* feel comfortable. Then, *they* will be willing to openly discuss *their* problems with *them*.

Clear: Doctors and patients must have good relationships. **Doctors** must be friendly and relaxed so that **their patients** feel comfortable. Then, **the patients** will be willing to openly discuss their problems with **them**.

Using Demonstrative Pronouns to Avoid Repeating an Entire Phrase

It can only represent a noun or noun phrase. *This* must be used to represent an idea or process.

Examples

> *Doing research in the library* requires some planning and preparation. However, **it** is an enjoyable process once you get started.

> We first subjected the samples to extreme heat. **This** took twelve hours.

Make sure that the pronouns you use agree with the nouns they refer to (singular/plural agreement and subject-verb agreement).

Example

> We experienced *numerous problems* in our experiment. **They** delayed our results so much that we could not publish our article in September as we had planned.

Using Synonyms for Reference

Good writing uses synonyms to avoid repetition. They are often used with demonstrative pronouns *this, that, these, those* or with the reference word *such*. Remember that few words in English have <u>exactly</u> the same meaning. Be sure you know the precise meaning of any synonyms you choose. For instance, the words in each of these groups might be used as alternatives for each other in certain contexts.

- *situation, condition, event, circumstance, process*

- *concept, idea, theory, opinion, hypothesis, perspective, argument, claim, reasoning, position*

- *problem, obstacle, challenge, difficulty, complication*

- *issue, question, matter, topic, subject*

- *characteristic, property, aspect, feature, quality*

<u>Examples</u>

We experienced numerous *problems* in our experiment. **These obstacles** delayed our results so much that we could not publish our article.

Her professor asked her to explain *the relationship between the global economy and the local unemployment rate*. She had never before considered **such an issue** and found the question extremely difficult.

Other words, such as *one, another, a/the first, a/the second, the former, the previous, the latter,* may also be used to refer back to previous ideas.

. . . .

Exercise 5.6: Using Reference Words to Avoid Repetition

WB Ex. 5.12

Revise the sentences to avoid repetition and/or correct errors in pronoun usage. Answers may vary.

1. Scientists often experience setbacks in their research. The scientists should not feel discouraged, however, because setbacks can help scientists make new discoveries that might have been overlooked.

2. There are two advantages of having friends who are different from ourselves. One advantage is that you can share different opinions. A second advantage is that they will learn a lot and help each other because they have different qualities than us.

3. Employees must take occasional vacations to reduce stress and stay efficient. Some employers encourage employees to take vacations, but some employers discourage taking vacations.

4. Since the first settlers arrived in South America, Brazil has gone through three main periods in Brazilian history. In the first main period, from the discovery of Brazil until about 1822, Brazil was a Portuguese colony.

5. The lifestyle of people who live in cities is totally different from the lifestyle of people who live in small towns or rural areas. People who live in cities often walk quickly and speak quickly because they are under pressure. Time is money for them. However, people who live in small towns do everything more slowly.

6. Public libraries are often faced with the difficulty of dealing with problem users. Problem users generally means users who cause difficulties in libraries by their offensive behaviors, such as eating, drinking, loitering, staring at others, or talking in a loud voice.

F. Reducing Wordiness

In good writing, being concise is valued. Wordiness represents a lack of skill. Wordiness includes repetition of ideas and redundancy. The two basic guidelines for reducing wordiness are:

- Do not use more words than necessary.
- Avoid unnecessary repetition.

Examples

Weak: **The majority of the time** that type of course takes place after 10 AM **in the morning.**

Better: That type of course **usually** takes place **after 10 AM.**

Weak: Professor Rouleau **teaches** at the university, where **he is the instructor** of the **introductory course** in Chemistry that is **designed to prepare students for later courses.**

Better: Professor Rouleau **teaches** the **introductory course** in Chemistry at the university.

. . . .

Exercise 5.7: Reducing Wordiness

WB
Ex. 5.13,
5.14

Reduce the wordy expressions in the essay. Be sure to keep the meaning of the original even if you make grammar changes. Paragraphs are numbered only for reference in this exercise. Answers may vary.

Disposing of Garbage

1. Garbage in the modern world is becoming a serious problem and is invading our lives nowadays. In the past, people used to be thrifty. They did not waste anything in those days but used all leftovers for some purpose; for example, cardboard was used for fires and heating, or containers were reused. People used to create less trash and waste in former times. Nowadays, unfortunately, we make a lot of waste. The quantity of garbage that we generate and throw in the trash is much more than the quantity of food we consume. Consequently, we are having problems and difficulties getting rid of garbage, which has started overwhelming our lives, nature, and the air we breathe. However, as we go forward into the future which is to come, we can find ways and means of exploiting garbage and using it positively.

2. The bad effects of garbage are not limited to the personal lives of individuals and families. In fact, the effects have spread out immensely to become a social and global phenomenon affecting the whole earth and the whole universe. Garbage has invaded and threatened our lives. Pollution and toxic chemicals and substances, some of which are the result of garbage, are threatening our existence.

3. Yet there are some solutions that could prevent the increase of the bad effects of garbage and reduce pollution. Some countries have developed very sophisticated ways of exploiting their garbage and extracting energy from it. In other countries, there are some initiatives to exploit garbage by recycling it or using it as compost for fertilizing seeds and plants.

4. Nowadays, people have become aware of the danger garbage can put their lives in. Consciousness of the bad, negative, injurious effects has increased. They have figured out smart ways of disposing of garbage without creating harmful side effects such as pollution. People have discovered how to manage their garbage and use it intelligently to make their lives easier and cleaner at the present time.

AT SENTENCE LEVEL

G. Parts of a Sentence

Clauses

A clause is a group of words in a sentence that contains a subject and a verb. There are two types of clauses: independent and dependent.

Independent Clauses:

1. contain a **subject** and a **verb**
2. convey a complete idea

> Examples
>
> The **northeastern region** of the United States **has** a temperate climate.
>
> Carefully **remove** the solid from the liquid.
>
> (In this sentence, as in most imperative sentences giving instructions, the subject is understood to be **you**.)

Dependent Clauses:

1. begin with a pronoun (*who, which, that, when, why, where, how*) or subordinator (see pages 244–248 for a list of these) followed by a subject and verb
2. do not convey a complete idea on their own

> Examples
>
> I don't know the man **who** *is sitting next to her.*
>
> (Notice that *who is sitting next to her* begins with a pronoun and is **not** a complete idea.)
>
> **Because solar panels are so expensive to produce**, manufacturers are reluctant to invest in them just yet.
>
> (Notice that *Because solar panels are so expensive to produce* begins with a subordinator and is **not** a complete idea.)

Exercise 5.8: Identifying Independent and Dependent Clauses

Identify whether each clause is independent or dependent. Write IC if the clause is independent, DC if the clause is dependent (and so a fragment, NOT a complete idea).

Example:

_IC_   You should not buy a new computer if you haven't done any research first.

1. _____ When it comes to the positive impact of preschool on children.

2. _____ Advances have been made in developing crops that mature faster.

3. _____ Although in a democracy people can vote to express their views and impact government, a large percentage of the population in democratic countries does not actually vote.

4. _____ What she was going to say.

5. _____ The information that CNN reported last night.

6. _____ Prior to 1980, personal computers could rarely be found in the home of most individuals.

7. _____ Because animal testing has proven to be extremely useful in determining the safety of new drugs.

8. _____ The reasons why people become addicted to gambling are varied.

Phrases

Phrases do **not** contain a subject and a verb but consist of words that go together in a sentence to form a unit. They may begin with a noun, preposition, adverb, or adjective.

<u>Example</u>

Trying to find a product online can be overwhelming.

(This sentence begins with a noun phrase that is acting as the subject of the sentence.)

<u>Example</u>

The library is located **to the left of the student union**.

(The two prepositional phrases in this sentence, one beginning with the preposition **to**, one beginning with the preposition **of**, provide location information.)

<u>Example</u>

After explaining the procedure, the professor let the students attempt it.

(This sentence begins with an adverbial phrase describing **when** something happened.)

<u>Example</u>

Cold as an icicle, her nose felt like it might fall off.

(This sentence begins with an adjectival phrase, describing something, *her nose.*)

H. Subject-Verb Agreement

Subject and verb must agree in **number**: a singular subject must have a singular verb form; a plural subject requires a plural verb form. Don't make the mistake of thinking that a plural verb has an *–s* at the end. In some cases, extra care must be taken to ensure agreement because the sentence structure or type of subject may make it more difficult to determine. Give extra attention to subject-verb agreement in these cases:

- If a prepositional phrase comes between the subject and the verb, be careful <u>not</u> to make the verb agree with the noun in the prepositional phrase.

  Wrong: **The president**, along with three new cabinet ministers, **are** going on a world tour.

  Correct: **The president,** along with three new cabinet ministers, **is** going on a world tour.

- Use a singular verb with a singular indefinite pronoun, even when the pronoun implies more than one person. The most common such pronouns are *each, every, everyone, everybody, everything, someone, somebody, nobody, anybody, no one, anything, another.*

  Wrong: **Each** of the new college students on this campus **are** required to register for courses today.

  Correct: **Each** of the new college students on this campus **is** required to register for courses today.

- When a compound subject is joined by *either . . . or*, or by *neither . . . nor*, the verb agrees with the noun closest to it.

  Wrong: **Neither** the professor **nor** the students **is** in the classroom.

  Correct: **Neither** the professor **nor** the students **are** in the classroom.

- When the grammatical subject is *there*, the verb agrees with the noun that follows it (the true subject).

  Wrong: **There are**, among the many new books, **an excellent one** that is a handbook for writers.

  Correct: **There is,** among the many new books, **an excellent one** that is a handbook for writers.

- Some nouns referring to subjects of study are singular even though they end in -*s* and look as if they are plural, such as the nouns *mathematics, economics, statistics, linguistics, electronics,* and *physics.* The noun *news* is also singular. These nouns require singular verb agreement.

    Wrong: The **news** about those towns **are** much more positive now.

    Correct: The **news** about those towns **is** much more positive now.

- Collective nouns, such as *team, family, series, jury, group,* and *class,* have singular verb agreement unless it is very clear from the meaning that the writer is thinking of the members of the group as separate from each other. However, note that there is a lot of variation in this usage: American English uses singular verb agreement for collective nouns in most cases, but British English uses more plural agreement. The examples, and items in the exercise, follow American English usage.

    Wrong: The family were not willing to accept the offer.

    Correct: The family **was** not willing to accept the offer.

    Wrong: The family was quarreling among themselves.

    Correct: The family **were** quarreling among **themselves**.

    (The plural pronoun *themselves* shows that the writer is thinking of each family member as an individual.)

WB
Ex. 5.15,
5.16

Exercise 5.9: Practicing Subject-Verb Agreement

Circle the correct form of the verb in the sentences.

1. The soldiers, accompanied by one officer who was experienced in this kind of situation, **was/were** taken to a new location.

2. Everybody, including the cook and his assistants, **was/were** invited to the party at the manager's house.

3. Neither the teachers nor the director of the city schools **is/are** in the room.

4. There **is/are** only one or two possible explanations for the recent, sudden changes in the weather pattern.

5. Economics **is/are** among the sciences that are primarily observational, like astronomy.

6. My family **is/are** traveling to Egypt to see the pyramids.

7. The class **is/are** going to make individual speeches to develop spoken language skills.

8. The class **is/are** going on a visit to a clothing factory to learn about the manufacturing process.

I. Run-On Sentences and Sentence Fragments

Every grammatically complete sentence or independent clause must have a subject and a verb and must express a complete idea. Two common errors in writing are run-on sentences and sentence fragments.

Run-On Sentences

Run-on sentences occur when two or more independent clauses are not connected with appropriate conjunctions or punctuation. The error is that the two complete sentences run on into each other, forcing the reader to check back to understand where one sentence ends and the other begins.

Run-ons can be corrected in any of these ways:

- Use a period between the independent clauses.
- Use a semicolon between the independent clauses.
- Use a comma and a **coordinating conjunction** such as *and, but,* or *or* to connect the independent clauses.
- Use a **subordinating conjunction** such as *because, when,* or *although* to make an independent clause subordinate. (Note that when the dependent clause comes first, it is followed by a comma, as in the example.)

Example

> *Wrong:* He was driving 65 mph in a 35 mph zone, the police stopped him.
>
> *Correct:* **Because he was driving 65 mph in a 35 mph zone, the police stopped him.**

Sentence Fragments

Fragments are sentences that are not grammatically complete; they do not contain a complete idea and are not connected to an independent clause. For instance, they may be phrases or subordinate (dependent) clauses that are punctuated as if they are complete sentences.

Types of Phrases or Clauses Commonly Written as Fragments

- **Subordinate clauses** beginning with subordinating conjunctions such as *when, whenever, while, after, before, although, even though, because, since,* or *as soon as*

  <u>Example</u>

  > *Wrong:* Angeline was happy. Because Maurice arrived.
  > *Correct:* **Angeline was happy because Maurice arrived.**

- **Prepositional phrases** beginning with, for example, *in, on, at, of, for, above, under, despite, because of, due to*

  <u>Example</u>

  > *Wrong:* Despite the rainy weather. The group of tourists walked around the city.
  > *Correct:* **Despite the rainy weather, the group of tourists walked around the city.**

- Noun phrases or clauses that have a noun followed by some type of clause or phrase but contain no main verb for the subject

  <u>Example</u>

  > *Wrong:* The man who sat next to me on the bus. He talked the whole way.
  > *Correct:* **The man who sat next to me on the bus talked the whole way.**

Exercise 5.10: Correcting Run-On Sentences

WB
Ex. 5.17

Insert correct punctuation, if needed, in the sentences.

1. The passengers on the airplane put their seatbelts on as soon as all of the luggage was aboard, the airplane took off.

2. We realized in the middle of the experiment that we had lost some equipment we really needed.

3. Engineers understand how much force travels from the ground through the shoe to the foot as a result they are able to design shoes that provide maximum comfort to the wearer.

4. Earthquakes have become a much more common phenomenon in recent years for example, over the past decade, Asia has experienced 30 percent more earthquakes than in previous decades.

Exercise 5.11: Correcting Sentence Fragments

WB
Ex. 5.

Correct any sentence fragment errors in the paragraph.

Advertisements and propaganda are used very systematically for political matters today. For example, advertising on TV to gain votes. Because of their very strong influence on people. Therefore, politicians sometimes hire an advertising specialist. However, the advertisement strategy is not just a way to attract people's attention in modern times. Was also used in the 17th century. We can find many historical examples. The advertising strategy of the famous French king, Louis 14th, called the Sun King by his people.

J. Comma Splice

Comma splice errors occur when two or more independent clauses are connected only by a comma. This creates a run-on sentence (see page 190). The error is that the two complete sentences are joined (or spliced) by means of a mark of punctuation that is not correct for this purpose.

Comma splice errors can be corrected in any of these ways:

- Use a period between the independent clauses.
- Use a semicolon between the independent clauses.
- Use a coordinating conjunction such as *and, but,* or *or* to connect the independent clauses.
- Use a subordinating conjunction, appropriate to the intended meaning, such as *because, when,* or *although* to make one of the independent clauses subordinate.

Example

> **Wrong:** If you like to have fun and to enjoy nightlife in the evening, a town like Stuttgart is the right place for you to live in, there are many possibilities for entertainment like theaters, cinemas, and restaurants.

Correction 1—Using a Period

> If you like to have fun and to enjoy nightlife in the evening, a town like Stuttgart is the right place for you to live in. There are many possibilities for entertainment like theaters, cinemas, and restaurants.

Correction 2—Using a Semicolon

> If you like to have fun and to enjoy nightlife in the evening, a town like Stuttgart is the right place for you to live in; there are many possibilities for entertainment like theaters, cinemas, and restaurants.

Correction 3—Using Coordination

If you like to have fun and to enjoy nightlife in the evening, a town like Stuttgart is the right place for you to live in, **for there are many possibilities for entertainment like theaters, cinemas, and restaurants.**

Correction 4—Using Subordination

If you like to have fun and to enjoy nightlife in the evening, a town like Stuttgart is the right place for you to live in **because there are many possibilities for entertainment like theatres, cinemas, and restaurants.**

Exercise 5.12: Recognizing Comma Splices

WB Ex. 5.1

Correct the comma splice errors in the sentences by using the correction strategies provided. Answers may vary.

1. "Laughter is the best medicine," this is a well-known proverb, having a positive outlook on life has many health benefits.

2. A sense of humor reduces stress, there is less tension in personal relationships, a person with low stress and healthy relationships tends to live longer.

3. A person with a positive perspective encounters difficulties, she is more likely to see the benefits that these challenges bring to her life.

4. Moreover, researchers have found that people who are ill recover more quickly if they experience some laughter every day, therefore, some hospitals make an effort to bring humor into patients' lives.

5. Keeping a smile on your face brightens other people's days, it can help you have a healthier, longer life as well.

K. Adjective Clauses

Adjective clauses begin with a relative pronoun. The **relative pronouns** are: *who, whom, which, that, whose, when, why,* and *where.* Adjective clauses are used for two reasons:

1. to identify a specific noun (called an **identifying** or **restrictive clause**).
2. to add extra information about a noun (called a **non-identifying** or **non-restrictive clause**).

Identifying Adjective Clauses

These are used when the noun itself does not tell us "which one." This means that the adjective clause includes **necessary information** to identify the noun.

<u>Examples</u>

1. Situation: I have two brothers. One of them lives in Utah. One of them lives in Seattle.

   My brother **who lives in Utah** has one child. My brother **who lives in Seattle** does not have any children.

   My brother is the noun, but it could mean two different people. Therefore, the adjective clauses are necessary to identify **which** brother the writer is talking about.

2. Noam Chomsky is the man **who(m) most people** regard as the father of modern linguistics.

   The man is the noun, but these two words do not limit the noun to one man. Therefore we need the adjective clause after it to identify **which** man.

> ▸ ▸ ▸ **Usage Note**
>
> Use **that** only with identifying adjective clauses. **Which** can be used with either type of adjective clause but many people prefer that **that** be used for all identifying clauses.

Non-Identifying Adjective Clauses

These are used when the noun in the independent clause is identified by its name or some other identifier. This means that the adjective clause provides **extra information**. For these clauses, you must have punctuation at the beginning of the clause and at the end of the clause.

<u>Examples</u>

1. Harvard University, **which is located in Boston**, is famous worldwide.

   Harvard University is a name, so it makes this noun unique to one place. The adjective clause simply provides additional information about it. This is shown by having punctuation before and after the clause.

2. Yesterday I visited Joan's house, **which she recently renovated**.

   Joan's house narrows the noun *house* to one particular one—Joan's—so this is a non-identifying clause. In this case, it's at the end of the sentence, so a comma is placed before the clause and a period after it.

3. Yesterday I got to see my father, **whom I hadn't seen for almost a year**.

   My father is a unique person, making this is a non-identifying clause.

In informal writing or speech, the relative pronouns **that** and **which** are often omitted in identifying clauses where the pronoun is not the subject.

> The movie **(that)** I saw last night was really sad.
>   (Obj) S V
> The book **(that)** I have to buy for class is quite expensive.
>   (Obj) S   V

WB
x. 5.20

Exercise 5.13: Comma Use in Adjective Clauses

Decide whether or not to add commas to the sentences. Be prepared to explain your choices.

1. The Statue of Liberty which is in New York City is visited by millions of people every year.

2. Seoul, Korea where she grew up has a population of about 10,000,000.

3. We participated in a service project in Jamaica where the hurricane hit two weeks ago.

4. He has always wanted to visit the Metropolitan Museum of Art which is in New York.

5. The city where I was born is Rio de Janeiro, Brazil.

6. The author's most recent book which people think is her best is the only one translated into Chinese.

7. If you need a letter of recommendation, you should ask a teacher whom you talk to frequently and who knows you personally.

8. *Tom Sawyer* which I read last year is one of my favorite novels.

9. I cannot remember the year when it happened.

10. People who want to broaden their outlook by experiencing other cultures should study or work for some time in one or more foreign countries.

L. Parallel Structure

Words, phrases, and clauses that are linked in a series or joined in a sentence by coordination (for example, using *and* or *or*) must be expressed using **parallel structure.** Each item in the list of coordinated elements requires the same structural or grammatical form. Common coordinators are *and, or, nor, for, but, either . . . or, neither . . . nor, both . . . and, not only . . . but also.*

Parallel Word Forms

> *Wrong:* On weekends my sister spends time reading, hiking, **or** swim.
>
> *Correct:* On weekends my sister spends time reading, hiking, **or** swimming.
>
> Gerunds are parallel.

Parallel Phrases

> *Wrong:* He is **neither** a good student **nor** does he work hard.
>
> *Correct:* He is **neither** a good student **nor** a hard worker.
>
> Noun phrases are parallel.

Parallel Clauses

> *Wrong:* Students who eat junk food **and** by not getting enough sleep may have poor health.
>
> *Correct:* Students who eat junk food **and** (who) do not get enough sleep may have poor health.
>
> Relative clauses are parallel; repeating who is optional in this sentence.

Parallel Coordinate Conjunctions and Paired Words

> *Wrong:* I am **more** anxious **than** I feel excitement about this new job.
>
> *Correct:* I am **more** anxious **than** excited about this new job.
>
> Adjectives are parallel.

Exercise 5.14: Creating Parallel Structures

Correct the parallelism errors in each sentence.

1. Because he was sick and because of being discouraged, Lee quit his job.

2. To earn some extra money while I was in college, I worked as a computer technician, as a secretary, and I babysat.

3. That executive is known for her kindness, and she is honest in her business.

4. The bones in the body not only give the body shape but also to protect the heart, lungs, and brain.

5. During our vacation, we relaxed on the beach every day and swimming every day was enjoyable.

6. Statistics is a field of study concerned with the collection, organization, summary, and analyzing data.

7. By carrier pigeons, the telegraph, wired telephones, and cell phones are all ways people have been using to communicate for many years.

8. Neither putting off difficult tasks nor if you think without acting will help you get your work done.

9. James wanted to be either a lawyer or have a career in banking.

10. Both teaching in the public schools and working as a nurse in a hospital were types of employment that Felicity had at different times in her life.

M. Sentence Combining

To avoid making errors, writers sometimes write many simple sentences in succession. Even if such writing is grammatically correct, it is not effective and can be difficult to read. Combining simple sentences in various ways makes your writing clearer and more coherent.

However, be careful when combining simple sentences. You may unintentionally change the meaning of the sentences in some way. You need to be sure that your combined sentences express the exact meaning you intend.

Sentences can be effectively combined by use of coordination, subordination, **parallel elements**, **appositives**, and **participial phrases**.

- Use **coordination** to form compound sentences consisting of two or more independent clauses. The coordinators for this purpose are *and, or, nor, but, for, yet, so.*

  Example

  Original simple sentences: Traveling can give you unforgettable memories. You can learn many things from it. Through traveling you can even change your thinking about other cultures.

  Combined by coordination: Traveling can give you unforgettable memories, **and** from it you can learn many things. Through traveling you can even change your thinking about other cultures.

- Use **subordination** to form complex sentences consisting of independent and dependent clauses. A **subordinator** will begin the dependent clause. Different subordinators are used to show different relationships between sentences (see Table 5.1).

  Example

  Original simple sentences: Traveling can give you unforgettable memories. You can learn many things from it. Traveling can even change your thinking about other cultures.

  Combined by subordination: Traveling can give you unforgettable memories. You can learn many things from it as well **because** it can change your thinking about other cultures.

- **Combine parallel elements** of different sentences, such as subjects, verbs, objects, phrases, and clauses.

  Example

  > *Original simple sentences:* Traveling can give you unforgettable memories. You can learn many things from it. You can even change your thinking about other cultures.

  > *Combined parallel clauses:* Traveling can give you unforgettable memories, and from it you can **learn** many things **and** even **change** your thinking about other cultures.

- Use **appositives** to combine ideas from different sentences. Appositives are words or phrases that explain or restate previously mentioned ideas.

  Example

  > *Original simple sentences:* Traveling can give you unforgettable memories. You can learn many things from it. You can even change your thinking about other cultures.

  > *Combined with an appositive phrase:* Traveling, **a way of learning many things and even changing your thinking about other cultures**, can give you unforgettable memories.

- Use **participial phrases** to combine ideas from different sentences. Participial phrases are verb forms ending in *-ing* or *-ed*.

  Example

  > *Original simple sentences:* Traveling can give you unforgettable memories. You can learn many things from it. You can even change your thinking about other cultures.

  > *Combined using a present participle:* **By traveling**, you can gain unforgettable memories, learn many things, and even change your thinking about other cultures.

Table 5.1: List of Subordinators for Connecting Ideas	
Relationship	**Subordinating Conjunctions**
Time	*when, while, since, after, before, until, (as soon as, once*—one action immediately after the other), *now that* Example: **Now that** we have found some research, we can begin writing our paper.
Place	*anywhere, everywhere, wherever (where)* Example: I can find Pittsburgh Steelers fans **wherever** I go.
Condition	*if, unless, even if, only if, if only* Example: Your proposal will be accepted **only if** you follow the exact content and formatting requirements.
Cause/Effect	*because, as, since* Example: **Because** air pollution is a global issue, countries around the world are trying to establish policies aimed at lessening it.
Contrast	*although, even though, whereas, now, while* Example: **Although** efforts are being made to reduce air pollution, many companies are still ignoring regulations resulting from these efforts.

WB
x. 5.22,
5.23

Exercise 5.15: Combining Sentences with Subordinators

For each sentence identify the relationship between the ideas. Then choose a subordinator from Table 5.1 and use it to combine the two sentences into a dependent clause plus an independent clause (or independent clause + dependent clause). Note that use of *may* or *might* implies a conditional relationship.

Example:

Cell phones are often a distraction. Teachers often prohibit their use in the classroom.

Relationship: ___cause/effect___

Because (As, Since) cell phones are often a distraction,

teachers often prohibit their use in the classroom.

1. I finished my homework. At the same time, my roommate made dinner.

   Relationship: _____

   _____

   _____

   _____

2. Mark was speeding on the highway. The policeman did not give him a ticket.

   Relationship: _____

   _____

   _____

   _____

3. Judith might write a good paper for her sociology class. A good paper means she will get an A in the class.

   Relationship: _____

   _____

   _____

   _____

4. Recycling is one of the most effective ways to reduce garbage and improve our environment. We should increase penalties on households that do not obey local recycling policies.

Relationship: _____

_____

_____

_____

5. You may have questions about the writing assignment. You should talk to the teacher after class.

Relationship: _____

_____

_____

_____

6. School districts rarely see even one case of the measles per year. Our local elementary school reported seven cases last year.

Relationship: _____

_____

_____

_____

7. Carrie got home from the movies. Immediately, she realized that her house had been robbed.

Relationship: _____

_____

_____

_____

N. Sentence Variety

WB
x. 5.24

Effective writing uses a variety of sentence structures. This means that within one paragraph a writer uses not only simple sentences (**subject + verb + object**), but also compound sentences (**two or more independent clauses**) and complex sentences [**independent clause(s) + dependent clause(s)**].

You can also shape your sentences in other ways to make your writing more interesting and varied, for example, by using active or passive voice, inverting the order of the subject and verb, changing the order of independent and dependent clauses, and using modifiers (words, phrases, or clauses that give additional information about other parts of a sentence).

Varying the Positions of Modifiers

Many modifiers in sentences can be placed in different positions.

- **Beginning of sentence**

Dependent clause

> **Even though I wasn't feeling well,** I decided to go to the party.

Infinitive phrase

> **To get to my friend's house on time,** I had to drive very fast.

Adverb

> **Unfortunately** I was pulled over for speeding.

Participial phrase (-ing or -ed adjective phrase)

> **Seeing that I was ill,** the police officer had pity on me.

> **Worried by my lateness,** my friends called me on my cell phone.

> ▶ ▶ ▶ **Usage Note**
>
> Be careful: The "understood" subject of the participial phrase **must be the same as** the subject of the main clause.

Prepositional phrase

> **With the officer standing right next to my car,** I decided to ignore my ringing cell phone.

• **Mid-sentence**

Appositives (used to explain or restate previously mentioned ideas)

> My friend Carlos, **the host of the party,** was happy when I arrived at his apartment.

Participial phrase

> His girlfriend Anna, **noticing my stressed state,** brought me a glass of water.

• **End of sentence**

Participial phrase

> I walked toward the living room, **wondering why they were whispering behind me.**
>
> I nearly dropped my glass of water, **shocked to see all of my friends with a birthday cake!**

Changing Emphasis with a Divided Sentence

To emphasize a specific part of a sentence, it can be divided into two parts, each with its own verb. The initial part of the sentence focuses attention on the second part as the main idea. Usually this is done by using *it* or a *wh-* word.

> I realized then that this was a surprise birthday party for me.
>
> *Changed emphasis:* **It was then that** I realized that this was a surprise birthday party for me.
> (focus on *then*)
>
> Carlos had been planning this party for weeks, and I hadn't known it.
>
> *Changed emphasis:* **What I hadn't known was that** Carlos had been planning this party for weeks.
> (focus on *what I hadn't known*)

Example Paragraph and Revision

This paragraph expresses ideas clearly, but the writing style of the original is very simple and somewhat boring because most of the sentences follow the same pattern of **subject + verb + modifier**, with repetition of subject words. Notice how the paragraph is improved in revision on the next page by varying the sentence structure so that it flows more smoothly and is more interesting.

ORIGINAL:

I visited Boston last summer. Boston is a very beautiful and comfortable city. People there sit on chairs or lie on the lawn when they are watching performances on the street. People read their books or don't do anything. Everyone looks like they are taking a vacation. People walk slowly and wear casual clothes. I asked them some questions, and they always helped me. I think that Boston is the oldest city in America. It is also the most beautiful city in America. There are lots of historical sites, such as some old churches, and famous schools, like M.I.T. and Harvard. I could see and enjoy the views when I walked on the streets. I think that I will go to Boston again when I take a vacation some day.

REVISED:

Last summer I visited the city of Boston, which is a very beautiful and comfortable city. People there always sit on chairs or lie on the lawn when they are watching performances on the street. As they relax, reading their books or not doing anything, Bostonians look like they are taking a vacation. I observed that many people walk slowly and wear casual clothes. Moreover, when I asked them some questions, they always helped me in a friendly way. Home to many historical sites, Boston is not only the oldest city but also the most beautiful city in America. A number of famous schools, such as M.I.T. and Harvard, are located in Boston. What I particularly enjoyed was seeing the lovely views when I walked on the city streets. I think that I will go to Boston again when I take a vacation some day.

SECTION 6

PUNCTUATION

A. Period .
B. Question Mark ?
C. Exclamation Point !
D. Comma ,
E. Semicolon ;
F. Colon :
G. Hyphen -
H. Dash —
I. Double Quotation Marks " "
J. Single Quotation Marks ' '
K. Parentheses ( )
L. Brackets [ ]
M. Apostrophe '
N. Ellipsis . . .
O. Capital Letters **ABC**
P. Indentation of Paragraphs and Quotations
Q. Abbreviation Period

6

Punctuation marks are conventional symbols used in writing. Many are essential indicators of sentence structure and meaning: the text cannot be correctly understood if such marks are left out or wrongly used. Other punctuation marks are less important for grammar and meaning but must also be used accurately in a well-written composition or research paper.

Some punctuation rules are applied very strictly with no variation, but in other cases variation is possible. For example, U.S.A. may be written with periods, but the form without periods, USA, is also common. The guidelines provided in this section are widely accepted, but if you are unsure of any punctuation usage, refer to a style guide or dictionary. Ask your instructor if there is a preferred guide for your field, such as APA or MLA style (see pages 129–165).

In this section, exercises are provided for the following marks: period, question mark, exclamation point, comma, semicolon, and colon.

A. Period [.]

End of Sentence

A period is used to mark the end of a sentence.

> Examples
>> The flowers are blooming.
>> Carry this box inside.
>> Please water the plants.
>> She asked where we had gone.

WB
Ex. 6.1,
6.2, 6.6

Exercise 6.1: Period at End of Sentence

The periods have been left out of this paragraph. Add periods and capitalize the word after the inserted period.

More and more these days, people all over the world are eating insects for many reasons crickets, for example, provide a lot of protein, they are also very inexpensive and a sustainable source of food it takes much less water and land to raise crickets for food than to raise livestock crickets also emit almost no greenhouse gases finally, the overall nutritional value of crickets is very high they are a real "super food."

Decimals

A period shows where the decimal point goes in numerals.

Example

3.14 (three point one four / three and fourteen hundredths)

WB
Ex. 6.3

Exercise 6.2: Period with Decimals

Use numerals, and put the periods in the correct places to express the amounts.

1. eleven and four hundredths _____

2. ninety-seven and thirty-one hundredths _____

3. one thousand and thirty-three point zero one six _____

B. Question Mark [?]

A question mark comes at the end of a sentence and indicates that a sentence is to be understood as a question. Even if the grammatical structure of the sentence is not in question form, **intonation** could be added to a sentence to make it a question. When a question mark is used, do not also add a period. **Do not use a question mark with a reported or indirect question (in other words, with a sentence that is not an exact quotation of a question).**

Examples

Who will volunteer to carry this box?

Is that the reason?

That is the reason? [with emphasis on rising intonation on **that**, perhaps because the speaker is surprised or shocked]

He asked if we were going to the party. [no question mark because this is a reported question]

. . . .

Exercise 6.3: Question Mark and Period

WB
Ex. 6.4
6.6

Place question marks and periods in the correct places in the dialogue. (Each part is numbered for reference only.) Remember that a question mark is not placed after indirect (reported) questions.

1. *Anna:* Are you traveling to Paris today

2. *Jose:* No Are you

3. *Anna:* Yes, I was told that Guillaume would be there, so I want to go there also

4. *Jose:* Why is Guillaume going there

5. *Anna:* He wouldn't tell me at first Then I asked him whether it was true that he was going to visit his aunt in Paris He next asked me why I wanted to know and added that it was none of my business So I stopped questioning him Later, he admitted that he would be visiting his aunt there Do you think that I should follow him

6. *Jose:* That depends on why you would want to do so Have you met his aunt

C. Exclamation Point [!]

An exclamation point comes at the end of a sentence and indicates a strong feeling, such as anger or surprise. The exclamation point frequently appears after short words or short phrases (Yay! Wow!); it is rarely used at the end of a long sentence. When an exclamation point is used, do not also add a period.

<u>Example</u>

What an amazing opportunity!

> ▶ ▶ ▶ **Usage Note**
>
> Do not use too many exclamation points so that the strength of emphasis is not lost.

WB
Ex. 6.5,
6.6

Exercise 6.4: Exclamation Point

The end punctuation of the sentences or phrases has been omitted. Decide which ones express strong feeling, and place exclamation points after them. Use a period where appropriate. If either is possible, explain why.

1. Her dog is very friendly

2. This is so exciting

3. She was sick all weekend

4. What gorgeous weather

5. What a surprise

6. Yesterday I finally heard from my brother overseas

D. Comma [,]

After Introductory or Transitional Words or Phrases

Place a comma after introductory or transitional words and phrases that begin a sentence.

Examples

As a result of the bad weather, we cancelled our trip.

However, we had a pleasant time relaxing at home.

. . . .

Exercise 6.5: Comma with Introductory or Transitional Words or Phrases

WB
Ex. 6.7

Place commas, if needed, after the introductory or transitional words and phrases in the sentences.

1. All things considered the event was a success.

2. The photographer fell out of the tree from which he was trying to see over the wall.

3. In summary there are many good reasons for studying the foreign languages in today's world, in which international exchange of information is so important.

4. Nevertheless Halima decided to buy the new car.

5. Mr. Roh and Ms. Kim traveled by train from Istanbul to Paris even though they preferred to fly.

6. By the third week of the semester Ching had discovered her great interest in neuroscience.

After Introductory Clauses

When a dependent clause begins a sentence, place a comma after it.

> ### Example
>
> **When Ali arrived at the house, Ahmed left.**

WB
Ex. 6.8

Exercise 6.6: Comma after Introductory Clauses

Decide where the introductory clause ends, and add a comma in each sentence.

1. So that the dinner does not burn we must be sure to keep an eye on the stove.

2. Even though the route through downtown would have been shorter Luma drove around the city center in order to avoid heavy traffic.

3. Because we wanted the party to be a surprise we asked the guests to park on the next street.

4. Since you began to study in this school your English has improved greatly.

5. While Svetlana made the cake and prepared the food Irina put up the decorations.

Before Conjunctions

When a sentence consists of independent clauses joined by a coordinating conjunction *(and, or, nor, but, for, so, yet)*, place a comma before the conjunction. However, when both clauses are very short (five words or less), it is acceptable to leave out the comma to emphasize a strong connection between the clauses.

<u>Example</u>

We thought it would be an easy exercise, **but** we found that it was quite difficult.

. . . .

Exercise 6.7: Comma before Conjunctions

WB
Ex. 6.9

Add commas, if necessary, before the conjunctions in the sentences.

1. I wanted to go to the movie or the concert.

2. Yi-Lin neither wanted to go directly to college nor did she want to get a job immediately.

3. He worked hard to prepare for the audition but he did not get the part.

4. Dr. Bennett, who was in charge of the emergency room, called to the nurse to move quickly and she then began to examine the patient.

5. Luis won the game easily but the spectators did not applaud.

In Lists of Words, Phrases, or Clauses

In a list of three or more words, phrases, or clauses separate these elements from each other by placing commas between them. If the items themselves include commas, use a semicolon to separate them (see semicolon rules on pages 224–225).

Example

The books, journals, indexes, **and** catalogs are all in the library.

WB
Ex. 6.10

Exercise 6.8: Comma with Lists of Words, Phrases, or Clauses

Separate the items in lists using commas.

1. Hearing touch taste smell and sight are the five senses of perception.

2. The next time I buy a car, it will have heated seats satellite radio and all-wheel drive.

3. How to prepare a speech how to deliver it how to adjust to audience reaction and how to learn from one's mistakes are all dealt with in the website on public speaking.

4. Many people are involved in the production of a good play, including the following: the actors the director the writer the makeup artist the costume designer and the set designer.

5. In spite of many difficulties, such as illness lack of money attacks by enemies and loss of public support the mayor decided to run for election.

With Coordinate Adjectives

When more than one coordinate adjective comes before a noun, separate the adjectives from each other by placing commas between them. Do not place a comma between the last adjective and the noun.

Each coordinate adjective equally modifies the noun; coordinate adjectives can be joined by *and*. Cumulative adjectives do not equally modify the noun; they often modify the following adjectives or the following adjectives plus the noun; cumulative adjectives cannot be joined by *and*; they are not separated by commas.

> Examples
>
> Senator Adamson is a tough, frequent, outspoken critic of the President's foreign policy. [coordinate—commas needed; each adjective can separately modify the noun *critic*]
>
> Senator Adamson wore a dark green jacket at the town meeting. [cumulative—no commas between *dark* and *green*; the adjective *dark* modifies the following adjective *green*]

- -

Exercise 6.9: Comma with Coordinate Adjectives

WB
Ex. 6.11

Separate coordinate adjectives as necessary by placing a comma between them.

1. Gabrielle said that her new computer was a wonderful valuable timesaving machine.

2. The squirrel climbed the big green tree quickly.

3. The citizens wanted an effective cheap program for repairing the old bridges, but the mayor said that it would be expensive.

4. The experienced calm kind teacher waited for the students to finish the project.

5. It was the most extensive evergreen forest in the southern region.

With Quotations

Commas separate the words of a direct quotation from the rest of the sentence. At the end of the direct speech, punctuation marks are placed inside (before) the final quotation mark.

<u>Examples</u>

Kumiko said, "I don't want to go until the very end."

"I don't want to go," said Kumiko, "until the very end."

"I don't want to go until the very end," Kumiko said.

Exercise 6.10: Comma with Quotations

Place commas before and after the direct quotations (the words actually spoken). Leave out the comma when a quotation begins or ends a sentence and when the quotation ends with a question mark or exclamation point.

1. Christina commented "That movie was very sad."

2. "The university that I want to go to is in Venezuela" announced Lyudmila.

3. "John" the boy's mother asked "When will you clean your room?"

4. She said "I like to study in the park because the fresh air helps me think."

5. "There are too many sheep in the north field. Please move some of them" said the farmer to the shepherd.

With Some Abbreviations

If one of these abbreviations is used in a sentence and the sentence continues after the abbreviation, place a comma before and after the period of the abbreviation:

e.g. (for example)
i.e. (that is)
etc. (and others, and so forth)
et al. (and other authors, and other people)

<u>Example</u>

I have visited many countries, **e.g.,** Korea, Thailand, Australia, and Egypt.

Although the rule given above is widely followed, there is some variation: some styles do not require a comma after the period of these abbreviations in mid-sentence. Also, in some styles, these abbreviations are used only in parentheses or **footnotes** but not in the text itself, where the full forms are preferred.

Avoiding Common Errors

1. Do not confuse *i.e.* and *e.g.* The former means "that is," and the latter means "for example."
2. Do not add *and* before *etc.* because *etc.* itself includes the meaning of *and*.
3. Do not add a period after the word *et* in *et al.*

WB
Ex. 6.13

. . . .
Exercise 6.11: Comma with Abbreviations

Place commas after the periods of the abbreviations if the sentence continues after the abbreviation.

1. We packed our bathing suits, towels, sunscreen, etc. to go to the beach.

2. Some of the approaches to social organization, e.g. communism and capitalism, are thought to be incompatible.

3. There are many interesting things at the aquarium, e.g. sting rays, jellyfish, penguins, and dolphins.

4. Dr. Burns wrote that extensive research on the cause of the disease was conducted by Jones et al.

5. To start the computer, press the "on" button, i.e. the red one at the side of the machine.

With Interrupting Expressions

Words, phrases, or clauses that are contrasting or interrupting or that need separation for clarity are set off by (surrounded by) commas. The most common examples are shown.

Appositive

<u>Example</u>

Dr. Yamaguchi**, the chief minister,** developed a new plan.

Direct Address

<u>Example</u>

Sam**,** I need you to come here.

Dates

Commas separate two words or two numbers that directly follow each other. Commas are not needed when a word is followed by a number.

Example

Sandra left for Greece on Friday, June 6, 2017.

Sandra arrived in Greece in June 2017.

Addresses or Place Names

Example

Miss Sondhi has a business office in London, Ontario, as well as one in London, England.

Our home address is 125 Lake Street, Burlington, VT 05401.

Parenthetical Expressions

Example

This is, of course, the right thing to do.

Non-Identifying Phrases or Clauses

Example

Sir Isaac Newton, who was a genius, discovered many scientific laws.

Transitional Words or Phrases

Example

In addition, I prepared a long speech.

Contrastive Elements

Example

My motorcycle, though new, has broken down.

Final Gerund Phrase

Example

The tornado struck the city center, causing great devastation.

WB
Ex. 6.14

Exercise 6.12: Comma with Contrasting or Interrupting Elements or Those Needing Separation for Clarity

Place a comma before and after contrasting or interrupting elements or those needing separation for clarity.

1. Unlike clarinets and oboes which are wind instruments flutes do not need reeds.

2. Luna I urge you to stop right away!

3. The revolution began in July 1789; to be more precise, it was July 14 1789.

4. The Oakdale Corporation has its office at 4701 Shadow Lane Houston Texas.

5. The whale as far as I know is the largest sea creature.

6. Lagos which is the largest city in Nigeria started as a small fishing and farming settlement.

7. Therefore the square of the hypotenuse is equal to the sum of the squares of the other two sides.

8. The morning flight not the evening one is what she prefers.

9. My party withdrew from the election ending interest in its reform proposals.

E. Semicolon [;]

A semicolon is thought of as a strong comma or a weak period, but it can only be used in the ways noted. It cannot be substituted for any other uses of the comma or period. A semicolon does not mark a new sentence (even though it can substitute for a period); therefore, it is not followed by a capital letter.

With Independent Clauses

A semicolon can be used to separate two independent clauses whose ideas are closely related.

> Example
>
> Alina traveled to France; Jean stayed at home.

. . . .

Exercise 6.13: Semicolon with Independent Clauses

WB
Ex. 6.1

Use a semicolon to separate the closely related independent clauses.

1. Mr. Wang bought a new house last month he has already sold it.

2. I looked everywhere for my punctuation workbook surprisingly it was on the back seat of my car.

3. Piradee is not feeling well she has a headache.

When Separating Elements with Internal Commas

When items or independent clauses in a list have internal commas, a semicolon is used to separate them.

> Examples
>
> On the cover of the catalog there were pictures of an electronic clock, which was selling for only $10; a steam iron, which cost $22.99; a gift-wrapped box, with no indication of what was inside it; and a camera.
>
> When you arrive for your first day at work, go and see the supervisor's assistant; and then, after she has checked your identity and given you an identity card, use your new card at the security point when entering and exiting the building.

WB
Ex. 6.16

Exercise 6.14: Semicolon Separating Elements with Internal Commas

The semicolons have been left out of the sentences. Add them in the appropriate places.

1. At the picnic, we will have, in addition to everything else, apples, brought by Tom oranges, brought by Tina pears; brought by Harry and watermelon, brought by Jane.

2. These packages need to be shipped take them to the post office today.

3. Sharon and Sherman had an accident while riding their bikes she was fine but he broke his wrist.

4. Hans found that his punctuation workbook contained rules and exercises for the use of the period, referred to as a full stop in British English the comma, which he realized had the greatest variety of uses and all the other marks that he needed to know about.

5. Ivan wanted to leave Moscow because of the cold, which affected his health and, as a consequence of that, his work but Natasha, who enjoyed cold weather, was hoping it would get colder.

F. Colon [:]

Before a Series

A colon is used to introduce a series (a list) of items.

Example

They took lots of equipment for the camping trip: tents, food, camp beds, portable stoves, and much more.

Before Long Quotations

Long quotations (more than four lines) are introduced by a colon.

Example

In their introduction to the book *Emotions, Community, and Citizenship*, Kingston et al. write:

Some researchers suggest that, physiologically, the human experience of emotion is unique, with the cortical regions playing an important role and with greater possibility of flexibility and compensatory processes in the functioning of human brains than in the brains of animals. So while it may be conceded that both humans and animals have similar forms of background and/or primary emotions, the greater complexity of the human mind allows for different types of secondary emotions (or emotions about our emotions—for example, shame, pride, and guilt), which have no counterpart in the animal world." (2017, p. 9)

Before Short Quotations

Short quotations, if formal or dramatic, can be introduced by a colon.

Example

Confucius made a statement that has become proverbial: "The journey of a thousand miles begins with the first step."

Before the Second Part of Sentence

The second part of a sentence can be introduced by a colon when it restates, further explains, or exemplifies the first part.

Example

Mr. Harvey always reads two magazines each week: *Time* and *Newsweek*.

With a Salutation

In a formal letter, the salutation is followed by a colon (in American usage).

Example

Dear Ms. Moore:

Our records show that you have not paid your most recent bill, even after repeated reminders from us. Unless you pay some or all of the amount due within the next two weeks, we will be forced to take legal action against you.

In Bibliographic References

In bibliographic references, a colon is used to separate place of publication from the publisher.

Example

Cologne: Taschen Press.

In Time Expressions

A colon is used to separate hour from minutes in an expression of time.

Example

9:00 AM

In Ratios

A colon is used to separate the first number from the second number in ratios (statements of proportion).

Example

3:2 (three to two)

. . . .

Exercise 6.15: Colon

WB
Ex. 6.17

Add colons in the appropriate places in the sentences.

1. According to one analysis, there are four stages in human development childhood, youth, adulthood, and old age.

2. In describing the elements that have influenced the pronunciation of Brazilian Portuguese, María Porter explains

   The Semana de arte moderna, also led by Andrade, represents a major turning point in the landscape of Brazilian culture. The movement stressed the belief that Brazilian folklore and cultural roots were the foundation of national identity and encouraged other Brazilian artists to reject European models and embrace their own heritage. This idea of a national identity was the same as that of the *Normas*, as the document is commonly called. The *Normas* were not intended as strict rules or "laws," but rather as "norms" or suggestions for pronunciation. (2017, p. 4)

3. President John F. Kennedy said "Ask not what your country can do for you; ask what you can do for your country."

4. "Your punctuation," said the reader to the writer, "is very confusing it does not help to clarify the sentence structure and meaning."

5. When Josephine Lewis received the letter from the government agency, she saw that it began with the words

   Dear Ms. Lewis
   We are pleased to inform you that you have been awarded a scholarship for the continuation of your studies. . . .

6. This is the book citation in APA style Porter, M. (2017). *Singing in Brazilian Portuguese*. Lanham, MD Rowman & Littlefield Press.

7. The next flight is due at 1015 AM not at 1115 AM

8. Mix yellow and green in the ratio of 21 (two to one).

G. Hyphen [-]

A hyphen is written with no space between it and the words or letters before or after it.

With Compound Nouns

A hyphen is used to show the close connection between the words of many compound nouns (a noun consisting of two or more parts).

Example
Alphonse's mother-in-law is a lawyer.

With Compound Adjectives

A hyphen is used for compound adjectives (an adjective consisting of two or more parts) that come before a noun. However, the same adjectives are not joined with a hyphen in other (non-compound) grammatical forms.

Examples [compound adjectives before a noun]
Long-time workers at this company have good benefits.
She was holding the hand of a four-year-old child.

Examples [same adjectives in non-compound forms]
Dr. Mowicki has worked at this hospital for a long time.
My child is four years old.

With Prefixes

Hyphens sometimes are used when a prefix (such as *pre-, pro-, semi-, ex-*) is added to a word.

Example
They found the injured animal in a semi-wooded area.

With Fractions

Hyphens are used when a fraction or the numbers 21 to 99 are written in words.

<u>Examples</u>

Two-thirds of the students got an A.

It took me thirty-three minutes to complete the race.

With Syllable Division

A hyphen is used between syllables of a word when the word must be divided at the end of a line. Most dictionaries indicate syllable division for words of more than one syllable.

<u>Example</u>

After much discussion with my teachers and parents, I submitted an application to three colleges.

H. Dash [—]

When typing, use a double hyphen to make the dash symbol if your keyboard does not have a separate dash symbol. Some computer programs automatically convert a double hyphen into a single dash symbol.

A dash is written with no space between it and the words before or after it.

With Strong Interrupting Element

A dash can be used (instead of commas or parentheses) to give very strong emphasis to an interrupting expression. (Refer to pages 221–222 for an explanation of interrupting.) Use two dashes if the expression is in the middle of the sentence; use one dash if it is at the end.

<u>Examples</u>

We ate at a fine restaurant—an expensive one—last
week.

A writer must think of punctuation as a crucial tool—a
vitally important element of written communication.

With Change in Flow of Ideas

A dash is used to indicate a sudden or dramatic change in the flow of ideas.

<u>Example</u>

The president quietly walked to the center of the stage, discussed some new proposals—and announced his resignation!

With Introductory Series

A dash is used to separate an introductory series from a clause that explains or refers back to it.

<u>Example</u>

Flour, yeast, water, and oil—this is all you need to make pizza dough.

Before Items Listed in a Category

A dash is used when a list of items in a category follows the naming of the category in a sentence.

<u>Example</u>

We needed many things for the move—boxes, newspaper, and packing tape.

I. Double Quotation Marks [" "]

The closing mark of double quotation marks is placed **after** a period or comma.

With Direct Quotations

Double quotation marks are used to show the exact words spoken or written by someone. These are called **direct quotations**. The marks are placed before and after the original words. (For more examples and information on using quotations, refer to pages 112–119 and 126–128.)

<u>Example</u>

> Gomez and McFarlane (2017) assert that "there is often a simultaneous reliance on and denial of the past wherein problems with race and gender are acknowledged yet at the same time are represented as being unimportant or overcome."

> "[T]here is often a simultaneous reliance on and denial of the past wherein problems with race and gender are acknowledged yet at the same time are represented as being unimportant or overcome" (Gomez & McFarlane, 2017, p. 373).

In the second example, the brackets in *[T]here* indicate that the word did not start with an uppercase letter in the original source. However, since this word begins a sentence in this example, it should be capitalized.

With Long Direct Quotations

In some punctuation styles, a passage of several paragraphs is indicated by double quotation marks (without block indentation). The marks are placed at the beginning of each paragraph and at the end of the last paragraph.

<u>Example</u>

> Stillman and Stillman (2017) draw interesting comparisons between Generation X and Generation Z in order to explain the changing attitudes in the U.S. toward the value of a college education:

>> "Our worries about the economy have led to real conversations about what we can and should do to prepare for our futures. One issue on the table is the value of college. More than just our parents' struggles, we have watched how Millennials at such a young age are straddled with so much debt. All we hear about is how expensive college is. Northeastern University found that 67 percent of Gen Zers indicate their top concern is being able to afford college.

>> "Gen Z is more hesitant about going to college or the value of the four-year degree. It might be hard to blame them. More than just hearing about how crippling college debt can be, Gen Z hears from the Bureau of Labor Statistics that one in eight recent college grads are unemployed and that one-half of those employed hold jobs that do not even require college degrees.

"For Boomers, a college degree was still the shiniest bullet on the resume and even debt wasn't going to stop them from pushing their Millennial children to graduate from college. What do Gen Z's moms and dads have to say about it? For Gen Xers who have always been more open to alternative routes, debt for a degree might not seem as worth it. So the message they have been giving their Gen Z children is that if you are going to go to college, make every dollar count."

> ▶ ▶ ▶ **Usage Note**

In most academic styles, such as APA, long quotations are block-indented without quotation marks.

For Reference to Language Use

In some punctuation styles, a term, word, or expression that is referred to as a word or expression can be indicated by double quotation marks. (Frequently this is also done by typing the word or expression in italics.)

Example

The idiom "a piece of cake" means the job referred to is very easy.

For Special Meaning

Double quotation marks are sometimes used to indicate that a word or expression has a special meaning different from its usual one.

Example

John's "explanation" for his absence left us even more confused about where he had actually been.

J. Single Quotation Marks [' ']

The closing mark of single quotation marks is placed **after** a period or comma.

With Direct Quotations

Single quotation marks are used to show the exact words of a quotation within another quotation. The marks are placed before and after the original words.

> Example
>
> In his statement before the judge, Walters explained, "While I was questioning her, she said, 'I was there when it happened,' and then she kept quiet and refused to answer any more questions."

K. Parentheses [( )]

With Interrupting Expressions

Parentheses are used to enclose interrupting words or expressions. This is similar to one of the uses of the comma, but parentheses indicate a stronger interruption than commas and information that is less related to the rest of the sentence. What is in parentheses does not affect the grammatical completeness of the sentence.

> Example
>
> Dr. Yousef had to choose between several research methods (survey, direct observation, experiment, and self-report) before proceeding with his study of how athletes prepare psychologically for important games.

With Numbers

Parentheses are used to enclose numbers, dates, and citations in a sentence.

> Example
>
> The students agreed to (1) make an appointment with the professor, (2) file a complaint about the unfair test, and (3) ask to take a revised and improved test.

With Dates

Parentheses are used to enclose dates.

Example

Bruce Lee (1940–1973) was a Chinese American who became famous for his acting in martial arts movies.

With Citations

Parentheses are used to enclose textual citations.

Example

One of the leading authorities in international diplomacy claims that the United Nations is the only organization that can lead the world to a peaceful future (Gomez, 2017, pp. 263–265).

L. Brackets [[ ]]

To Show Added Words

Brackets are used in a quoted passage to show words that have been added by the person quoting it or by an editor. The added words are usually to explain or clarify what might not be understood.

Example

Ella claimed, "It is because they [the students] were so eager to learn about the subject that they came to extra classes in the evening."

To Show Errors in Quoted Passage

Brackets are used with the word *sic* (meaning "thus") to show that an apparent error in a quoted passage is exactly how it was in the original and is not a mistake made by the person quoting it.

Example [including original's spelling error]

Samuel wrote about his early life: "I never understood how much the school principle [sic] tried to help me."

To Show Omitted Words

Brackets are sometimes used to enclose ellipsis marks (indicating omitted words) in a quoted passage.

Example

> On page 37 of their recent history book, Barbour and Fromkin write, "The battle was begun at dawn on a Monday [. . .], and surprisingly lasted only until Friday of the same week."

M. Apostrophe [']

With Contractions

An apostrophe is used in contractions, such as *will not* written as the contraction *won't.*

Example

> "They're doing well," said Pierre, "but don't visit them until tomorrow."

To Show Possession

Apostrophes, together with an *s,* are used to show singular and plural possession.

Singular: Add an apostrophe and an s.

Example

> The vehicle's engine was the source of the pollution in the air.

Plural: Add an apostrophe after the plural –s of the noun.

Example

> The vehicles' engines were the sources of the pollution in the air.

Examples

> The secretary went into his boss' office.
> The secretary went into his boss's office.

When the noun ends in an **s**, the apostrophe alone ('s) or the apostrophe with an additional s (s's) can be used.

N. Ellipsis [. . .]

To Show Omitted Words

Use an ellipsis (three periods with a space between each one) to show that some words in a quoted passage have been left out. The ellipsis is sometimes enclosed in brackets. Some computer programs automatically add spaces between the periods when three periods are typed.

The singular (referring to one set of three periods) is **ellipsis** and the plural is **ellipses**.

<u>Example</u>

According to McKibben, "In the end, global warming presents the greatest test we humans have yet faced [. . .]. It's our coming-of-age moment, and there are no certainties or guarantees" (*National Geographic*, 2017, p. 36).

O. Capital Letters

Capital letters are also called uppercase letters, in contrast with (the usually smaller) lowercase letters.

At the Beginning of a Sentence

As a mark of punctuation, a capital letter is used at the beginning of a sentence. (Do not use a capital letter after a semicolon in a sentence.)

<u>Example</u>

You should start your journey from here. It's the best route.

As Part of Spelling

In the written form of individual words (spelling), various uses are shown.

Proper names

   <u>Examples:</u> **Adriana, Chen, Stefan**

Titles used with names

   <u>Examples:</u> **Doctor Chang, Professor Lequieu**

Organizations

   <u>Examples:</u> **United Nations, Berlin School of
                Architecture**

Geographical names

   <u>Examples:</u> **Iguazu Falls, Mount Everest, South China Sea**

Countries and nationalities

   <u>Examples:</u> **Algeria, Algerian; Ecuador, Ecuadorian**

Languages

   <u>Examples:</u> **Swahili, Portuguese, Arabic, Korean**

Religions

   <u>Examples:</u> **Hinduism, Islam, Buddhism, Christianity**

Compass directions referring to regions but not general direction

   <u>Examples:</u> the people in the **North**
                to travel north

Days of the week, months of the year

   <u>Examples:</u> **Wednesday, September**

Periods in history

   <u>Examples:</u> **Middle Ages, Ming Dynasty, Second
                World War**

Names of traditional holidays

> <u>Examples:</u> **Thanksgiving, Kwanzaa, Independence Day**

Names of college courses but not the general subject name

> <u>Examples:</u> . . . registered for **Biology 201** next term
> . . . studying **biology**

Abbreviations of organizations and titles

(Periods with each letter are optional in some styles.)

> <u>Examples:</u> **UNESCO, BA, PhD [U.N.E.S.C.O., B.A, Ph.D.]**

P. Indentation of Paragraphs and Quotations

First Line of Paragraphs

In printed essays, indent the first line of each paragraph five to seven spaces (or one tab on a keyboard). The example is an excerpt of two paragraphs from a student paper.

<u>Example</u>

Additionally, only if the economic situation is good can people have money for buying houses and the government entities have money for building facilities. As the economy improves, the demands of people will increase gradually. That will boost the development of real estate too. Thus, its rapid economic development requires and enhances real estate development of new houses in China.

On the other hand, in the United States, the speed of economic development is stable and the living conditions of people have been very good. Therefore, there is comparatively less need for new houses.

Block Indentation of Long Quotation

A long quotation of more than four or five lines is given a block indentation format in many academic styles. The indentation is five spaces or one inch, and the quotation has the same line spacing as the rest of the text. It has **no** quotation marks. The example is from a student research paper; this indented quotation is in the middle of the paper's final paragraph.

<u>Example</u>

In conclusion, creative thinking in the theory of human security has been remarkable because it sheds light on reasons why people have not received care from their governments, but it has not been well implemented at the practical level because of its ambiguity. The theory is sometimes misused. Therefore, as Lopez argues:

> Much more analysis and discussion of the human security approach is necessary, especially regarding its implementation across national boundaries. We need to know whether it is truly applicable across most of the globe. The strength of nationalism may interfere with implementing it even though it is particularly urgent in times of conflict over resources. (2006, p. 23)

Although more and more projects implementing the human security notion are being started, this theory needs to be cultivated since it is still in transition from academic idea to practical instrument in the field of development.

Q. Abbreviation Period

This mark is also sometimes referred to as the *abbreviation point*.

A period is used with many abbreviations, but be careful because this usage is variable! Fewer abbreviation periods are now being used, especially with the increasing influence of electronic communications and the tendency of editors of publications to prefer a less cluttered look in page design. Style guides may differ from each other, and American and British styles also vary. Check with your instructor to see if there is a preferred style for your course or field of study, and consult a recent dictionary for additional information.

Abbreviations are formed in different ways, such as using the beginnings of words (*prof.* for *professor*); different letters from the word (*blvd.* for *boulevard*); the first letters of each word in a phrase (*UN* for *United Nations*); and other languages (*e.g.* for *for example*, from a Latin phrase).

Abbreviations formed using the initial letters of words are called **acronyms**. They are sometimes pronounced as whole words (*UNESCO* for *United Nations Educational, Scientific, and Cultural Organization*) and sometimes as initial letters (*BA* for *Bachelor of Arts).*

Some abbreviations are written with capital (uppercase) letters, especially when they have been formed using the initial letters of a phrase (*AC* for *air conditioning*). The punctuation of these examples is accepted by many instructors (but note the information above about style variation).

Examples

Dr.—Doctor

Mr.—Mister

Mrs. (title of married woman)

Ms. (title of woman, not a word abbreviation)

etc.—and so on (from a Latin phrase)

i.e.—that is (from a Latin phrase)

Mt.—Mount

St.—Street

Ave.—Avenue

Rd.—Road

in.—inch

ft.—foot/feet

Sgt.—Sergeant

Capt.—Captain

NASA—National Aeronautical and Space Administration

RSVP—please reply (from a French phrase)

QUICK REFERENCE

7

A. Connections between Ideas

It is important to have clear, logical connections between ideas within sentences, paragraphs, and sections of a text. As you are writing, ask yourself what exact relationship there is between ideas and choose the best connections to express that relationship. Many possible expressions—transitions, conjunctions, prepositions, and other forms—make logical connections. Some examples are given in the list and Table 7.1. See also Section 3 for more examples of expressions that connect ideas.

Examples of Appropriate Expressions for Connecting Ideas

Time

> **As** you perform this diagnostic, **at the same time** it is important to. . . .
>
> **Whenever** there is a thunderstorm. . . .

Space

> **Where** these results will have the most impact is. . . .
>
> **In** the south of Spain. . . .
>
> **Adjacent to** the building there is. . . .

Means

> We performed the experiment **using** a commonly accepted form.
>
> We achieved the best results **by** double-checking all of the procedures and **by** immediately recording the. . . .
>
> We performed the experiment **with** a beaker and a. . . .
>
> **Through** wise distribution of resources, we were able to. . . .

Comparison/Contrast

> **Whether** she chooses to take the written test **or** decides that the oral one is. . . .
>
> Her first novel had interesting characters and a complex plot. Her short stories, **on the other hand**, were. . . .

Concession

> **Although** these plants do not grow well in rainy areas, it is **still** possible to. . . .
>
> **Despite** the climatic conditions, these plants. . . .

Cause/Reason

> **Because of** the hurricanes, gas prices are. . . .
>
> **As a result of** the rainy weather, we. . . .

Condition

> **If** this study were to be expanded upon, some areas to work on would be. . . .
>
> **Unless** we act on this information immediately, many people. . . .
>
> He must follow the doctors orders carefully; **otherwise**, he might. . . .

Elaboration/Analysis

> As we can see, there are **many issues to consider** when building. . . . **With respect to** materials, . . .
>
> **More specifically**, we must consider the **particular issue** of the economic effects that. . . .

Referring to a Specific Point in the Text

> The **following section** describes some outcomes of. . . .
>
> **As mentioned earlier,** we can increase taxes or. . . .
>
> **As mentioned above,** there are good reasons to. . . .
>
> **Taking this into consideration,** we can assume that. . . .

Table 7.1: Examples of Logical Connections				
Type of Logical Connection	Connecting Word/Phrase	Coordinating Conjunction (connects independent clauses)	Subordinating Conjunction (begins dependent clause)	Verb, Preposition, Adverb, and Other Forms
Adding an Idea	also furthermore in addition moreover another point is that . . .	and		additionally not only . . . but also both . . . and
Describing Process/ Chronological Order	first then next last after that at the same time before while after		after as as soon as before since until when while	subsequently
Describing Means Used				by with in such a way that through using
Comparison	also similarly in the same way similar to compared to			is/are similar in that . . . is/are alike
Contrast/ Concesssion	however in contrast to/with on the other hand alternatively in comparison to/with when comparing X to/with Y	but yet	although even though though whereas while	differ with respect to is/are different differ from each other despite in spite of

Table 7.1 (cont'd)				
Type of Logical Connection	**Connecting Word/Phrase**	**Coordinating Conjunction (connects independent clauses)**	**Subordinating Conjunction (begins dependent clause)**	**Verb, Preposition, Adverb, and Other Forms**
Cause or Reason	the reason for this was taking this into consideration	for	because since as	due to the consequence/result of because of
Condition			if unless	
Effect/Result	as a result consequently one effect of this is as the above facts show therefore	so		bring about lead to produce generate create contribute to is/are responsible for result in
Elaboration or Restatement	that is for example looking at this information, we can see that as for x with respect to with regard to indeed in fact more specifically specifically more precisely		who whom that which	

Table 7.1 (cont'd)				
Type of Logical Connection	Connecting Word/Phrase	Coordinating Conjunction (connects independent clauses)	Subordinating Conjunction (begins dependent clause)	Verb, Preposition, Adverb, and Other Forms
Conclusion	therefore thus hence as you can see briefly in brief in short above all taking all this into account taking the above into consider-ation, we conclude that results show/ indicate/ imply given this information			
Example	for instance for example to illustrate			
Alternative		or		either . . . or neither . . . nor another way is an alternative is alternatively
Emphasis				actually indeed in fact

B. Words Often Confused

Correct word choice is essential in writing, so take special care with words that are often confused. The words and phrases in this list may be confused because their spellings or pronunciations are similar or because of their meanings. Short definitions or explanations are provided. Consult your dictionary for more information about these words and the differences between them. Remember: your word processor's spelling and grammar check function will probably not find errors you make with these words. Do not forget to proofread!

---

aggravate = to make a situation or condition worse than it already is
annoy/irritate = to make a person upset or angry

all ready = fully ready; entirely prepared
already = by this time; previously

all right = completely fine; without problem
alright = satisfactory; acceptable

all together = all at once; simultaneously
altogether = on the whole; completely

any more = additional
anymore = any longer; at the present time

any one = any single item of a group of items
anyone = any person

between = in the space or time that separates two things or people or from one to another
among = amid; surrounded by; in the space that separates more than two things or people

borrow = to take temporarily with the intention of returning (verb)
lend = to give temporarily with the intention of getting it back (verb)
loan = something given temporarily that is to be returned (noun) (*Loan* is also a verb.)

bored = feeling uninterested
boring = causing (someone) to feel uninterested

bring = to come (here) with
take = to go (away) with

cloth = fabric; material
clothes = clothing; garments; outfits

compose = to constitute; to make up
comprise = to include; to be made up of

criterion = standard; measure; condition (singular noun)
criteria = standards; measures; conditions (plural noun)
Also note these singular/plural pairs: **phenomenon/
phenomena, datum/data, medium/media**

custom = a tradition or practice that is common to a
　　　　　culture or group of people
habit = a frequent behavior or practice of an individual,
　　　　often done unconsciously or without thought

e.g. = for example
i.e. = in other words

eager = having strong desire to do something; enthusiastic
anxious = nervous; worried; concerned

effect = a result or outcome (noun) or to bring about; to
　　　　make happen (verb)
affect = to influence; to have an effect on or to imitate; to
　　　　pretend (verb)

every one = every single item; each one
everyone = everybody; all people

excuse = a justification for wrongdoing or absence
reason = an explanation; a rationale

famous = well-known; prominent; celebrated
notable = remarkable; distinguished; outstanding
notorious = famous, but in an unfavorable or negative
　　　　　way; infamous

farther = a greater distance
further = an additional extent or degree

former = the first thing previously mentioned in a set of two items

latter = the second thing previously mentioned in a set of two items

fun = describes something that is enjoyable or entertaining (like a party)

funny = describes something or someone that makes one laugh (like a joke)

guilty = having done wrong; feeling of having done wrong

ashamed = painful feeling of having done something against good or honorable behavior

embarrassed = feeling self-conscious or distressed

immigrate = to enter a new country that is not one's native country in order to live there

emigrate = to leave one's native country in order to live in a new place

migrate = to move from one country or place to another

imply = to indirectly indicate

infer = to conclude from existing evidence

interested = feeling of being curious or having one's attention drawn to something

interesting = causing (someone) to feel curious or attend to something

last = the previous; the preceding

latest = the most recent; the newest

listen = pay attention to; try to hear

hear = perceive with the ears (not intentionally)

look = to direct attention with the eyes

see = to perceive with the eyes; not intentionally

watch = look at something in action for a period of time (like a movie or a play)

make = to create; to manufacture (usually used for producing things)

do = to perform; to accomplish (usually used for actions)

on the contrary = in contrast; in opposition to what has been stated
on the other hand = conversely; alternatively

place = an area or part of an area
space = an empty area
room = enough space for a particular purpose

remember = to recall; to keep in mind
remind = to make someone remember

say = to speak; to utter
tell = to inform; to notify

sensible = reasonable; rational; level-headed
sensitive = easily upset or hurt; vulnerable

shade = shelter from the sun; darkness created by objects (like trees and buildings) that block sunlight
shadow = darkness in the image of an object (like a person) that blocks light

site = location; position
sight = the ability to see; something that is seen
cite = to use as an example or an authority

skill = an ability that has been gained through prolonged study and/or practice (such as learning a language or being an athlete)
talent = a natural ability (such as musical or artistic ability)

too = excessively; exceedingly; overly OR also; in addition to
very = extremely; especially
enough = the amount or quantity that is needed or appropriate

uninterested = not interested; not concerned
disinterested = neutral; not biased; impartial

used to = something done regularly in the past that is no longer done now
get used to = to grow accustomed to; to become comfortable with
be used to = to be accustomed to; to be familiar with

C. Active and Passive Voice

Writers are often advised to avoid using the passive voice whenever possible because it is said to be less vivid than the active or to have less force. While this may be true in personal essays, there is often good reason to use the passive in expository writing.

The main difference between these verb forms is that in an active sentence the subject is doing the action expressed in the verb, and in a passive sentence the subject is receiving the action.

In general, use the active form whenever possible because it is simpler, more direct, and easier for the reader to understand quickly. But the passive is sometimes more appropriate, especially in scientific and technical writing.

- When it is important to know **who** or **what is doing the action**, the **active** is necessary.
- When it is **not important** to know who or what is doing the action, the **passive** may be more effective.

Compare these sentences:

> **Active**: In her memoir, she **described** her personal experiences working in different cultures.
> (essential to know whose personal experiences)

> **Passive**: In the history textbook, important cultural sites around the world **are described** in detail.
> (not necessary to know who wrote the description)

In these cases, the passive is appropriate.

1. Describing steps in research or a process:

   One sample **was grown** in temperatures exceeding 30 degrees Celsius, while the other **was grown** in temperatures below freezing.

   As soon as the papers **were graded**, they **were sent** to the office so the grades **could be recorded**.

2. Making recommendations for future processes:

   The behavior of the two groups of students **must be compared** in another controlled study to discover more about successful study habits.

   Samples **need to be** randomly **selected** in order to avoid bias.

3. Describing cause and effect:

   When atoms **are heated**, electrons **are released**.

   If the instructions **are not followed** carefully, the project **may be considered a failure**.

D. Verb Tenses

The list of verb tenses and examples in Table 7.2 provide a brief overview and a quick reference on verb form and function. Refer to a grammar reference book for more details.

Table 7.2: Verb Tenses with Examples	
Simple Present **V (base form)** I **like** broccoli.	**Simple Past** **V -ed (or irregular V form)** I **walked** ten miles last week.
Present Continuous **be [present tense form] + V -ing** I **am talking** on the phone right now.	**Past Continuous** **was/were + V -ing** I **was typing** my paper when the phone rang.
Present Perfect **has/have + V -ed** During the past year she **has performed** several successful experiments.	**Past Perfect** **had + V -ed** By the time I was eight years old, I **had traveled** to four countries.
Present Perfect Continuous **has/have been + V -ing** I **have been working** in this job since January.	**Past Perfect Continuous** **had been + V -ing** I **had been speaking** for ten minutes before I was interrupted.
Future **will/shall + V (base form)** Next week I **will travel** to Brazil. **be going to + V (base form)** Next week I **am going to travel** to Brazil. **V (base form) [Simple Present]** Next week I **travel** to Brazil. **be + V -ing [Present Continuous]** Next week I **am traveling** to Brazil.	
Future Continuous **will be + V -ing** I **will be working** in my new job next week.	
Future Perfect **will have + V -ed** As of next year, we **will have worked** on this project for four years.	
Future Perfect Continuous **will have been + V -ing** As of next year, we **will have been working** on this project for four years.	

Simple Present

- used for actions involving current facts, habits, general truths
- sometimes refers to actions in future
- in a research paper, used to refer to general processes
- used to give citations in papers

    Jason **speaks** Mandarin very well.

    The weekly flight to Oslo **leaves** every Tuesday at 8:30 AM.

    Pierre and Michele **leave** the country tomorrow on an early flight.

    According to Donovan, this procedure **provides** valuable information to the researcher.

    Based on their long-term study, the researchers **believe** they have found a cure for the disease.

Simple Past

- action in the past at a specific time
- action begun and completed in the past

    While installing the new computer application, the laptop **crashed**.

    After analyzing the data, we **determined** that several steps need to be added to make the process run more smoothly.

Present Continuous

- action happening and continuing in or near the present time

    Giovanni **is writing** a research paper that is due very soon.

    The solution that Jones and Wells **are working** on right now seems to offer the best hope of a remedy for the problems in this software.

Past Continuous

- action continuing during a period of time in the past

    Yoko **was working** at an interesting job in Kobe before she left to study in Canada.

    The fact that the liquid **was** not **boiling** at its usual boiling point led us to believe that environmental factors **were affecting** the experiment.

Present Perfect

- past action that is still true and might continue in the future
- past action at unspecified point in time
- recent past action, emphasizing its present effect

    After our latest discussion, we **have decided** to postpone the next meeting.

    The federal government **has reported** that over one million children in America do not have health insurance.

    The general population **has become** increasingly dependent on TV as a form of entertainment.

Past Perfect

- action began and ended in the past before another action or before a specific time

    Pedro **had worked** in Venezuela for five years when he decided to leave for Chile.

    Jan's printer ran out of ink before she **had finished** printing her paper.

Present Perfect Continuous

- action begun in the past and still continuing at present, with emphasis on duration (how long the action has been going on)

    Alex **has been training** to be a chef for more than a year.

    Scientists **have been studying** this problem for only two years, yet they have already come up with several good solutions.

Past Perfect Continuous

- action in the past that was continuing before another
  action or time in the past, sometimes with emphasis
  on duration (how long the action has been going on)

  > Angelina **had been considering** engineering as
  > her major, but she decided on chemistry instead.

  > Keith **had been playing** tennis for twenty years
  > before he became a professional coach.

Future

- action in the future

  > This summer we **will travel** to New York and then
  > we **will fly** to Argentina.

  > Rika and Nina **will take** time off work and **will
  > have** a vacation in Rio.

Future Continuous

- action that will begin and continue in the future

  > Mac **will be performing** on stage at the Gemini
  > Theater for one month.

  > Santosh **will be visiting** his grandparents in
  > Nantucket this summer.

Future Perfect

- action in the future that will end before a specific time

  > Within fifteen years self-driving cars **will have
  > become** the norm.

  > The earth's population **will have increased** greatly
  > by the year 2050 over what it is today.

Future Perfect Continuous

- action in the future that will end before a specific time
  with emphasis on duration (how long the action has
  been going on)

  > By the time Helen leaves for Korea she **will have
  > been teaching** English for more than three years.

  > Next year the satellite **will have been orbiting** the
  > earth for seven years.

E. Irregular Verb Forms

Regular verbs form their simple past tense and past participles by adding -ed to the end of the verb, sometimes with a change in spelling, as in *walk, walked* or *bury, buried*. However, there are many irregular verbs that form their past tense and past participles in other ways, as shown in Table 7.3.

The past participle is used to form the present perfect and past perfect tenses (*have/had walked*) and the passive voice (*was buried by*). It is also sometimes used as an adjective (*buried treasure*).

Table 7.3: Common Irregular Verbs		
Base Form	**Past Tense Form**	**Past Participle Form**
arise	arose	arisen
be	was/were	been
bear	bore	borne
beat	beat	beaten
become	became	become
begin	began	begun
bite	bit	bitten
blow	blew	blown
break	broke	broken
bring	brought	brought
build	built	built
buy	bought	bought
catch	caught	caught
choose	chose	chosen
come	came	come
cut	cut	cut
do	did	done
draw	drew	drawn
drink	drank	drunk
drive	drove	driven
eat	ate	eaten
fall	fell	fallen
feed	fed	fed
feel	felt	felt
find	found	found
fly	flew	flown
forget	forgot	forgotten
freeze	froze	frozen
get	got	gotten
give	gave	given
go	went	gone
grow	grew	grown

have	had	had
hear	heard	heard
hide	hid	hidden
hold	held	held
keep	kept	kept
know	knew	known
lay	laid	laid
lead	led	led
leave	left	left
lend	lent	lent
let	let	let
lie	lay	lain
lose	lost	lost
make	made	made
meet	met	met
pay	paid	paid
read	read	read
ride	rode	ridden
rise	rose	risen
run	ran	run
say	said	said
see	saw	seen
sell	sold	sold
send	sent	sent
set	set	set
shake	shook	shaken
shine	shone/shined	shone/shined
shrink	shrank	shrunk
sing	sang	sung
sit	sat	sat
sleep	slept	slept
speak	spoke	spoken
spend	spent	spent
spring	sprang	sprung
stand	stood	stood
steal	stole	stolen
swim	swam	swum
take	took	taken
teach	taught	taught
tear	tore	torn
tell	told	told
think	thought	thought
throw	threw	thrown
understand	understood	understood
wear	wore	worn
win	won	won
write	wrote	written

F. Gerunds and Infinitives

Gerunds and **infinitives** are frequently used after verbs, but there are no rules that can be relied on in deciding whether a verb can be followed by only a gerund, only an infinitive, or either one. Try to become familiar with the usage of these forms with each verb separately. For more detailed descriptions and explanations on the correct use of gerunds and infinitives, consult a grammar reference or textbook series like *Clear Grammar* (by Keith Folse, University of Michigan Press).

Gerund Functioning as a Noun

It is formed by adding an **-ing** ending to the base form of a verb.

- A gerund can be used as the subject or object of a verb:

     Taking notes is a useful skill to practice.

     I enjoy **swimming** and **playing** golf.

- A gerund can follow a preposition as its object:

     I'm excited **about going** to Seattle this weekend.

     He started driving **without looking** at the map.

Infinitive Functioning as a Noun

It is formed by adding **to** before the base form of the verb. (This use of *to* is an infinitive marker, not a preposition.)

- An infinitive can be used as the subject or object of a verb:

     To follow her advice is very important.

     I want **to visit** all seven continents.

- Some verbs require a noun or pronoun before the infinitive:

     Claude **begged his parents to let** him get a kitten.

- Occasionally the *to* is omitted, such as after the verbs *have*, *let*, and *make*:

     I **let** my son **paint** his bedroom green. (not **to paint**)

> ▸ ▸ ▸ **Usage Notes**
>
> - Never combine the infinitive and gerund forms!
>   I went <u>to shopping</u> after work. ➔ I went **shopping** after work.
> - Only the gerund can act as a subject; the base form of a verb cannot act as a subject!
>   <u>Look</u> for a job is difficult. ➔ **Looking** for a job is difficult.

Common Verbs Followed by the Gerund

The citizens **supported passing** the new law.

admit	dislike	imagine	regret
appreciate	enjoy	keep (**continue**)	resist
avoid	feel like	mind (**object to**)	suggest
consider	finish	propose	support
deny	go	recommend	

Common Verbs Followed by the Infinitive

We all **arranged to meet** before the game.

agree	deserve	learn	refuse
arrange	expect	need	seem
ask	help	offer	wait
attempt	hesitate	plan	want
choose	hope	prepare	would like
decide	intend	promise	

Common Verbs Followed by the Gerund or the Infinitive

Henry **continued studying** German for five years.
Henry **continued to study** German for five years.

begin	hate	prefer	start
continue	like	regret	stop
forget	love	remember	try

Common Adjectives (Usually Followed by the Infinitive)

He was **delighted to tell** his friend the good news that he had been accepted by the college.

afraid	eager	hesitant	sad
delighted	easy	likely	surprised
determined	glad	pleased	
disappointed	happy	ready	

G. Using Prepositions

Prepositions can be used in many ways in English.

Phrasal Verbs

A **phrasal verb** consists of a verb and one or more prepositions that **change the meaning of the verb**. This change of meaning is what makes phrasal verbs different from other verb + preposition combinations. For example to *drop in* means to visit someone unexpectedly: the preposition *in* changes the meaning of the original verb *drop*, making this a phrasal verb. Phrasal verbs must, therefore, be learned as individual items because there is no way to predict how the meaning of the verb will change when the preposition is added. Many grammar books have a list of phrasal verbs and an explanation of their form and usage. Consult a grammar reference for more information. A few examples with their meanings are given here.

back up (support)	*put off* (postpone)
break down (become upset)	*shop around* (compare prices)
call on (visit)	*stick to* (continue)
check out (investigate)	*turn down* (refuse)
give in (surrender)	*try out* (test)
let down (disappoint)	*work out* (be successful)

> ▸ ▸ ▸ **Usage Note**
>
> Remember that phrasal verbs are **often an informal way of expressing an idea**. They are commonly used in everyday speaking and writing, but when writing or speaking in an academic or professional setting, try to use more formal alternatives.
>
> *cut down on/cut back on* → *reduce*
> *look forward to* → *anticipate*
> *put off* → *postpone, delay*
> *put up with* → *tolerate*
> *start up* → *commence, begin*

Verb + Preposition Combinations

Many verbs can occur in combination with a certain preposition, but **if the basic meaning of the verb is not changed**, these are not considered phrasal verbs. Some examples are:

admit to	*choose among*	*plan on*
advise against	*complain about*	*search for*
apologize for	*feel like*	*talk about*
approve of	*insist on*	*think about*
believe in	*object to*	
choose between	*pay attention to*	

Adjective + Preposition Combinations

It is helpful to notice and remember adjective + preposition combinations. A few examples are:

accustomed to	*different from*	*responsible for*
famous for	*excited about*	*satisfied with*
angry about	*fond of*	*sorry about*
ashamed of	*good at*	*surprised at*
aware of	*interested in*	*worried about*
capable of	*opposed to*	
concerned about	*proud of*	

Common Preposition + Noun Phrases

Many noun phrases in English include prepositions and are used in a variety of ways. It is helpful to remember their correct form and usage. A few examples are:

on the way	*in time*	*for example*
on my own	*by the way*	*at present*
for sure	*by chance*	*in the future*

SPECIAL TYPES OF WRITING

A. Email Guidelines

For many people, email is the primary means of communication, particularly in professional and academic contexts. A list of guidelines when composing email messages follows. These guidelines apply mainly to email sent to people you do not know or people with whom you are being **formal** (in other words, not your family members and friends).

Email *Do's*

- **Do** always include a short but specific subject in the subject line, preferably in reference to the content of the message. Vague or very general subject lines like *question* or *hello* or *class* do not give the recipient much information, and your message could be ignored or discarded as spam, especially if the person you're writing to does not know you. If you are replying to a message, keep the same subject line as the original message.
- **Do** always use a proper greeting, usually title + last name.

Examples

> **Dear Professor Roberts,**
>
> **Dear Amanda Rogers,**
>
> **Dear Jim Taylor,**
>
> **Dear Dr. Johnson,**

- **Do** use an appropriate title (Dr., Ms., Mr.). If you must use Mr. or Ms. but you do not know if the person is a man or a woman, try to find out before sending your message. Avoid a general greeting like *Dear Sir or Madam* if possible.
- **Do** identify yourself clearly. Make sure that your full name appears in the message somewhere—either in the From line, the first line of your message, or the signature block. Do not assume that the reader knows who you are from your email address or your first name alone.
- **Do** write clearly and concisely. Email messages are usually fairly short. If you have many thoughts to communicate or several questions to ask, organize your writing into short paragraphs, each addressing one topic or issue. This will

help to ensure that the reader sees the most important points or questions in your message. Remember that most people receive a lot of email every day and want to get through their messages quickly, so they may skim through without reading carefully.

- **Do** use an appropriate closing. This will depend on your relationship with the person you are writing to. For example, *Regards* is very business-like and unemotional, while *Cheers* is very informal and more personal. Take care to choose the right closing for the situation.

- **Do** proofread your message before you hit Send. Just like any other piece of writing, you want to make sure that you have made no grammar or spelling errors and that your writing is clear and understandable.

- **Do** reply in a reasonable amount of time to a message someone has sent you. How quickly you respond will depend on the urgency of the message, but a good general rule is to respond within 24 hours from the time that you receive a message (not including weekends and holidays).

- **Do** give your reader time to respond to your message. Even if you think the message is urgent, do not send another email unless a long time (at least several days) has passed. Remember that most people do their best to respond to you as soon as they can, but they may have many other things to do before they can write back to you.

Email *Don'ts*

- **Don't** use a person's first and last name with Mr., Mrs., Ms., or Dr. (for example, *Dear Dr. Norah Johnson* should be *Dear Dr. Johnson*).

- **Don't** misspell the name of the person you are sending the message to. Double-check the spelling to make sure it's correct before you send the message.

- **Don't** write in all capital letters or all lowercase letters. Using all capital letters makes it seem like you are shouting; using all lowercase letters may make it appear that you are being careless or too informal. Use proper punctuation, including capitalization, as if you were writing a message by hand.

- **Don't** make jokes or try to be sarcastic. Your intentions may not be understood by the reader, and you could offend without meaning to.

- **Don't** send attachments that are too large or that are unnecessary. You may cause a problem in the recipient's email system, such as an overflow in his or her Inbox. Also, make sure that any attachments you send are free of viruses.

- **Don't** discuss very private information through email. You cannot be sure that email is completely secure. It is better to make an appointment to talk face-to-face or over the phone with someone about personal matters. Also, do not send confidential information (such as credit card numbers or passwords) through email.

- **Don't** use abbreviations (BTW, IMO, FWIW) or words that are shortened or that have alternative spellings (*thanx, 2, u*). The reader may not understand you or may find it inappropriate. Remember that you are using a different style from what you use to send email or text messages to your friends.

- **Don't** use emoticons like smiley faces in your messages, especially to people you do not know. They are too informal and may make you seem unprofessional. Similarly, do not overuse punctuation to emphasize something (e.g., *Thank you very much!!!!!!!!!* would be better with just one exclamation point). Avoid multiple exclamation points and question marks.

- **Don't** write your message as if you are having a conversation on the telephone (e.g., *My name is Henry. How are you today?*)

Each of the email messages that follow was written by a student to a professor.

Sample Emails

Examples of Well-Presented Email Messages

Subject: Help with assignment

Good morning Professor,
I would like to ask for some help with the assignment for
class that is due next week. I read the instructions, but I do
not understand everything well. Can I meet you to ask some
questions? I have time available after our class tomorrow. Is that
okay for you? Thank you very much for your time and help.
Sincerely,
Akiko Iwai

Subject: I would like to join class

Dear Dr. Williams:
I was a student in your English class last semester. I would like
to join your class this semester, but it is already full. I tried to sign
up, but I could not do it because there were no spaces left. Is it
possible for me to sign up with your permission? I enjoyed your
class and I would like to be in your class again. Thank you.
Best regards,
Harry Li

Examples of Poorly Presented Email Messages

Subject: (No subject)

Hey Carina-
this is Juan from your english class, you remember me? i hope u
didnt forget your favorite student =)
i have a question,i want to get new id card so i can use the city
bus.
i think I lost my old one so u know where
I can get the new one?
it will be helpful for me haha =)
thank u very much...
Yours,
Juan

Subject: Hello

Hi Teacher Jones Gabriela!
It is to let you know that today for class I am leaving early before
it is finished. It is because i want to call my mother to tell her for
my travel plans home for vacation and i think she will be home
that time. I will try to be quiet when i leave your class!! but i
wanna talk to her soon so I am sorry :-(
Have a nice day today!!
Jenny

B. Resumes

A resume (sometimes called a *curriculum vitae* or *CV*) is a brief summary of your educational and career experience. It can also include information such as special skills and interests that you have, honors that you have received, and leadership positions that you have held. The purpose of a resume is—in the space of just one or two pages—to introduce yourself to an employer and to persuade the reader to interview and/or hire you. Therefore, a resume must describe your experience and interests clearly, succinctly, and impressively. Although the terms are sometimes used as synonyms, a curriculum vitae is normally longer than a resume and more academic, with publications and conference presentations listed.

A resume should be organized, written, and formatted in a way that makes it easy to read and emphasizes the most significant things you have done.

It is helpful to look at example resumes to see what format looks attractive and fits your particular experience and career goals. Many websites have good tips, templates, and example resumes, and most universities and companies have career centers where you can receive help in developing a strong resume.

Length

- A resume should be limited to 1–2 pages.
- A CV should be a longer document that details your academic and career accomplishments more extensively.

General Formatting

- Although you can adjust the margins and font size in order to fit more information on the page, it is important to leave enough space and to use a large enough font so that your resume is easy to read and pleasing to look at.
- Be sure that the headings and sections are noticeable and easy to distinguish.

Content

- Focus on the things you have done well. Emphasize your strengths.
- Be sure to include current contact information with an alternate address if you will be changing addresses or are not living in a permanent location.
- If you are sending your resume to apply for a job, it is common to write an objective at the beginning of your resume. This is a one-sentence statement summarizing the type of position you want or your overall career goals.
- A resume usually contains at least three major categories: education, work experience, and activities (school- or community-related). You can add other categories that best express your interests and strengths.
- **Optional categories** include:
  › Honors (scholarships, honor societies, academic or community awards)
  › Languages (include proficiency level—fluent or conversational, for example)
  › Skills (could include language ability or computer expertise, for example)
  › Interests (only if there is space, and if these add to an overall positive impression)
  › Coursework (if your work experience is limited, this can give a clearer picture of your knowledge and experience. List only courses relevant to your field.)
  › Experience abroad (list countries, dates, and purpose of travel—research, employment, study abroad, for example)
  › Professional organizations in which you have a current membership
  › Publications (provide complete bibliographic information, and a brief description of the content if there is space)
  › Presentations (list the name of the conference, title of the presentation, date, location, and a brief summary if there is space)

Language

A resume must be professional, clear, and concise. This requires a particular style of language and type of vocabulary. Since a resume is such a short document that contains a lot of information, every word is important.

- Your sentences should be short, so they are easy to read. Your grammatical structure should be simple and clear. Long sentences and complex grammar are not a good way to communicate in a resume because your reader will be skimming quickly for important points. Also, every sentence should provide new, important information. Since space is quite limited, do not repeat any information and choose each word carefully.

- Use formal language—avoid slang, contractions, or informal vocabulary. Use positive, descriptive words in providing details about your personality, experience, and activities. Some descriptive nouns, adjectives, and verbs that are useful in a resume are shown in Table 8.1. Most of the adjectives and nouns can be changed and used in either form (adjective or noun).

Table 8.1: List of Descriptive Words for Resumes

Nouns	Adjectives	Verbs	
ability	capable	achieve	exhibit
ambition	exceptional	assist	facilitate
confidence	honest	create	implement
energy	loyal	collaborate	improve
enthusiasm	notable	complete	initiate
excellence	organized	conduct	manage
ingenuity	proficient	coordinate	organize
integrity	reliable	design	participate
innovation	responsible	demonstrate	plan
opportunity	significant	develop	produce
recognition	sincere	direct	streamline
success	thoughtful	establish	supervise
	vital	evaluate	

- Use the simple past tense in a resume, unless it is an activity that you are currently involved in. Also, do not include the subject *I*. Instead, simply start your sentences with the verb.

Sample Resumes

Two sample resumes are given. The first format is suitable for someone with not much work experience, like a recent college graduate. The second format is suitable for a person with work experience in a technical field.

Resume of Person with Not Much Work Experience

Christine Koehler
981 Hunter Avenue, Morristown, OH 12218
Phone: 409-555-3110 Email: ckoehler@email.net

EDUCATION
    Bachelor of Arts in International Studies   May 2016
    Summa cum laude, Minors in French and German
    Grandville College, Grandville, Pennsylvania

LANGUAGES
    Fluent in German, both written and oral
    Advanced conversational ability in French
    Some study of Latin, Chinese, and Japanese

INTERNATIONAL EXPERIENCE
    Swaziland ~ English teaching and community   2016–2017
    development work

    France ~ Semester of home-stay, study, and travel   Spring 2015
    (Université de Strasbourg)

    Germany ~ Volunteer service, home-stay, and   Summer 2014
    independent travel

EMPLOYMENT
    Private Tutor in French and German, Grandville, PA   2012–2016
    Worked with university students of French and
    German to improve their skills in reading,
    pronunciation, conversation, and vocabulary

    Peer Tutor, Grandville College Writing Center   2014–2016
    Assisted undergraduate students in improving their
    writing skills in a one-on-one setting; specialized in
    working with international and ESL students

    Office Assistant, Morristown Family Practice,   Summers 2012–2015
    Morristown, OH
    Helped with typing, filing, scheduling, and
    general office management in a private physician's
    practice

VOLUNTEER AND COMMUNITY EXPERIENCE

Student Representative for Department of Politics, Grandville College	2015–2016
Chair of Annual "Grand Race" Fundraiser for Cancer Research	2014–2016
Volunteer Tutor for middle school student, Kids Extra Learning Program, Grandville	2012–2016

HONORS

Student of the Year Award ~ Presented to one outstanding graduating senior each year by the Grandville Alumni Association, based on scholarship, service, and character.	May 2016
Lincoln Scholar ~ Four-year honors program requiring an honors thesis, on-campus leadership experience, and community service	2012–2016

Resume of Person with Work Experience in a Technical Field

NICOLO ALVARETTI
2055 Napoleon Rd
Golden Town, CA 12345
nicoalva@school.edu   604-555-2547

EDUCATION & TRAINING

Golden Town University – Summer Program in Quantitative Methods of Social Research (Summer 2016)
- Completed courses in Mathematics of Social Science and Applied Multilevel Modelling Techniques.

Grand State University – Bachelor of Arts (2013 – May 2017)
- Major: Sociology, Minor: Education Studies
- Received scholarship award for Outstanding Junior in Social Sciences
- Relevant Technical Skills courses: Research Methods, Research Statistics, Quantitative Methods, Quantitative Sociology Capstone, Intro. Demographic Techniques, Statistical Packages.

RELATED WORK & RESEARCH EXPERIENCE

Inter-collegiate Consortium for Social Science Research, Research Intern (Summer 2016)
- Attended seminars and skill development sessions on Unix scripting, data processing & dissemination, data ethics, and data & research funding & infrastructure, curated studies for public download and analysis and online SDA analysis.
- Developed an independent research project under Dr. Lionel Holton using SPSS and SAS.

GSU Department of Sociology, Undergraduate Research Assistant (Fall 2015 – Spring 2016)
- Paid position funded by an NSF grant under (PI) Dr. Ramona Switzer.
- Developing familiarization with SAS, multi-wave Add Health data, and conducting rigorous literature reviews.
- Paper (in preparation) examined family SES and school aggregate SES interaction effects when predicting violent perpetration.

GSU Department of Education, Undergraduate Teaching Assistant (Fall 2014 – Present)
- Served for six consecutive semesters under Dr. Patricia Vermian.
- Assisted students with literature review assignments based on academic journal article readings.
- Provided instructional support to graduate student staff in the facilitation of lecture and recitation sessions.
  - Currently designing a mixed methods survey instrument to evaluate students' learning outcomes.

Business Professionals of America National Office, Intern (Summer 2014)
- Conducted historical research investigating key BPA historical figures and events for BPA's 50th anniversary.
- Collecting and reviewing official documents and records, identifying significant names and events.

Educators in the Community, Member (Fall 2013 – Present)
- Completed 110 hours of teaching field experience in California schools.
- Visited innovative charter schools in Detroit, MI; Chicago, IL; Oklahoma City, OK; New York, NY; and Oakland, CA.
- Served on the ECCO Executive Board for six consecutive semesters.
  - Assisted with the coordination of the 2014 Annual ECCO Conference.

PRESENTATIONS

"We Don't Need No Education": High School Dropouts, the GED, and Pathways to Economic Capability in the Transition to Adulthood (August 9, 2016).
- Presented at Student Research Symposium, Golden Town University.
- Examined differing economic returns of family formation, and occupational and educational attainment for high school dropouts.

Violent Perpetration and the Interplay of Family and School Socioeconomic Segregation (April 23, 2016).
- Presented at: GSU Undergraduate Symposium for Research and Scholarship, paper version currently being prepared for publication.
- Examined how individuals' relative socioeconomic position with their high schools relates to their trajectories of violent behavior.

The Relationship Between Teacher Regard and Expectations for College Attendance: Social Class and Racial-Ethnic Differences (March 12, 2016).
- Presented at: National Undergraduate Sociology Symposium, Valley State University, Received 1st place award for best poster.
- Examined school climate variables as they relate to students' expectations and aspirations for their academic future.

Educational Processes in Singapore, Urban China, and the United States: A Comparative Analysis of Social Influences and Career Decision-Making (March 14, 2015).
- Presented at: National Undergraduate Sociology Symposium, Valley State University.
- Examined how Westernization and the aging East Asian population are causing conflict in youths' career choices.

SELECTED REFERENCES:

Dr. Ramona Switzer - research mentor
Professor
Department of Sociology
Grand State University
rswitz@school.edu
(409) 555-8054

Alma Lopez - internship supervisor
Program Manager: ICPSR Summer Internship
Inter-collegiate Consortium for Political and Social Research
Institute for Social Research, Golden Town University
alopez@university.edu
(234) 555-7765

Bharani Asuri - data processing mentor and internship supervisor
Data Curation Supervisor
Inter-collegiate Consortium for Political and Social Research
Institute for Social Research, Golden Town University
basuri@university.edu
(234) 555-7763

C. Cover Letters

When you are applying for a job, it is customary to send a cover letter along with your resume. While your resume describes your experience and skills, the cover letter explains why you are especially suitable for the position that you are applying for. In the cover letter, point out your experience and skills that exactly match the qualifications that are described in the job posting, along with any other reasons that you feel show why you are particularly qualified for the position and state why you are interested in the position.

- Always follow a standard business letter format. (See the example on page 280 or one of the many available online or in a career center.)
- Use complete titles and addresses, not abbreviations. Write directly to the person in charge of hiring if at all possible.
- The opening paragraph should specify which position you are applying for or if you are simply inquiring as to the availability of job openings at the company.
- The middle paragraph highlights your skills and experience that are most closely matched to the job description. Be careful, though, not to simply restate information contained in your resume. Make the reader want to read the resume.
- The closing paragraph requests action from the reader, most commonly an interview appointment and/or a phone call.
- Remember to put the word *Enclosure* below your typed name to indicate that your resume is enclosed.
- Do not forget to sign your name.

Sample Cover Letter (Formal, blocked)

Nicolo Alvaretti
2055 Napoleon Road
Golden Town, CA 12345
Email: nicoalva@school.edu
Phone: 604-555-2547

Mr. Joe Shmough, Personnel Manager
Educational Innovations, Inc.
4598 Corporate Boulevard
Tech Town, CA 12543

May 25, 2017

Dear Mr. Shmough:

I am writing to you in response to your recent posting for a data manager at Educational Innovations, Inc. specializing in educational data. As you can see from my enclosed resume, my experiences and qualifications are a good match for this position's requirements.

I recently graduated from Grand State University with a BA in Sociology and a minor in Education Studies. During my four years at GSU, I have gained valuable research experience in data collection, processing, and analysis. Additionally, my course work in social sciences and quantitative methods has given me solid foundational knowledge as well as practical experience in working with various kinds of data for research purposes. This is particularly evident in the summer course I completed at Golden Town University, on Quantitative Methods of Social Science Research. I have worked on multiple projects in which I have demonstrated initiative and leadership in guiding a team towards successful completion. In addition, my many semesters as a teaching assistant have provided valuable experience helping students with course material in small groups and one-on-one. My success with working with people is yet another skill that makes me a good candidate for this position. Together with my experience in social science data analysis and background in education, I feel that I could benefit your company.

Thank you for your time and consideration. I look forward to the opportunity to meet with you in person to discuss why I am particularly well suited for this position. You can reach me by telephone at 604-555-2547 or by email at nicoalva@school.edu.

Sincerely,

Nicolo Alvaretti
Nicolo Alvaretti

Enclosure

D. Personal Statements

When applying to college or a graduate school or when applying for a scholarship, you are often required to send a personal statement describing why you are applying. The statement provides you with an opportunity to introduce yourself in a more personal way to the admissions officers or scholarship committee.

First, think about a focus for the personal statement:

- Why do you want to go to graduate school?
- Where did your interest come from?
- What do you hope to do with the degree?
- What are some experiences that have influenced you?
- What research have you participated in?
- What do you think is important for the reader to know about you?
- What qualities do you have that will enable you to succeed in this area?

Guidelines

1. Be sure to answer any specific questions you are asked.
2. The general organization is usually from past to present.
3. An anecdote at the beginning can help the reader to see you as an individual to help set you apart from all the other applicants.
4. Avoid beginning with a cliché like, *Ever since I was a child, I have wanted to study X.*
5. Be specific. For instance, instead of saying: *If we don't protect the environment, there will be nothing left for our children,* say: *Every year, more than 30 pounds of hazardous material is generated by the average home. This means that by the year 2050, we will have nowhere to put our garbage.*
6. Know important facts about the university you are applying to:

   - Use the name of a professor that you would like to work with and say why.

   - Know what areas the department you are applying to is focusing on to help determine what you include in the essay and provide a focus for your personal statement.

7. Be sure to provide some information on what you can contribute to the university or program. What makes you valuable to the school? Focus on your particular skills, experience, research interests, or background.

8. Ask someone such as a professor or writing center consultant to read your personal statement and provide some feedback.

   • Remember, your statement reflects your writing skill. It must have unity and coherence (see pages 48–52).

Sample Personal Statement

I remember when I was about seven years old, a friend of the family asked me what I wanted to be when I grew up. My grandmother immediately answered, "As smart as she is, she wants to be a doctor or lawyer of course!" However, I knew that what I really wanted was to teach. In fact, as the oldest of four children and the oldest in the neighborhood, I certainly got plenty of opportunity to practice patience and management skills in my family and with friends. When I graduated from high school, I actively sought a school with an excellent teaching program, Wells College, to help me achieve my goal of becoming a teacher.

As I am finishing my certification in elementary education, however, I have realized that while I do want to teach, I also want to do more in the broader field of education. My experience student teaching has opened my eyes to many of the pitfalls that exist in public schools, where underprepared children are slipping through the cracks because of financial concerns. Currently, I am a student teacher for a 3rd grade class where 9 of the 24 children in the class could not pass a reading proficiency exam. However, they will be passed on to 4th grade for funding reasons. Because of situations like this, I am applying to the Department of Administration and Policy Studies, with the intention of earning a Master of Education degree. I feel I can better serve students by becoming involved in the making of policies that place a serious value on education in schools rather than a value on getting the statistics needed to obtain funding from the government.

Realistically speaking, I realize that it is difficult for one person to make a huge difference, but I believe that small influences can exert power over time. An example that has proven this to me is a state and locally funded undergraduate project at the school where I am student teaching. After noticing the problems my students were having with reading and realizing that they were not the only grade with this problem, I began an after school program at the elementary school. Twice a week, students who scored below accepted grade proficiency levels on an administered reading exam participate in one-and-a-half-hour sessions alternating between a classroom or a computer room. There are four classrooms with eight students each and two computer rooms with twelve computers each. Six specially trained teachers on staff at the school participate, with one in charge of each room. In the classroom, students undertake activities as suggested by current pedagogical theories of literacy promotion. The most recently available literacy software is used in the computer rooms to encourage improvement in computer skills, as well as improvement in reading skills. After completing the six-week project, the students took a post-test on which their reading scores showed dramatic improvement.

I am eager to continue research in areas such as literacy, policy-making and administration in order to develop more such projects. Specifically, Dr. Novath's studies with respect to ways in which the community can become more directly involved in the education process particularly interest me as I believe that this is a crucial and often overlooked component to making our schools more effective. I look forward to sharing my experiences with other students and to working with your highly recognized faculty.

COMMON CORRECTION
SYMBOLS FOR EDITING

→| (indent)	Indent the paragraph by one tab or ten spaces.
→ (move)	Move this word or phrase to a different place in the sentence or paragraph.
↔	Reverse or compare these two words or ideas.
X or ~~delete~~ (delete)	Remove the word(s) that are crossed out.
[ ] (not necessary)	Remove this phrase or sentence.
( ) (optional)	The word(s) in parentheses are not necessary, but not incorrect.
add or ∧ (insert)	Something is missing and needs to be added.
? or unclear	The meaning is confusing or not clear and needs to be stated differently.
awk (awkward)	Sentence structure or grammar needs to be improved for better flow.
vague	Choose more specific words to explain this idea.
red (redundant)	This information has already been stated and should be removed.
ex (example)	Add some examples to support your point.
trans (transition)	Add or change a transition to make the connection between ideas clearer.
wc (word choice)	Incorrect word choice; select a word with more accurate meaning.
wf (word form)	The word form (adjective, noun, verb, adverb, etc.) is incorrect.
par or // (parallelism)	Word form needs to be changed to match others in a list.
agr (agreement)	Change number, word form, verb tense, etc., to correct agreement.

pro (pronoun)	Pronoun antecedent is unclear—what does the pronoun stand for?
art (article)	The sentence is missing *a* or *the*, or the wrong article is used.
pl (plural)	Change the word to plural form.
sg (singular)	Change the word to singular form.
vt (verb tense)	Verb tense is incorrect.
punct (punctuation)	Punctuation is missing or incorrect.
ro (run-on)	Two clauses are improperly combined into one sentence and must be divided into two sentences.
frag (fragment)	This is not a complete sentence.
sp (spelling)	Spelling is incorrect.
cap or <u>c</u> (capitalize)	Capitalize the letter indicated.
no cap or <u>C</u> (no capitalization)	Change the capitalized letter to lower case.
cs	Correct a comma splice.
poss	Make a word possessive.

GLOSSARY

The definitions given here are related to writing essays and research papers. Not all terms appear in this book. Some of the words and terms have other meanings in different contexts.

abstract—summary of a research paper or other academic text; frequently given at the beginning of the text and in indexes

alphabetize—to arrange words, such as names in a research paper's list of works cited, in order of the letters of the alphabet, from A to Z

argument—a presentation of different, possibly opposing points of view; a process of reasoning

audience—the person or people who will read a text

block indentation—setting the left margin for a group of lines further into the text than the standard left margin for the whole text; used for long quotations in most formatting styles

chronological—in time order

cite (noun: **citation**) —to name the source

clarity—a quality of style referring to how easy the text is to understand

classify—to arrange according to categories or groups

coherence—the quality of having meaningful connections between all parts of a text

compose—to use language to create a text

content—the information presented in a text

coordinating conjunction—a word that joins two grammatically equal clauses, phrases, or words; the coordinating conjunctions are *and, or, nor, but, yet, for, so*

coordination—the process of using a coordinating conjunction to connect two independent clauses

dependent clause—a part of a sentence that contains a subject and a verb and that is not a grammatically complete sentence; an example is *if he arrives*

development—the order of information and its organization in a text; the part of an essay or paper following the introduction and continuing up to the conclusion (also called the *body*)

dialogue—a conversation between two or more people

draft—a version of an essay or research paper

edit—to correct errors in a written text, typically focusing on spelling, punctuation, and grammar

evidence—the information on which a proof or judgment is based

expository writing—a text that aims to present information and facts in a clear and well-organized manner; a research paper is an example

footnote—a comment, note, or reference written at the bottom of a page

foreshadowing—the part of an introduction that indicates for the reader the main ideas that will be discussed in the development of an essay or research paper

indent—to start a line of writing further into the text than the standard left margin for the whole text; indentation is used to indicate the start of a new paragraph

independent clause—a group of words that contains a subject and a verb and that is a grammatically complete sentence; an example is *She wrote an essay.*

indirect (reported) quotation—not an exact quote from a person or source but a report of what the person or source said

intonation—the pattern of change in pitch (varying between high and low tones) in spoken language to express some aspect of meaning or attitude of the speaker; an example is *question intonation*, which in English is often expressed by a rising intonation toward the end of a sentence

key words—(a) words in a writing assignment's instruction that indicates how the assignment should be organized or the way to write the assignment; examples are *compare, argue for, present evidence against, trace the development of*; (b) concept words that are important in an essay or research paper and that may be repeated for emphasis

logical reasoning—the process of presenting proper arguments and evidence that lead to a conclusion

metaphor—a descriptive comparison in which items are directly compared without the use of words of comparison such as *like* and *as*; an example is *The boring musical performance was a sleeping pill.* (Compare this with the definition of *simile.*)

outline—a plan of the content and organization of an essay or paper, typically written at or near the start of creating a text

pagination—numbering of pages in a written text

paraphrase—restatement of the ideas of a source using different words and sentence structures; used frequently in research papers to report ideas of other writers

perspective—point of view about a subject

phrasal verb—combination of verb and one or more additional words, usually prepositions; the meaning of a phrasal verb as a whole unit is different from each of its parts; the whole phrasal verb functions as a verb; examples are *put up with* meaning *tolerate*; *get across* meaning *communicate something successfully*; *do away with* meaning *abolish* or *eliminate*

phrase—group of two or more words that does not contain a finite verb and is inferior grammatically to a clause or sentence

plagiarism—using the language or ideas of a source as if they are one's own

prompt—writing assignment instruction

quotation (**direct quotation**)—exact repetition of someone's words

reference words—words that refer to a previously mentioned specific noun, such as *these, they, some of which, he, she, it*

revise—to change a written text's content or organization

research question—a question focused on what you want to learn about; also the reason for writing the paper

rhetorical pattern—a specific way of organizing ideas in an essay or paper; examples are *narration, comparison, cause and effect*; an essay or research paper typically uses a combination of rhetorical patterns

shaping—process of creating a definite form or organization for an essay or paper

simile—a descriptive comparison in which items are compared using words of comparison such as *like* and *as*; an example is *The boring musical performance was like a sleeping pill.* (Compare this with the definition of *metaphor.*)

source—origin of the ideas and information in a text; in an academic paper sources are always mentioned and accurately cited

subordinating conjunction—a word or phrase that joins an independent (main) clause to a dependent (subordinate) clause; some examples are *because, although, if, in order that*

subordination—the process of using a subordinating conjunction to connect two ideas

summarize—to write a shortened version of a text, usually including only the main ideas

synonym—a word whose meaning is similar to that of another word

thesis statement—the sentence in an essay or research paper that expresses its main idea

topic—subject of an essay or paper

topic sentence—the sentence in a paragraph that expresses its main idea; sometimes a paragraph has an implied main idea and no specific topic sentence

transition—word, phrase, clause, sentence, or paragraph that provides a logical connection between parts of a text; some common transition words and phrases are *however, on the other hand, furthermore, in addition, next, second, third, consequently, as a result, in conclusion*

unity—the quality of having all parts of an essay or paper effectively combined, giving the reader an impression of all the parts being well connected with each other in both ideas and organization

ANSWER KEY

Section 1. The Writing Process

Exercise 1.1: Thinking about Composing (page 2)
Answers will vary.

Exercise 1.2: Reflecting on the Composing Process (page 3)
Answers will vary.

Exercise 1.3: Identifying Key Words in Writing Assignments (page 10)

1. <u>Describe</u> and <u>identify the function of</u> the major elements of a plant cell: cell wall, central vacuole, and plastids (including chloroplasts, chromoplasts, and leucoplasts). <u>Compare</u> the structure of plant cells to animal cells and <u>explain</u> why these differences exist. [Botany]

2. <u>Examine</u> a movie that was adapted from a book that you've read. <u>List</u> several changes that were made in adapting the book for the screen and <u>explain</u> why you think the director made these changes. <u>Assess</u> whether the book and the movie have the same impact on the audience and <u>discuss</u> which version you prefer. [Film Studies/Literature]

3. Choose a space telescope to <u>investigate</u>. Your investigation should include: (a) a brief <u>review</u> of the history of this telescope (launch date and lifespan); (b) a <u>description</u> of the telescope's components and how it works (i.e. the optics of its telescope and cameras); (c) a <u>summary</u> of the telescope's purpose and any major discoveries it has made; and (d) an <u>analysis</u> of the impact of this particular telescope on the field of astronomy. [Astronomy]

4. <u>Compare</u> and <u>contrast</u> the Italian Renaissance with the Renaissance in Northern Europe, particularly with regard to the arts. Use specific works to <u>support</u> your analysis. [European History]

5. <u>Discuss</u> the importance of memory as a brain function. <u>Define</u> explicit and implicit memory and <u>explain</u> three main stages in the formation and retrieval of memory. [Psychology]

Exercise 1.4: Generating Ideas (page 18)
Answers will vary.

Section 2. Essay Structure

Exercise 2.1: Topic and Perspective (page 21)

1. Students who want to learn another language may find software programs to be very effective tools.
2. University students should be sure to make time for social activities in addition to time for studying.
3. Social media can be very distracting.
4. Engineers are working on many new technologies to improve automobile emissions.
5. Small liberal arts colleges offer many benefits to students that larger universities cannot.

Exercise 2.2: Topic and Development Sentences (page 22)

Bilateral aid, the direct transfer of specific resources of money between two countries (definition), has several key features, both for the donor country and the receiving country. Bilateral aid is rarely a grant of money (explanation). It is usually a low-interest loan (explanation). In many cases, however, it is a tied loan (explanation), which means that the recipient country is required to purchase goods and services from the donor country (definition). For example, the United States may decide to give a tied loan for the construction of a steel mill (example). Under the terms of agreement the receiving government will have to buy the needed material and technical assistance from the donor country (explanation).

Exercise 2.3: Ordering Information (pages 30–31)

1. *Chronological*
   _2_ Experiment with ways to make your idea a reality.
   _5_ Discover one method that is successful.
   _7_ Seek out a way to produce your invention for sale to the general public.
   _6_ Patent your invention.
   _1_ Develop an idea that meets a need.
   _3_ Experience failure in your creative experimentation.
   _4_ Return to the idea phase and explore other ways of developing your idea.

2. *Importance—least to most*

___3___ It can summon help in an emergency situation.

___2___ It can save you time and frustration when looking for a friend in a busy place.

___1___ It is convenient for staying connected with friends.

3. *Familiarity—most to least*

___1___ A hammer allows you to pound in the picture hanger.

___3___ A stud-finder locates the sturdy beams within the walls.

___2___ A level helps to make sure that your picture is hung straight.

4. *Generality—most to least*

___2___ There are two main categories of trees: deciduous (which lose their leaves for part of the year) and evergreen (which keep their leaves year-round).

___1___ Every tree has a root system, a trunk, and branches with leaves. Its leaves absorb carbon dioxide and release oxygen into the air.

___4___ Red Maple, Silver Maple, and Sugar Maple are several of the varieties of maple trees that are popular for their shade and the fall colors of their leaves.

___3___ A small family of deciduous trees, maple trees are common in the temperate zones of the Northern Hemisphere.

Exercise 2.4: Key Words and Organizational Patterns in Writing Assignments (page 33)

Typical patterns for these topics are given here, with descriptions of appropriate organizational patterns.

1. Topic: Your company is deciding whether or not to switch to electric cars for business trips. <u>Analyze</u> the situation and offer an <u>opinion</u> as to which you would choose, being sure to <u>support</u> your choice with evidence and examples.

Patterns: comparison/contrast, description, cause/effect, argument

*Using a gas car must be **compared** to using an electric car to **analyze** the situation. There must be a **description** of each type, including the **effects** the switch would have on the company. Then an **argument** must be made for the opinion presented in the paper.*

2. Topic: <u>Explain</u> <u>what</u> friendship <u>is,</u> and give <u>examples</u> from <u>your own life</u> that reflect it.

Patterns: analysis, narration, examples

The word explain *means there must be an **analysis** and definition of the idea of friendship; events from the writer's own life must be **narrated** (story); **examples** are required.*

3. Topic: Professors are increasingly utilizing technology in the university classroom. <u>Describe</u> the changes in teaching methods, including classroom activities, that <u>you think</u> this use of technology is <u>causing</u>.

Patterns: Description, cause/effect, narration and/or process, argument

***Description** must be used to describe the changes. **Cause and effect** must be used to show how the technology is causing the changes. **Narration** and/or **Process** may be used to explain the process of classroom activities using technology. **Argument** might be used as you are choosing the causes that **you think** are happening.*

4. Topic: <u>Describe</u> someone who has had a big <u>influence</u> on <u>your life</u> <u>and tell how</u> that person has influenced you.

Patterns: description (person), narration, cause and effect, process

The word describe *requires telling about the person; saying how the change happened in the writer's life means giving a **narrative** (story) of what happened and the **process** of the influence, showing **cause and effect**.*

Exercise 2.5: Writing Descriptive Sentences (page 36)
Possible answers are:

1. the moon—The full moon is a pale glowing disk shimmering on the horizon.
2. your phone—My phone's blank black screen illuminates at the touch of a button, and suddenly a fascinating, glittering world is at my fingertips.
3. a favorite professor—Dr. Carrey was distinguished yet personable, with a funny brown mustache on his top lip.
4. a flower garden—A wild rainbow of color surrounds me: brilliant reds, glowing yellows, luscious greens, and deep purples.
5. your best friend—My best friend has wise, hazel eyes and a kind smile, and she wears long silver earrings that jingle when she laughs.
6. a concert—The rock music was agitated, dissonant, and deafening.
7. your breakfast this morning—The rich golden yolk of the over-easy egg oozes across the plate and soaks into the buttery triangle of toast.

Exercise 2.6: Description: Similes and Metaphors (page 38)
A. Sample sentences with similes and metaphors

1. My hometown is like a huge family, where everyone knows the best and the worst of your life. (simile)
2. The forest was alive and breathing, watching us as we stumbled through its shadowy green belly. (metaphor)
3. Our family celebrations during the holidays are as chaotic, noisy, and exuberant as a street carnival. (simile)
4. War is a many-limbed monster that reaches families of all cultures and classes and leaves their lives shrouded in grief. (metaphor)
5. The internet is like a vast spider web connecting people across the entire globe. (simile)
6. The children playing were as carefree as kittens tumbling beneath their mother's watchful eye. (simile)
7. The dark cloud of grief appeared at unexpected moments, throwing a shadow over every thought and emotion. (metaphor)
8. Language can connect or divide, like a gate between neighbors that can be opened or closed. (simile)

B. Sample descriptive paragraph: "Grief." Metaphors are shown in bold; similes are in italics; descriptive adjectives are underlined.

A <u>defining</u> event in Julie's life was the death of her mother when Julie was only eleven years old. As a child, the loss of her mother had **launched her into a vast sea** of confusion and grief. For months, she **floated** aimlessly through life, *like a boat loose from its moorings*, without direction or motivation, but the grief subsided as time passed. Years later, the pain of her loss still resurfaced sometimes, **darkening her thoughts** *like a storm cloud on the horizon.* But then a simple joy—a <u>brilliant</u> sunset, a <u>cheery</u> phone call from her sister, a <u>small</u> child's <u>carefree</u> laughter—would lift her spirits and she would be reminded of her mother's <u>bright</u> smile and <u>compassionate</u> spirit. At such times, Julie loved to make a <u>fresh</u> loaf of bread from her mother's recipe. She would then sit down with a <u>hot</u> cup of tea and savor each <u>comforting</u> bite of <u>warm</u> bread, letting the <u>sweet</u> memories of her mother *engulf her like the fragrant steam* emanating from the loaf in front of her.

Exercise 2.7: Writing Definitions (page 44)
Answers will vary.

Exercise 2.8: Writing Example Sentences (page 46)
Possible answers are:

1. If you want to make your diet healthier, there are several simple changes you can make. **For example**, <u>you can try to include two servings of fruits or vegetables at each meal</u>.
2. Mass transportation, **such as** <u>buses or subways</u>, is an important part of any major city's infrastructure.
3. The East African savannah is home to several large predatory animals. <u>The lion</u>, **for instance**, <u>hunts a variety of medium-sized animals for its food</u>.
4. Serious illness has a significant impact not only on the ill patient's life, but also on the lives of her immediate family and close friends. **For example**, <u>the patient's spouse or parent may have to quit his or her job in order to provide constant care for the patient</u>.
5. It is not difficult for college students to integrate volunteer activities **such as** <u>mentoring or tutoring children</u> into their lives.

Exercise 2.9: Using Examples in a Paragraph (page 48)
Answers will vary.

Exercise 2.10: Transition Words and Phrases (pages 50–51)
Possible answers are:

1. **sequence**
   When I decided to study in the U.S., there were many things I had to do. <u>First,</u> I had to decide on a university. <u>Then</u> I filled out an application. <u>Next,</u> I had to wait to be accepted.

2. **addition**
   Caffeine can impact the quality of your sleep at night. <u>In addition,</u> it can cause your body to crave it so that if you don't drink it, you will get a headache.

3. **cause and effect**
   So many people are eating out nowadays. <u>As a result,</u> restaurants are always busy, so service is often poor.

4. **exemplification**
   Companies who sell products online often send customers surveys to maintain customer service. <u>For example,</u> a week after you make a purchase online, you may receive an email asking you to answer questions about your satisfaction with the website, the delivery, and/or the quality of the product.

5. **emphasis**
   The governor said that the news reporter had called him a liar. <u>In fact,</u> the journalist had said no such thing; he had only claimed that the governor's statement should be carefully evaluated.

6. **comparison expressing similarity**
   An increasing number of people are calling Uber® if they need a ride rather than a taxi company. <u>Similarly,</u> people are also calling Lyft.®

Section 3. Patterns of Essay Organization

Exercise 3.1: Connecting Ideas in Narrative Writing (page 64)

Let me tell you about a scary day in the chemistry lab. It was the first experiment my partner and I had ever done. ① Before we performed the experiment, we checked all of our equipment to ensure it had been properly cleaned. ② Next, we poured our first solution into a beaker. ③ After adding this solution, we heated it. ④ Then we added a second solution to the first. ⑤ Suddenly, the color changed from yellow to green. ⑥ Simultaneously, it began to emit smoke. ⑦ Immediately, we dumped it down the sink, scared that it might explode! Unfortunately, we had obtained the correct reaction, but we got an F on the assignment since the professor had not seen our work. In the end, this was not only a scary day, but an unhappy one as well.

Exercise 3.2: Connecting Ideas to Describe a Process (page 70)
Part 1. a. 5 b. 1 c. 4 d. 2 e. 3
Part 2. Sample paragraph:

To begin with, a tropical depression takes warm air from the surface of the ocean and pushes it upward, causing rotating wind patterns to develop. After winds reach 39 mph, the system is labeled a tropical storm and given a name. In the next stage, the storm takes a cyclonic form, with an eye of moist, hot air in its center, and winds of at least 74 mph. It is now considered a hurricane. Subsequently, the hurricane continues to gain strength as it pulls moisture from the surface of warm waters (80 degrees F or warmer). The final stage in the life of a hurricane occurs when it moves over land or cooler water: it loses strength and its winds decrease until it is no longer considered a hurricane.

Exercise 3.3: Expressing Comparison or Contrast (page 78)
Possible answers are:

1. <u>Both</u> Professor Harrison <u>and</u> Professor Dukovich give very difficult examinations at the ends of their courses.
2. Ali and Ahmed are twins, <u>but</u> they do not behave <u>similarly</u> in all respects.
3. As forms of entertainment, watching television and going to the theater are <u>similar</u> in some ways and <u>different</u> in others.
4. <u>While</u> engineers are concerned with the soundness of a structure, architects are concerned with the aesthetic design.
5. Traveling to foreign countries to study the customs has many advantages; <u>nevertheless</u>, I want to point out some of the disadvantages.

Exercise 3.4: Creating a Cause-and-Effect Paragraph (page 84)
Answers will vary.

Exercise 3.5: Expressing Arguments (page 91)
Answers may vary.

1. <u>It seems evident that</u> temperatures on earth have been rising for the last decade.
2. <u>It is unreasonable to assume that</u> making civilian ownership of guns illegal will help lower the amount of violent crime in the United States.
3. <u>It is logical for people to think that</u> women and men who do the same job should make the same amount of money
4. <u>The proposition that</u> the family of murder victims should determine the punishment of the murderer <u>is easily refuted</u>.

Section 4. Research Paper

Exercise 4.1: Evaluating Sources (page 109)

Sample Answers

1. **An online journal**

   Title of journal: Addictive Behaviors

   Title of article: The evolution of internet addiction: A global perspective

   Author: All of the authors are professional psychologists and professors with several other publications, indicating they are experts. First author Mark D. Griffiths is a chartered psychologist and professor at the University of Trent, Nottingham, U.K., with many publications and is the head of the International Gaming Research Institute.

   Source: *Addictive Behaviors* is an international peer-reviewed journal, indicating that it is appropriate for a research paper.

   Relevance: This article gives an overview of the issue of internet addiction, which is the main topic of this paper. It will help us to define internet addiction and recognize some related issues to include in our paper.

   Accuracy of information: Because this is an article in a peer-reviewed journal, it should be trustworthy and accurate.

   Purpose: To provide an overview on internet addiction on a global scale—no bias indicated as these are scientists reporting on this topic, seemingly without an agenda.

   Currency: This article was published last year, so its information is still relevant and valuable, especially as it provides a basic overview.

   Use this source? Yes/ No/ Maybe

   This source is from a peer-reviewed journal and written by professional psychologists with many other publications. That means this information is trustworthy and expert and so would be good to include.

2. **A website**

   URL and title of website: http://www.addictionrecov.org/ Addictions/index.aspx?AID=43 "What is internet addiction?"

   Author: Unity Point Health Illinois Institute for Addiction Recovery

Source: Unity Point Health Illinois Institute for Addiction Recovery

Relevance: It defines internet addiction and offers warning signs and effects.

Accuracy of information: It is not a scholarly article, but it is from a medical institute so it should be fairly reliable.

Purpose: To help people recognize if they are addicted and advise them on when and how to seek help—a little bit biased since they provide services to addicts, but it is a medical institution that is supposed to help people.

Currency: There is no date on the website, but because it is a business, I assume that it is up to date. The information is mostly background information as well, so currency may not be a large consideration.

Use this source? Yes/No/(Maybe)

Because this is a business, I would use with caution. I would check facts and be sure it agreed with other sources before using.

Exercise 4.2: Recognizing Plagiarism of Language (pages 118–119)

1. Manu National Park, comprising over 6,000 square miles, covers the entire watershed of the Manu River, from high-altitude grasslands, on the eastern flank of the Andes, down through damp cloud forest to the rain forest in the lowlands of the westernmost Amazon Basin. (James, 2016, p. 42)
   Description: _____D_____

2. Butterflies of all sizes and colors flutter through the forest, and nearly one hundred species of bats fill the air at night. (James, 2016, p. 42)
   Description: _____B_____

3. Insects are so abundant in Manu National Park that at night, "the foliage sparkles in your headlamp with what looks like pixie dust" as the light hits the hundreds of thousands of insect eyes. (James, 2016, p. 42)
   Description: _____A_____

4. Peru's Manu National Park is a sumptuous, extravagant, overwhelming landscape traversed by tapirs, snakes, primates, and insects. (James, 2016, p. 42)
   Description: _____D_____

5. Tapirs, macaws, and snakes are among the species that fill Manu National Park, which comprises several habitats, from grassy highlands in the West to rain forest in the East. (James, 2016, p. 42)
   Description: _____B_____

Exercise 4.3: Thesis Statements: Argument or Report? (page 123)
1. A   2. R   3. A   4. R   5. A   6. A   7. R   8. A   9. A   10. R
   3. is not as effective
   5. the most crucial element
   6. need
   8. however; must be
   9. some may argue; if we do not; will become; resulting in

Exercise 4.4: APA References: Correcting Errors (pages 132–133)

1. **Book with one author**
   Gennett, P. (2015). *The benefits of walking:* What *your doctor never told you.* New York, NY: Pringle Press.

2. **Book with two or more authors, edition other than first**
   Salesh, B., & Jounell, G. (2017). *Giving up technology may just make your day* (2nd ed.). Chicago, IL: University of Chicago Press.

3. **Book by a group (corporate) author**
   World Bank. (2017). *Doing business: Equal opportunity for all.* Washington, DC: World Bank.

4. **Edited book, no author**
   Concueso, L. (Ed.). (2016). *Critical thinking: A collection of essays.* Stanford, CA: Stanford University Press.

5. **Journal article**
   O'Toole, R.S. (2017). The bonds of kinship, the ties of freedom in colonial Peru. *Journal of Family History,* *42*(1), 3–21.

6. **Chapter in an edited volume**
   Neruda, P. (2017). If you forget me. In M. Strand (Ed.), *100 great poems of the twentieth century* (pp. 21–22). New York, NY: W.W. Norton & Company.

7. **ebook**
   Kranz, M. (2017). *Building the internet of things: Implement new business models, disrupt competitors, transform your industry.* Retrieved from http://eds.a.ebscohost.com. authenticate.library.duq.edu/eds/ebookviewer/ebook/bmxlYmtfXzE0MDk4MDdfX0FO0?sid=78bd74b6-1bd3-4ebf-a41d-c5da0fdce15c@sessionmgr4009&vid=0&format=EB&rid=1

8. **Journal article (electronic)**
   Thomas, R. G. (2013). How to achieve world security. *Annual Review of Political Science, 6,* 205–232. doi: 10.1146/annurev.polisci.6.121901.085731

9. **Article from online periodical**
   Grossman, L. (2017). Milky Way's loner status is upheld. *Science News, 64.* Retrieved from https://www.sciencenews.org/article/milky-ways-loner-status-upheld?tgt=nr

10. **Online news article**
    Davis, N. (2017, Jun. 7). Suppressing the reasoning part of the brain stimulates creativity, study finds. *The Guardian.* Retrieved from https://www.theguardian.com/science/2017/jun/07/thinking-caps-on-electrical-currents-boost-creative-problem-solving-study-finds

11. **Non-periodical web document**
    Edmunds. (2016). *2016 hybrid buying guide.* Retrieved from https://www.edmunds.com/hybrid/buying-guide/

12. **Online encyclopedias and dictionaries**
    Fuel cell. (2017, Apr. 10). In *Encyclopaedia Britannica Online.* Retrieved from https://www.britannica.com/technology/fuel-cell

Exercise 4.5: MLA Works Cited: Correcting Errors
(pages 149–150)

1. **Book with one author, edition other than first**
   Renfrew, Stephen. ⸢*Tell Me a Story*⸣. 3rd ed., Scribner, 2015.

2. **Book with two authors**
   Springfield, Janice, ⸢and Simone Manchester⸣. *A History of Immigrants in the US.* W.W. Norton and Company, 2012.

3. **Book by a group (corporate) author**
   NASA. *A History of NASA.* ⸢2nd ed.,⸣ NASA, 2016.

4. **Edited book, no author**
   Ghost Stories from the Gore Orphanage. ⸢Edited by James Pierce,⸣ Ohio UP, 2014.

5. **Work in an anthology, reference, or collection / chapter in an edited volume**
   Vaira, Louis. "Some Aspects of Pittsburgh's Contributions to the Civil War." *Industry and Infantry: The Civil War in Western Pennsylvania,* edited by Brian Butko and Nicholas Ciotola, Historical Society of Western Pennsylvania, 2003, ⸢pp.⸣ 60–70.

6. **Journal article, more than two authors**
   Martinez-Austria, Polioptro F. et al. "Temperature and Heat-Related Mortality Trends in the Sonoran and Mojave Desert Region." *Atmosphere,* ⸢vol. 8, no. 3,⸣ 2017, pp. 1–13.

7. **ebook**
   Houston, Edwin J. *The Wonder Book of Volcanoes and Earthquakes.* Bolster Press, 2016. ⸢www.gutenberg.org/ebooks/43320.⸣

8. **Journal article with doi, obtained from a database**
   Clennett-Sirois, Laurence. "It's Complicated: The Social Lives of Networked Teens." *Canadian Journal of Communication,* vol. 39, no. 4, ⸢2014, pp. 663–665,⸣ *ProQuest Central,* dx.doi.org/10.22230/cjc.2014v39n4a2917.

9. **Article from online periodical**
   Lee, Robert. "Accounting for Conquest: The Price of the Louisiana Purchase of Indian Country." *The Journal of American History,* Mar. 2017, jah.oah.org/issues/march-2017/#articles.

10. **Chapter/section of a web document**
    The MLA Style Center. "Works Cited: A Quick Guide." *Modern Language Association,* style.mla.org/works-cited-a-quick-guide/.

11. **Email**
    Crettering, Kimberly. "Re: How to Find the Best Internships." Received by Humberto Gonzalez, 5 May, 2017.

Section 5. Grammar and Style

Exercise 5.1: Recognizing Word Form Errors (pages 168–169)

2. Progress in agriculture is essential for all societies.
3. The industrial revolution was based on learning how to harness the power of machinery.
4. They were speaking so loudly that I could not concentrate.
5. The impact of writing systems was profound because it allowed humans to communicate easily across great distances of time and space.
6. Oral history is part of many cultures, but written history is said to be the foundation of civilization.
7. Some experts claim that computer technology, as compared to all other inventions, has had the greatest influence on world history.
8. Electronic calculators have enabled modern commerce to progress in unexpected ways.
9. The astonishing advances in modern telecommunications will enable a new revolution to occur.
10. Technology today allows us to communicate instantaneously.
11. The most important question is whether humans can learn to use technology for peaceful purposes.
12. Inventions that we have not yet even dreamed of will be part of the normal life of future generations.

Exercise 5.2: Using Articles (page 173)

1. She would like to borrow **the** pencil on the desk.
2. **The** student sitting in **the** corner has an extra pencil.
3. Would you like **0** coffee or **0** tea?
4. He took **the** only maps that were left.
5. Our director announced, "**The** play has been cancelled."
6. She went to **0** Heinz Hall to listen to the symphony last night.
7. I bought **0** rice, **0** broccoli, and **a** pan at the store.
8. My daughter is learning to play **the/ 0** violin at school.
9. That restaurant is on **0** Fifth Avenue.
10. Seoul is **the** capital of Korea.
11. **0** President Costa defeated all his **0** opponents in the election.
12. I had an appointment with Mrs. Aldali, **an/the** accountant who works for **0** Baker, Zelie, and Sons, Ltd.
13. Marie ate some of **the** candy that I gave her.
14. **The/ a** human being is a mammal.

Exercise 5.3: Using Appropriate Prepositions (page 175)

① **In** my opinion the most important and useful everyday device ② **at** present is a computer. There are several reasons why I would suggest buying a computer first when you would like to furnish your apartment ③ **with** technical devices. Modern computers have enough multimedia and computational capabilities to perform all functions that such devices ④ **as** televisions, audio players, and video equipment can. In relation ⑤ **to** computer games, a computer can become the entertainment center ⑥ **of** your world. The internet as a source ⑦ **of** most news information, e-business, e-shopping opportunities, email, and videoconference communication is an advantage you can obtain only ⑧ **by** means ⑨ **of** a home computer. Finally, a great deal ⑩ **of** hiring ⑪ **for** modern jobs is done ⑫ **by** using computers. Having a computer ⑬ **at** home helps you to get the necessary practice if you are a novice. If you are an experienced user, all these arguments are redundant because you already know the reasons! I am sure you will agree ⑭ **with** me.

Exercise 5.4: Using More Specific Words (page 177)

Answers may vary.

1. I am planning to <u>buy</u> a new car this year.
2. Eating nutritious food and getting enough exercise are the most important <u>principles</u> for a healthy lifestyle.
3. From the time she was a child, she has been a <u>skilled</u> soccer player.
4. I believe that Apple should add some new <u>features</u> to the next version of the iPhone.

Exercise 5.5: Using More Formal Words (page 177)

Answers may vary.

1. For her research, she will <u>examine</u> the effects of carbon monoxide emissions on the environment.
2. In order to <u>obtain</u> a driver's license, you have to take a computerized test and a driving exam.
3. The third chapter of the book <u>considers</u> the role of stereotypes in speech processing.
4. Mrs. Romero was a <u>generous</u> person; she always gave money to charities and helped individuals financially whenever she could.

Exercise 5.6: Using Reference Words to Avoid Repetition (pages 180–181)

Answers may vary.

1. Scientists often experience setbacks in their research. **They** should not feel discouraged, however, because **these problems** can help **them** make new discoveries that might have been overlooked.
2. There are two advantages of having friends who are different from ourselves. **One** is that **we** can share different opinions. **Another** is that **we** will learn a lot and help each other because **we** have different qualities.
3. Employees must take occasional vacations to reduce stress and stay efficient. Some employers encourage employees to take **such breaks**, but **others** discourage **this**.
4. Since the first settlers arrived in South America, Brazil has gone through three main periods in **its** history. In the **first**, from **its** discovery until about 1822, **it** was a Portuguese colony.

5. The lifestyle of people who live in cities is totally different from **those** in small towns or rural areas. **Those** living in cities often walk quickly and speak quickly because they are under pressure. Time is money for them. However, **those** in small towns do everything more slowly.

6. Public libraries are often faced with the difficulty of dealing with problem users. **Such people** are usually **those** who cause **problems** for **librarians** by their offensive behaviors, which include eating, drinking, loitering, staring at others, or talking in a loud voice.

Exercise 5.7: Reducing Wordiness (pages 182–183)

Some wordiness that could be eliminated from the original is indicated in italics below, followed by a sample answer with reduced wordiness. Notice that the sample answer is much shorter than the original.

1. Garbage *in the modern world* is becoming a serious problem and is invading *our lives nowadays. In the past,* people used to be thrifty. They *did not waste anything in those days* but *used all leftovers* for some purpose; for example, cardboard was used for fires and heating, or containers were reused. *People used to create less trash and waste in former times.* Nowadays, unfortunately, we make a lot of waste. The quantity of garbage *that we generate and throw in the trash* is much more than the quantity of food we consume. Consequently, we are having *problems and difficulties* getting rid of garbage, which has started overwhelming our lives, nature, and the air we breathe. However, as we *go forward into the future which is to come,* we can find ways and means of *exploiting* garbage and *using it positively.*

2. The bad effects of garbage are not limited to the *personal* lives of *individuals* and families. In fact, the effects have spread out immensely to become a social and *global* phenomenon *affecting the whole earth* and *the whole universe.* Garbage has invaded and *threatened our lives.* Pollution and toxic chemicals and substances, some of which are the result of garbage, are *threatening our existence.*

3. Yet there are some solutions that could prevent the increase of the *bad effects of garbage* and reduce *pollution.* Some countries have developed very sophisticated ways of exploiting their garbage and extracting energy from it. In other countries, there are some initiatives to exploit garbage by recycling it or using it as *compost* for *fertilizing* seeds and plants.

4. *Nowadays, people have become aware of the danger* garbage can put their lives in. *Consciousness of the bad, negative, injurious effects has increased.* They have *figured out smart ways of disposing of garbage* without creating harmful side effects such as pollution. People have *discovered how to manage their garbage* and use it intelligently to make their lives easier and cleaner *at the present time.*

Sample answer with reduced wordiness:

1. Garbage is becoming a serious problem and is invading our lives. In the past, people used to create less waste. They used all leftovers for some purpose; for example, cardboard was used for fires and heating, and containers were reused. The quantity of garbage that we generate now is much more than the quantity of food we consume. Consequently, we are having problems getting rid of garbage, which has started overwhelming our lives, nature, and the air we breathe. However, we can in the future find ways and means of exploiting garbage.

2. The bad effects of garbage are not limited to the lives of individuals and families. In fact, the effects have spread out immensely to become a social and global phenomenon. Pollution and toxic substances, some of which are the result of garbage, are threatening our existence.

3. Yet there are some solutions that could prevent the increase of the bad effects. Some countries have developed very sophisticated ways of exploiting their garbage and extracting energy from it. In other countries, there are some initiatives to exploit garbage by recycling it or using it as compost.

4. People have now become more conscious of the danger garbage can put their lives in. They have figured out smart ways of disposing of it without creating harmful side effects, making their lives easier and cleaner.

Exercise 5.8: Identifying Independent and Dependent Clauses (page 185)

1. <u>DC</u> When it comes to the positive impact of preschool on children.
2. <u>IC</u> Advances have been made in developing crops that mature faster.
3. <u>IC</u> Although in a democracy people can vote to express their views and impact government, a large percentage of the population in democratic countries does not actually vote.
4. <u>DC</u> What she was going to say.
5. <u>DC</u> The information that CNN reported last night.
6. <u>IC</u> Prior to 1980, personal computers could rarely be found in the home of most individuals.
7. <u>DC</u> Because animal testing has proven to be extremely useful in determining the safety of new drugs.
8. <u>IC</u> The reasons why people become addicted to gambling are varied.

Exercise 5.9: Practicing Subject-Verb Agreement (page 189)

1. The soldiers, accompanied by one officer who was experienced in this kind of situation, was / were taken to a new location.
2. Everybody, including the cook and his assistants, was /were invited to the party at the manager's house.
3. Neither the teachers nor the director of the city schools is /are in the room.
4. There is / are only one or two possible explanations for the recent, sudden changes in the weather pattern.
5. Economics is / are among the sciences that are primarily observational, like astronomy.
6. My family is / are traveling to Egypt to see the pyramids.
7. The class is / are going to make individual speeches to develop their spoken language skills. [The writer is here thinking of the members of the class as individuals.]
8. The class is / are going on a visit to a clothing factory to learn about the manufacturing process. [The writer is here thinking of the class as a single unit.]

Exercise 5.10: Correcting Run-On Sentences (page 192)

1. The passengers on the airplane put their seatbelts on. As soon as all the luggage was aboard, the airplane took off.

2. We realized in the middle of the experiment that we had lost some equipment we really needed. [NO CHANGE]

3. Engineers understand how much force travels from the ground through the shoe to the foot. As a result, they are able to design shoes that provide maximum comfort to the wearer.

4. Earthquakes have become a much more common phenomenon in recent years. For example, over the past decade, Asia has experienced 30 percent more earthquakes than in previous decades.

Exercise 5.11: Correcting Sentence Fragments (page 192)

Answers may vary.

Advertisements and propaganda are used very systematically for political matters today—for example, advertising on TV to gain votes. This is because of their very strong influence on people. Therefore, politicians sometimes hire an advertising specialist. However, the advertisement strategy is not just a way to attract people's attention in modern times. It was also used in the 17th century. We can find many historical examples. One is the advertising strategy of the famous French king, Louis 14th, who was called the Sun King by his people.

Exercise 5.12: Recognizing Comma Splices (page 194)

Answers may vary.

1. "Laughter is the best medicine" is a well-known proverb. Having a positive outlook on life has many health benefits.

2. A sense of humor reduces stress, and as a result, there is less tension in personal relationships. A person with low stress and healthy relationships tends to live longer.

3. When a person with a positive perspective encounters difficulties, she is more likely to see the benefits that these challenges bring to her life.

4. Moreover, researchers have found that people who are ill recover more quickly if they experience some laughter every day; therefore, some hospitals make an effort to bring humor into patients' lives.

5. Keeping a smile on your face brightens other peoples' days, and it can help you have a healthier, longer life as well.

Exercise 5.13: Comma Use in Adjective Clauses (page 197)

1. The Statue of Liberty, which is located in New York City, is visited by millions of people every year. [**The words "Statue of Liberty" make this noun unique, so the adjective clause is extra information. This means you need punctuation before and after the clause.**]

2. Seoul, Korea, where she grew up, has a population of about 10,000,000. [**Seoul, Korea, is unique, so the adjective clause is extra information. This means you need punctuation before and after the clause.**]

3. We participated in a service project in Jamaica, where the hurricane hit two weeks ago. [**The word "Jamaica" identifies the noun, so the adjective clause is extra information. This means you need punctuation before and after the clause.**]

4. He has always wanted to visit the Metropolitan Museum of Art, which is in New York. [**The words "Metropolitan Museum of Art" make this noun unique, so the adjective clause is extra information. This means you need punctuation before and after the clause.**]

5. The city where I was born is Rio de Janeiro, Brazil. [NO CHANGE because the clause is identifying which city: the one I was born in.]

6. The author's most recent book, which people think is her best, is the one that has been translated into Chinese. [**The words "most recent" identify the noun, so the adjective clause is extra information. This means you need punctuation before and after the clause.**]

7. If you need a letter of recommendation, you should ask a teacher whom you talk with frequently and who knows you personally. [NO CHANGE because the clause is identifying which type of teacher: the one with whom you talk with frequently and who knows you personally.]

8. *Tom Sawyer*, which I read last year, is one of my favorite classic American novels. [**The name of the book identifies it: "Tom Sawyer." The adjective clause is extra information. This means you need punctuation before and after the clause.**]

9. I cannot remember the year when it happened. [NO CHANGE because the clause is identifying which year: the one when it happened.]

10. People who want to broaden their outlook by experiencing other cultures should study or work for some time in a foreign country. [NO CHANGE because the clause is identifying which people: those who want to broaden their outlook by experiencing other cultures.]

Exercise 5.14: Creating Parallel Structures (page 199)

1. Because he was <u>sick</u> and <u>discouraged</u>, Lee quit his job.
2. To earn some extra money while I was in college, I worked as a <u>computer technician</u>, as a <u>secretary</u>, and as a <u>babysitter</u>.
3. That executive is known for her <u>kindness</u> and <u>honesty</u>.
4. The bones in the body not only <u>give</u> the body shape but also <u>protect</u> the heart, lungs, and brain.
5. Every day during our vacation, we <u>relaxed</u> on the beach and <u>enjoyed</u> swimming.
6. Statistics is a field of study concerned with the <u>collection</u>, <u>organization</u>, <u>summary</u>, and <u>analysis</u> of data.
7. <u>Carrier pigeons</u>, <u>the telegraph</u>, <u>wired telephones</u>, and <u>cell phones</u> are all ways people have been using to communicate for many years.
8. Neither <u>putting off</u> difficult tasks nor <u>thinking</u> without acting will help you get your work done.
9. James wanted to be either a <u>lawyer</u> or a <u>banker</u>.
10. Both <u>teaching</u> in the public schools and <u>working</u> as a nurse in a hospital were types of employment that Felicity had at different times in her life. [NO CHANGE]

Exercise 5.15: Combining Sentences with Subordinators (pages 203–204)

Example:

Cell phones are often a distraction. Teachers often prohibit their use in the classroom.

Relationship: <u>cause/effect</u>

<u>Because (As, Since) cell phones are often a distraction, teachers often prohibit their use in the classroom.</u>

1. I finished my homework. At the same time, my roommate made dinner.

Relationship: <u>time</u>

<u>I finished my homework while my roommate made dinner.</u>

2. Mark was speeding on the highway. The policeman did not give him a ticket.
Relationship: <u>contrast</u>
<u>Although/Even though Mark was speeding on the highway, the policeman did not give him a ticket.</u>

3. Judith might write a good paper for her sociology class. A good paper means she will get an A in the class.
Relationship: <u>condition</u>
<u>If Judith writes a good paper for her sociology class, she will get an A in the class.</u>

4. Recycling is one of the most effective ways to reduce garbage and improve our environment. We should increase penalties on households that do not obey local recycling policies.
Relationship: <u>cause/effect</u>
<u>Because/Since/As recycling is one of the most effective ways to reduce garbage and improve our environment, we should increase penalties on households that do not obey local recycling policies.</u>

5. You may have questions about the writing assignment. You should talk to the teacher after class.
Relationship: <u>condition</u>
<u>If you have questions about the writing assignment, you should talk to the teacher after class.</u>

6. School districts rarely see even one case of the measles per year. Our local elementary school reported seven cases last year.
Relationship: <u>contrast</u>
<u>Although school districts rarely see even one case of the measles per year, our local elementary school reported seven cases last year.</u>

7. Carrie got home from the movies. Immediately, she realized that her house had been robbed.
Relationship: <u>time</u>
<u>As soon as Carrie got home from the movies, she realized that her house had been robbed.</u>

Section 6. Punctuation

Exercise 6.1: Period at End of Sentence (page 211)

More and more these days, people all over the world are eating insects for many reasons. Crickets, for example, provide a lot of protein. They are also very inexpensive and a sustainable source of food. It takes much less water and land to raise crickets for food than to raise livestock. Crickets also emit almost no greenhouse gases. Finally, the overall nutritional value of crickets is very high. They are a real "super food."

Exercise 6.2: Period with Decimals (page 211)

1. 11.04   2. 97.31   3. 1033.016

Exercise 6.3: Question Mark and Period (page 212)

1. *Anna:* Are you traveling to Paris today?
2. *Jose:* No. Are you?
3. *Anna:* Yes, I was told that Guillaume would be there, so I want to go there also.
4. *Jose:* Why is Guillaume going there?
5. *Anna:* He wouldn't tell me at first. Then I asked him whether it was true that he was going to visit his aunt in Paris. He next asked me why I wanted to know and added that it was none of my business. So I stopped questioning him. Later, he admitted that he would be visiting his aunt there. Do you think that I should follow him?
6. *Jose:* That depends on why you would want to do so. Have you met his aunt?

Exercise 6.4: Exclamation Point (page 213)

1. Her dog is very friendly.
2. This is so exciting!
3. She was sick all weekend. (Both are possible.)
4. What gorgeous weather!
5. What a surprise!
6. Yesterday I finally heard from my brother overseas! (Both are possible.)

Exercise 6.5: Comma with Introductory or Transitional Words or Phrases (page 214)

1. All things considered, the event was a success.
2. The photographer fell out of the tree from which he was trying to see over the wall. [NO CHANGE]
3. In summary, there are many good reasons for studying the foreign languages in today's world, in which international exchange of information is so important.
4. Nevertheless, Halima decided to buy the new car.
5. Mr. Roh and Ms. Kim traveled by train from Istanbul to Paris even though they preferred to fly. [NO CHANGE]
6. By the third week of the semester, Ching had discovered her great interest in neuroscience.

Exercise 6.6: Comma after Introductory Clauses (page 215)

1. So that the dinner does not burn, we must be sure to keep an eye on the stove.
2. Even though the route through downtown would have been shorter, Luma drove around the city center in order to avoid heavy traffic.
3. Because we wanted the party to be a surprise, we asked the guests to park on the next street.
4. Since you began to study in this school, your English has improved greatly.
5. While Svetlana made the cake and prepared the food, Irina put up the decorations.

Exercise 6.7: Comma before Conjunctions (page 216)

1. I wanted to go to the movie or the concert. [NO CHANGE]
2. Yi-Lin neither wanted to go directly to college, nor did she want to get a job immediately.
3. He worked hard to prepare for the audition, but he did not get the part.
4. Dr. Bennett, who was in charge of the emergency room, called to the nurse to move quickly, and she then began to examine the patient.
5. Luis won the game easily, but the spectators did not applaud.

Exercise 6.8: Comma with Lists of Words, Phrases, or Clauses (page 217)

1. Hearing, touch, taste, smell, and sight are the five senses of perception.
2. The next time I buy a car, it will have heated seats, satellite radio, and all-wheel drive. [NO CHANGE]
3. How to prepare a speech, how to deliver it, how to adjust to audience reaction, and how to learn from one's mistakes are all dealt with in the website on public speaking.
4. Many people are involved in the production of a good play, including the following: the actors, the director, the writers, the makeup artist, the costume designer, and the set designer.
5. In spite of many difficulties, such as illness, lack of money, attacks by enemies, and loss of public support, the mayor decided to run for election.

Exercise 6.9: Comma with Coordinate Adjectives (page 218)

1. Gabrielle said that her new computer was a wonderful, valuable, timesaving machine.
2. The squirrel climbed the big green tree quickly. [NO CHANGE]
3. The citizens wanted an effective, cheap program for repairing the old bridges, but the mayor said that it would be expensive.
4. The experienced, calm, kind teacher waited for the students to finish the project.
5. It was the most extensive evergreen forest in the southern region. [NO CHANGE]

Exercise 6.10: Comma with Quotations (page 219)

1. Christina commented, "That movie was very sad."
2. "The university that I want to go to is in Venezuela," announced Lyudmila.
3. "John," the boy's mother asked, "when will you clean your room?"
4. She said, "I like to study in the park because the fresh air helps me think."
5. "There are too many sheep in the north field. Please move some of them," said the farmer to the shepherd.

Exercise 6.11: Comma with Abbreviations (page 221)

1. We packed our bathing suits, towels, sunscreen, etc., to go to the beach.
2. Some of the approaches to social organizations, e.g., communism and capitalism, are thought to be incompatible.
3. There are many interesting things at the aquarium, e.g., sting rays, jellyfish, penguins, and dolphins.
4. Dr. Burns wrote that extensive research on the cause of the disease was conducted by Jones et al. [NO CHANGE]
5. To start the computer, press the "on" button, i.e., the red one at the side of the machine.

Exercise 6.12: Comma with Contrasting or Interrupting Elements or Those Needing Separation for Clarity (page 223)

1. Unlike clarinets and oboes, which are wind instruments, flutes do not need reeds.
2. Luna, I urge you to stop right away!
3. The revolution began in July 1789; to be more precise, it was July 14, 1789.
4. The Oakdale Corporation has its office at 4701 Shadow Lane, Houston, Texas.
5. The whale, as far as I know, is the largest sea creature.
6. Lagos, which is the largest city in Nigeria, started as a small fishing and farming settlement.
7. Therefore, the square of the hypotenuse is equal to the sum of the squares of the other two sides.
8. The morning flight, not the evening one, is what she prefers.
9. My party withdrew from the election, ending interest in its reform proposals.

Exercise 6.13: Semicolon with Independent Clauses (page 224)

1. Mr. Wang bought a new house last month; he has already sold it.
2. I looked everywhere for my punctuation workbook; surprisingly, it was on the back seat of my car.
3. Piradee is not feeling well; she has a headache.

Exercise 6.14: Semicolon Separating Elements with Internal Commas (page 225)

1. At the picnic, we will have, in addition to everything else, apples, brought by Tom; oranges, brought by Tina; pears, brought by Harry; and watermelon, brought by Jane.

2. These packages need to be shipped; take them to the post office today.

3. Sharon and Sherman had an accident while riding their bikes; she was fine but he broke his wrist.

4. Hans found that his punctuation workbook contained rules and exercises for the use of the period, referred to as a full stop in British English; the comma, which he realized had the greatest variety of uses; and all the other marks that he needed to know about.

5. Ivan wanted to leave Moscow because of the cold, which affected his health and, as a consequence of that, his work; but Natasha, who enjoyed cold weather, was hoping it would get colder.

Exercise 6.15: Colon (page 228)

1. According to one analysis, there are four stages in human development: childhood, youth, adulthood, and old age.

2. In describing the elements that have influenced the pronunciation of Brazilian Portuguese, Marcía Porter explains:

> *The Semana de arte moderna*, also led by Andrade, represents a major turning point in the landscape of Brazilian culture. The movement stressed the belief that Brazilian folklore and cultural roots were the foundation of national identity and encouraged other Brazilian artists to reject European models and embrace their own heritage. This idea of a national identity was the same as that of the *Normas*, as the document is commonly called. The *Normas* were not intended as strict rules or "laws," but rather as "norms" or suggestions for pronunciation. (2017, p. 4)

3. President John F. Kennedy said: "Ask not what your country can do for you; ask what you can do for your country."

4. "Your punctuation," said the reader to the writer, "is very confusing: it does not help to clarify the sentence structure and meaning."

5. When Josephine Lewis received the letter from the government agency, she saw that it began with the words:

Dear Ms. Lewis:

We are pleased to inform you that you have been awarded a scholarship for the continuation of your studies. . . .

6. This is the book citation in APA style: Porter, M. (2017). *Singing in Brazilian Portuguese*. Lanham, MD: Rowman & Littlefield Press.

7. The next flight is due at 10:15 AM, not at 11:15 AM.

8. Mix yellow and green in the ratio of 2:1 (two to one).

INDEX